BARGAINING FOR WOMEN'S RIGHTS

BARGAINING FOR WOMEN'S RIGHTS

Activism in an Aspiring Muslim Democracy

ALICE J. KANG

University of Minnesota Press

Minneapolis

London

The University of Minnesota Press gratefully acknowledges financial assistance for the publication of this book from the College of Arts and Sciences at the University of Nebraska–Lincoln.

Portions of chapter 3 appeared previously in "The Effect of Gender Quota Laws on the Election of Women: Lessons from Niger," *Women's Studies International Forum* 41, no. 2 (2013): 94–102; reprinted with permission from Elsevier.

Published by the University of Minnesota Press
111 Third Avenue South, Suite 290
Minneapolis, MN 55401-2520
http://www.upress.umn.edu

Library of Congress Cataloging-in-Publication Data
Kang, Alice J.
Bargaining for women's rights : activism in an aspiring Muslim democracy / Alice J. Kang.
Includes bibliographical references and index.
ISBN 978-0-8166-9217-0 (hc : alk. paper)
ISBN 978-0-8166-9218-7 (pb : alk. paper)
1. Women's rights—Islamic countries.   2. Women's rights—Niger—Case studies.   3. Women—Political activity—Islamic countries.   4. Women in development—Islamic countries.   5. Nongovernmental organizations—Islamic countries.   I. Title.
HQ1236.5.I74K36 2015
305.4209767—dc23

                                                            2014032698

Printed in the United States of America on acid-free paper

The University of Minnesota is an equal-opportunity educator and employer.

— 21   20   19   18   17   16   15   10   9   8   7   6   5   4   3   2   1

TO SUNG SOOK SHIN

CONTENTS

ACKNOWLEDGMENTS

In the course of writing this book, I have become indebted to numerous individuals, associations, and institutions, though any errors in the pages that follow are mine alone. First and foremost, I am grateful to the women's activists, conservative activists, and state officials in Niger who received me in their homes and workplaces and talked with me about their work. Whereas some interviewees gave me permission to publish their names, others wished to be identified by their associational affiliation, arguing that their advocacy was done in the name of a broader collective. As a result, I refrain from naming individuals whom I interviewed and refer to their position in their associations or institutions instead.

This book dates back to when I was a doctoral candidate in political science at the University of Wisconsin–Madison. I thank Aili Mari Tripp for her constant support, feedback on draft proposals and chapters, and phone calls while I was in the field. Michael Schatzberg challenged me to read broadly, think about politics differently, and see things "from the other end of the telescope." Christina Ewig asked pertinent questions about this project from its inception to its defense and showed me where to look for answers. Scott Straus's advice throughout the project also made for a much better product, and Crawford Young was a delight with whom to discuss Nigérien politics. Jon Pevehouse, Asifa Quraishi, Christa Tiernan, and participants at the Comparative Politics Colloquium and International Relations Colloquium gave helpful feedback on the project. The Gender and Women in Social Science Writing Group, which included Valerie Hennings, Elizabeth Holzer, Kristy Kelly, Lauren McCarthy, Kimiko Osawa, and Aili Tripp, provided constructive criticism on early drafts of the dissertation. Fellow students of Africa Melinda Adams, Ladan Affi, Kelly Duke Bryant, Libbie Freed, Sarah Hardin, Brandon Kendhammer, Carmen McCain, and Naaborko Sackeyfio-Lenoch, along with the

University of Wisconsin African Politics Graduate Student Group, were a source of hope, merriment, and wisdom. In particular, conversations with Brandon influenced the development of this project.

Many individuals and institutions in Niger made conducting research for this book a joy. Fatouma Alidou, Ousseina Alidou, Robert Charlick, and Sue Rosenfeld helped me get my feet on the ground. The Department of History at Abdou Moumouni University and the Laboratory for the Study of Social Dynamics and Local Development (LASDEL) provided a lively environment for the study of Nigérien society and politics. Director Idrissa Yansambou and Ousmane Maman Idi of the National Archives stood at the helm of, to use the words of one scholar, "the best run public service in the country" and helped me, and countless other researchers, procure key documents. At LASDEL, Jean-Pierre Olivier de Sardan presided over an intellectually lively doctoral seminar, in which I developed a greater appreciation for socio-anthropological research methods and received incisive feedback on my project. Mahaman Tidjani Alou shared his perceptive observations about religion and politics with me, along with his good humor. Soumana Cissé of the American Cultural Center provided sound advice and helped put me in touch with key activists. Roukyatou Idrissa and I conducted several interviews together, which proved to be both fun and intellectually rewarding. A capable team of interpreters and translators worked with me in Kiota, Niamey, and Zinder. To Boubacar Almoustapha, Aminatou Hainikoye, Ousseini Maman, Moussa Nouhou, Mahaman Ragi, and Abdou Sanda, *na godé* and *ay saabu*.

For their camaraderie in Niger and in the United States, I am grateful to Fatouma Alidou, Claire Breedlove, Christine and Geoffrey Brinker, Soumana Cissé and his family, Maggie Fick, Roukyatou Idrissa, Brian Nowak, Antoinette and Mahaman Tidjani Alou, and the barmen of the Grand Hotel—Alio, Amadou, Bachir, and Salissou. Jennifer and Will Everhart, Sue Rosenfeld, Marc Seltzer, and Cezarina Trone fed and sheltered me for a significant duration in Niamey, as did Sambo Bodé and his family in Niamey and Zinder.

In transforming the dissertation to the book, I accumulated new debts of gratitude. At the University of Nebraska–Lincoln, Elizabeth Theiss-Morse and Amelia Montes provided warm encouragement, and Patrice McMahon commented on the entire first draft. Shimelis Beyene, Dawne Curry, Lori Janelle Dance, Kwakiutl Dreher, David Forsythe, Courtney Hillebrecht, Jeannette Eileen Jones, Patrick Jones, Nam Kyu Kim, Ari Kohen, Ross Miller, Dona-Gene Mitchell, Greg Rutledge, Mike Wagner, Sergio Wals, and Tyler White gave advice and created an enjoyable environment in which to write. The International Relations–Comparative Politics Brownbag of the Department of

Political Science gave excellent feedback on chapter 3, as did my undergraduate students in Women and Politics on chapters 2 and 3. Liv Tønnessen and anonymous reviewers for *Women's Studies International Forum* gave excellent feedback on an article, portions of which are found in chapter 3. Madeline Hoffer and Julia Reilly carefully read the manuscript; I am grateful to both for their acuity. For their reading of selected chapters and stimulating conversations, I thank Gretchen Bauer, Mala Htun, Abdourahmane Idrissa, Dörte Rompel, and Leonardo Villalón. Hadiza Moussa's scholarship on gender and society and incisive feedback on chapter 2 were invaluable. In 2013, Hadiza Moussa and graduate school friend Marie-Ange Bunga passed away; this book was written in their memory.

Comments from participants at the 2010 APSA Africa Workshop in Dar es Salaam, Tanzania; the 2012 workshop on quota policies and democratization in Africa organized by the Department of Comparative Politics at the University of Bergen and the Chr. Michelsen Institute in Norway; and numerous African Studies Association, American Political Science Association, and Midwest Political Science Association meetings were helpful. At the University of Minnesota Press, I am grateful to Pieter Martin and his assistant, Kristian Tvedten, for shepherding my manuscript through the publication process. I extend gratitude to Michael Bohrer-Clancy for his assistance in the various stages of production. Jamie Nan Thaman expertly copyedited the manuscript and Diana Witt prepared the index. Gretchen Bauer and Barbara Cooper provided critical and thoughtful feedback on the entire manuscript as external reviewers for the press.

Several sources provided financial assistance that allowed me to go to Niger and write up my findings. Above all, U.S. government funding to area studies materially supported the research conducted for this book. A Fulbright-Hays Doctoral Dissertation Research Abroad fellowship from the U.S. Department of Education allowed me to conduct fieldwork in Niger in 2007–8. Two Foreign Language Area Studies fellowships, also through the U.S. Department of Education, funded language training in Hausa in 2004–5 and 2005–6. My arguments do not necessarily reflect the views of the U.S. government or any of the organizations that supported this study. A Scott Kloeck-Jenson International Pre-dissertation Travel award from Global Studies at the University of Wisconsin, a Hyde Dissertation Research award from the Gender and Women's Studies Department at the University of Wisconsin, and two Senning awards from the Department of Political Science at the University of Nebraska–Lincoln are gratefully recognized. Dean Joseph Francisco of the College of Arts and Sciences at the University of Nebraska–Lincoln supported the professional preparation of the index through an ENHANCE CAS award.

Last, I am grateful for friends and family who cheered me on in this endeavor. They include Mi Hwa Hong, Joanne Hsu, Jackie Kang, Joon Hyun Kang, Chrissa LaPorte, Leah and Zachary Larson-Rabin, Jennifer Petersen, Naaborko Sackefiyo-Lenoch, the San Ramon Crew, and Sheila Dorsey Vinton. Daizaburo Shizuka helped care for our new son, read penultimate drafts, and pushed me to just turn the manuscript in. Most of all, I acknowledge the support of my mother, Sung Sook Shin, the first feminist I met, who instilled in me a deep desire to seek wisdom and practice compassion. I dedicate this book to her.

ABBREVIATIONS

Unless otherwise noted, translations from French into English are by the author.

ACOI	Association pour la Culture et l'Orientation Islamique (Association for Culture and Islamic Guidance)
ACTN	Association des Chefs Traditionnels du Niger (Association of Traditional Chiefs of Niger)
ADF	African Development Fund
ADINI Islam	Association pour la Diffusion de l'Islam au Niger (Association for the Diffusion of Islam in Niger)
AED	Academy for Educational Development
AEMUN	Association des Étudiants Musulmans de l'Université de Niamey (Association of the Muslim Students of the University of Niamey)
AFC	Alliance des Forces du Changement (Alliance of Forces for Change)
AFJN	Association des Femmes Juristes du Niger (Association of Women Lawyers of Niger)
AFMBD	Association des Femmes Musulmanes pour les Œuvres de Bienfaisance et de Développement (Association of Muslim Women for Charitable Works and Development)
AFN	Association des Femmes du Niger (Association of Women of Niger)
AFR	Association des Femmes Rahama (Association of Rahama Women)
AIN	Association Islamique du Niger (Islamic Association of Niger)
AJMN	Association des Jeunes Musulmans du Niger (Association of Young Muslims of Niger)
ANASI	Association Nigérienne pour l'Appel et la Solidarité Islamique (Nigérien Islamic Call and Solidarity Society)
ANAUSI	Association Nigérienne pour l'Appel à l'Unité et la Solidarité Islamique (Nigérien Islamic Call to Unity and Solidarity Society)

ANDDH	Association Nigérienne pour la Défense des Droits de l'Homme (Nigérien Human Rights Defense Association)
ANDP	Alliance Nigérienne pour la Démocratie et le Progrès (Nigérien Alliance for Democracy and Progress)
AOF	Afrique Occidentale Française (French West Africa)
ARCI	Association pour le Rayonnement de la Culture Islamique (Association for the Radiance of Islamic Culture)
ARFI	Association pour le Rassemblement et la Foi Islamique (Association for Rally and Islamic Faith)
AU	African Union
CASIN	Collectif des Associations Islamiques du Niger (Collective of Islamic Associations of Niger)
CCN	Conseil Consultatif National (National Advisory Council)
CDS	Convention Démocratique et Sociale (Democratic and Social Convention)
CEDAW	Convention on the Elimination of All Forms of Discrimination Against Women
CENI	Commission Electorale Nationale Indépendante (National Independent Electoral Commission)
CIDA	Canadian International Development Agency
CMS	Conseil Militaire Suprême (Supreme Military Council)
CNPCN	Commission Nationale Préparatoire à la Conférence Nationale (National Preparatory Committee for the National Conference)
CONGAFEN	Coordination des Organisations Non Gouvernementales et Associations Féminines Nigériennes (Coordinating Body of Women's NGOs and Associations of Niger)
CONIPRAT	Comité Nigérien sur les Pratiques Traditionnelles (Nigérien Committee on Traditional Practices)
CRN	Conseil de Reconciliation Nationale (Council of National Reconciliation)
CSC	Conseil Supérieur de la Communication (High Council for Communication)
CSRD	Conseil Suprême pour la Restauration de la Démocratie (Supreme Council for the Restoration of Democracy)
CSW	Commission on the Status of Women
ECA	Economic Commission for Africa
FAMEDEV	Réseau Interafricain pour les Femmes, Media, Genre et Développement (Inter-African Network for Women, Media, Gender and Development)

FIDH	Fédération Internationale des Ligues de Droits de l'Homme (International Federation for Human Rights)
FRDD	Front pour la Restauration et la Défense de la Démocratie (Front for the Restoration and Defense of Democracy)
GAIP/DS	Groupement des Associations Islamiques en matière de Planning Familial et Développement Social (Confederation of Islamic Associations Concerned with Family Planning and Social Development)
GAIPF	Groupement des Associations Islamiques pour les Activités en matière de Planification Familiale et de Promotion de la Femme (Confederation of Islamic Associations Concerned with Family Planning and the Advancement of Women)
HCR	Haut Conseil de la République
IDA	International Development Association
IPU	Inter-Parliamentary Union
MNSD	Mouvement National pour la Société de Développement (National Movement for the Development Society)
MP	Member of Parliament
MSA	Mouvement Socialiste Africain (African Socialist Movement; Sawaba Movement)
NDI	National Democratic Institute
NGO	Nongovernmental organization
OECD	Organization for Economic Cooperation and Development
OIC	Organization of the Islamic Conference
ORTN	Office de Radiodiffusion Télévision du Niger (Office of Radio and Television of Niger)
PNA	Parti Nigérien pour l'Autogestion (Nigérien Self-Management Party)
PNDS	Parti Nigérien pour la Démocratie et le Socialisme (Nigérien Party for Democracy and Socialism)
PNRD	Parti Nigérien pour le Renforcement de la Démocratie (PNRD)
PPN-RDA	Parti Progressiste Nigérien–Rassemblement Démocratique Africain (Nigérien Progressive Party–African Democratic Rally)
PR	Proportional representation
PSDN	Parti Social-Démocrate Nigérien (Nigérien Social Democratic Party)
RDFN	Rassemblement Démocratique des Femmes du Niger (Democratic Rally of Women of Niger)
RDP	Rassemblement pour la Démocratie et le Progrès (Rally for Democracy and Progress)

REFAM/P	Réseau des Femmes Africaines Ministres et Parlementaires (Network of African Women Ministers and Parliamentarians)
RSD	Rassemblement Social-Démocratique (Social Democratic Rally)
SNV	Netherlands Development Organization
SOAWR	Solidarity for African Women's Rights
SOS FEVVF	SOS Femmes et Enfants Victimes de Violence Familiale (SOS Women and Children Victims of Family Violence)
TANs	Transnational advocacy networks
UDR	Union pour la Démocratie et la République (Union for Democracy and the Republic)
UFMN	Union des Femmes Musulmanes du Niger (Union of Muslim Women of Niger)
UFN	Union des Femmes du Niger (Union of Women of Niger)
UN	United Nations
UNDP	United Nations Development Program
UNFPA	United Nations Population Fund
UNICEF	United Nations Children's Fund
UNIFEM	United Nations Development Fund for Women
UNIRD	Union Nationale des Indépendants pour le Renouveau Démocratique (National Union of Independents for Democratic Renewal)
UNIS	Union Nigérienne des Indépendants et Sympathisants (Union of Independents and Sympathizers)
UPFN	Union pour la Promotion de la Femme Nigérienne (Union for the Advancement of the Nigérien Woman)
USAID	United States Agency for International Development

INTRODUCTION

Women's Rights in an African Muslim Democracy

ON AN OTHERWISE TYPICAL DAY, the president of Niger's largest umbrella women's association, the Coordination des Organisations Non Gouvernementales et Associations Féminines Nigériennes (CONGAFEN, Coordinating Body of Women's NGOs and Associations of Niger), was at work when two plainclothes police officers came to her office.[1] The policemen asked to see her. Thinking that she was going to be arrested, her colleagues in the Office on the Advancement of Women in the Ministry of Social Development vacated the room, leaving the women's leader and two friends behind. The police officers, however, had not come to take the president of CONGAFEN into custody. Instead, they had come to deliver a message. Representatives of Niger's national women's associations were being summoned to meet with the country's new leader at the presidential palace the following afternoon.[2]

Days before, on April 9, 1999, the state radio's regularly scheduled program was interrupted with military marches—a musical signal that a coup d'état had taken place. The prime minister announced that in an "unfortunate accident," President Ibrahim Baré Maïnassara had been shot and killed as he was about to board a helicopter.[3] Commandant Daouda Malam Wanké, the ostensible head of Baré's personal security, became Niger's new head of state and set up a transitional government.[4] Wanké promised the Nigérien people and concerned foreign countries that he would stay in power temporarily and soon organize free and fair elections.[5]

When the police officers left her office, the president of CONGAFEN started thinking about her fast approaching meeting with the country's new leader. She reflected on her association's five-year-long push for the ratification of the Convention on the Elimination of All Forms of Discrimination Against Women (CEDAW), a treaty widely known as an international bill of rights for women. At the time, 163 countries had ratified CEDAW.[6] Niger, however, had yet to ratify the convention. To generate mass support for its ratification, women's activists organized informational seminars about CEDAW and reached out to public opinion leaders to garner their backing. The president of CONGAFEN thought the meeting would be an opportune time to bring the issue to Wanké's attention. She assembled a dossier about CEDAW—a copy of the treaty, along with a study of the treaty's compatibility with Islam, Niger's dominant religion—and went to sleep.

The next morning, representatives of national women's associations gathered at the presidential palace. When it was her turn to greet Wanké, the president of CONGAFEN placed the dossier with information about CEDAW into his hands and said, "On behalf of women in Niger, here is what we expect of you." Wanké took a quick glance inside the file and said that the transitional government would examine it. Following that encounter, the minister of foreign affairs and the minister of social development—both women—kept after Wanké about the status of the convention. On August 13, 1999, approximately four months after the meeting at the presidential palace, Wanké's government ratified CEDAW by military decree. In doing so, the state made a legally binding commitment to eliminate discrimination against women in the predominantly Muslim country of Niger.

When Are Women's Rights Policies Adopted?

Gender equality in predominantly Muslim countries has been in a state of intense debate over the past decades. Women in some societies have fought for and won new access to education, political representation, and reproductive health. In other times and places, women's efforts to secure their rights have been thwarted. Scholars from a variety of disciplines have examined these debates, with some concluding that women are less likely to gain equality in Muslim-majority countries—particularly poor, agrarian countries—as long as men and women remain attached to what they call Islamic doctrine and traditional values.[7] Others argue that there is no inherent reason why Muslim women cannot enjoy their basic human rights, pointing to the agency of Muslim women artists, political party activists, religious scholars, and working-class women.[8] More important for others is understanding why some authoritarian Muslim-majority states collude with religious and traditional leaders whereas others do not.[9]

Few analysts have examined debates over women's rights in predominantly Muslim democracies, where enhanced freedoms to speak and assemble have opened up space for autonomous women's and religious organizing. Precisely how Muslim-majority democracies address women's issues—that is, who puts issues on the national agenda, how issues are framed, and who has the final say—has mostly gone without comment by social scientists.[10] The lack of research on women's rights policymaking in Muslim-majority democracies is an important gap not just for understanding gender equality in Muslim-majority societies but also for understanding state responsiveness to social movements and the spread of international norms.

This book addresses this gap by examining women's rights debates in the Muslim-majority African country of Niger. Landlocked between the Mediterranean countries of Algeria and Libya and the coastal countries of Benin and Nigeria, Niger forms part of the semiarid Sahel. More than 90 percent of Niger's 13.7 million people are Muslim.[11] Since its first transition to multiparty politics in the early 1990s, Niger has seen vibrant and at times vitriolic debates take place over what the state ought to do about gender inequality. In a country consistently ranked as one of the poorest in the world, analysts would expect what they call religious and traditional values to dominate discussions over women's rights to the point of forestalling reform. Yet some debates in Niger have resulted in far-reaching policy change, while others, to repeat an oft-used expression, have remained in the drawers.

Of numerous debates over women's rights, this book focuses on the conflict that arose over four proposed women's rights reforms in Niger since its first democratic transition. Two proposals to help improve women's lives were adopted by the Nigérien state: (1) the ratification of CEDAW in 1999, and (2) the adoption of a gender-based affirmative action law for all elected offices, positions in the executive cabinet, and promotions in public administration in 2000. In contrast, Niger has yet to complete its (1) revision of its overarching policy on marriage, divorce, and inheritance law, and (2) ratification the African Union's regional treaty on women's rights. The challenge is to explain policy change as well as continuity; policy adoption as well as rejection. This challenge drives the book's central question: *Under what conditions do states adopt women's rights policy?*

The Impact of Mobilization

This book argues that both *how civil society mobilizes* and the *domestic political context* are central to understanding Niger's seemingly inconsistent record of women's rights policy adoption. I break this argument down into three claims. When women's activists mobilize, states are more likely to adopt women's rights policy. Women's activists, however, do not operate in isolation or in a political vacuum. When conservative activists mobilize against reforms, states are less likely to adopt them. Last, the adoption of women's rights policy hinges on the domestic political context.

To give a definition, women's activists mobilize in the name of women, claiming to represent women's interests. By women's activists, I mean women in civil society and in the state. On the former, scholars of women's movements in Africa such as Aili Mari Tripp have focused their analytic lens on the rise and impact of women's activists.[12] A major concern of such scholars was with whether women in society are autonomous from the state. This focus on women's independence from the state was and remains relevant. Women are better able to exert influence when they form their own organizations, when the organizations set their own agendas, and when the organizations select their own leaders. Without these powers, women's activists remain under the thumb of the state, their central purpose being limited to advancing the state's priorities. In the extreme, states repress autonomous women's organizing. Such was the case in authoritarian Nigeria under Ibrahim Babangida, whose government imprisoned the head of the Country Women Association of Nigeria following a confrontation with the Better Life for Rural Women Program, an association led by Babangida's wife.[13]

Autonomous women's associations help advance women's rights reforms, but they rarely work alone. A consensus finding among scholars of social movements is that activists are more likely to succeed when they form alliances with actors with direct control over policymaking, such as political party leaders, parliamentarians, and high-ranking civil servants.[14] A comparative study of women's movements in Europe and Latin America finds that women's interests are more effectively defended when women's activists, politicians, and civil servants form a "triangle of empowerment."[15] Amy Mazur's assessment of the scholarship on feminist policy concludes that women's coalitions are vital to understanding variation in feminist policy outcomes.[16] Mozambique's "extremely progressive" family law reform would not have been adopted without combined pressure from women parliamentarians; the regional women's organization Women and Law in Southern Africa (WLSA); and women's organizations such as Forum Mulher, the Association of Women Lawyers (AMMCJ), and Women, Law, and Development (MULEIDE).[17] Women in civil society, academia, and political parties formed a "triple alliance" in South Africa to lobby for a constitutional article that prioritized gender equality over so-called tradition in 1994 and the adoption of a Domestic Violence Act in 1998.[18] This book similarly suggests that when women in and outside the state mobilize in predominantly Muslim contexts, they are more likely to influence policy adoption.

Indeed, the distinction between civil society and the state may blur in ways that help advance women's interests, as Lee Ann Banaszak demonstrates in her study of feminist bureaucrats in the United States.[19] Women, like the president of CONGAFEN introduced at the beginning of this chapter, may simultaneously work for a state agency and lead a women's organization, facilitating communication between state and civil society. Feminists in state bodies such as Chile's Servicio Nacional de la Mujer (SERNAM) may provide women's movements with a focal point around which to organize, in addition to proposing women's rights policy.[20] Women who begin their careers in the state may later become leaders in civil society, taking their knowledge of how the state works with them. Having close ties with the state, however, may delegitimize the women's movement and deradicalize women's demands. Women's movements may falter if too many of their leaders take up positions in the government or parliament.[21] Nevertheless, when working in concert with women in civil society, women inside the state play a key role in advancing women's rights policy.

Having identified who women's activists are, we can now examine the major ways in which activists influence policy. One important way that women's activists in and outside the state help make reform possible is by putting issues on the national agenda. The importance of this work of making problems public cannot be underestimated. In the absence of women's mobilization, practices that discriminate against women may remain taken for granted or seen as part of the so-called natural order. In the pages that follow, I show that women's activists were the first to name inequality in the family and underrepresentation in elected office as matters of political import, requiring national-level policy change. Attention to women's issues, moreover, may dissipate. Thus, women's repeated mobilization may help keep issues from permanently falling off the national agenda.

Another major way women's activists help advance policy change is by presenting policy proposals as politically legitimate or, to use a term developed by Michael Schatzberg, "thinkable."[22] That is, women's activists propose specific solutions to the problem that they have named. Policy solutions have different meanings; they can be interpreted in multiple ways. In their efforts to make reforms thinkable, women's activists invoke what Schatzberg calls "politically valid subjacent concepts." These concepts may come and go or change depending on the specific historical context. In democratic Niger, women's activists were relatively successful when they were able to tie their proposed reforms to local conceptualizations of democracy and fairness. In addition to appealing to politically legitimate concepts, activists may use salient symbols and causal stories to further make change imaginable. These concepts, symbols, and stories are often deployed through the media and in public rituals. If successful, women's demands become part of the mainstream discourse and appear to represent the will of the public.

The persistent mobilization of women's activists in and outside the state plays a vital role in helping make the adoption of women's rights policy possible. Policy adoption often occurs only after women mobilize around an issue—not in a one-off event but over years or, in some cases, decades. This is because at any point in the policymaking process, women's demands may be derided, ignored, or silenced. Over multiple iterations, women's activists may adjust their demands, form new alliances, and modify their tactics to overcome derision and be heard. Thus, continuing in spite of difficulty over a prolonged period helps make women's rights policy adoption more likely.

The impact of women's movements on policymaking in Muslim-majority countries has not been explored enough. By examining how and under what conditions women's mobilization in Muslim-majority countries influences the uptake of women's rights reforms, this book contributes an important set of case studies to the comparative scholarship on women's movements. Women's mobilization has been found to influence reform in the so-called advanced industrialized world, including the United States.[23] Women's activism has been shown to be an important driver of reform in religiously diverse or predominantly Christian African countries such as Cameroon, Mozambique, South Africa, and Uganda.[24] Scholars have documented the rise, diversity, and dynamism of women in Muslim-majority societies such as Bangladesh, Indonesia, and Morocco, but few have systematically examined the policy impact of women's mobilization in predominantly Muslim societies.[25]

This book's second claim is that the persistent mobilization of opposing activists in and outside the state also plays a vital role in women's rights policymaking. Despite a swell of research on the mobilization of women around the world, little is known about the resistance that women's activists encounter in their efforts to improve women's lives through state channels.

The conservative or opposing actors of interest here are conservative religious activists. Religious activists mobilize in the name of religion, claiming to represent the interests of a religious community. Conservative religious activists are a particular overlapping subcategory of religious activists and conservative activists in that they seek to promote so-called traditional religious values. In Niger, conservative Muslim activists are commonly referred to as Islamists. Because the phenomenon of anti-women's rights mobilization is not limited to Muslims, I prefer to use the broader term *conservative activism*. Like women's activists, conservative activists are more effective in shaping women's rights policy outcomes when they mobilize against women's rights policy repeatedly. In the early years of the democratic transition, conservative activists in Niger were met with disdain by the mainstream press. Over time, however, mainstream newspapers and radio stations treated conservative activists more favorably, inviting conservatives to publish or air long opinion pieces. As a result, conservative activists carved out a space for the articulation of arguments against women's rights reforms in the public sphere. It was through an iterative process that conservative activists avoided marginalization and began to influence women's rights policymaking.

Just as women's advocates rely on having activists inside the state, conservative activists are more successful in influencing women's rights policy debates when they form alliances with statist actors. In Niger, an important state-based source of support for conservative activists is the Association Islamique du Niger (AIN). The AIN, created by President Kountché's government in 1974, is considered the closest entity to a state church. In the democratic transition, the AIN formally became an independent association, but it acts as a quasi-state body. AIN's leaders are often called on by the state to open major religious ceremonies, and the central headquarters in Niamey serves as a semiofficial family law court and civil registry.[26] Conservative activists are better able to sway policymakers when they have the support of the central Islamic association. When conservative activists and the AIN are divided over a women's rights issue, conservative activists struggle to advance reform.

Akin to women's activists, conservative activists play an important role in women's rights policymaking by putting new issues on the national agenda. Though not inherently at odds, conservative activists may place their issues in competition with the concerns of women's activists. In Niger, conservative activists made secularism, or *laïcité*—the state's stance as a secular republic—a public problem. At the end of authoritarian rule, conservative activists demanded that the new constitution identify Niger as a Muslim country. They opposed any inclusion of the term *état laïc,* arguing that the constitution ought to reflect the realities (in their words) of the majority of the Nigérien people.[27] In subsequent years, conservative activists would frame women's demands for family law reform as part of an anti-Muslim, pro-secularist plot.

Recall that a policy proposal can take on multiple meanings. Conservative activists can also influence policymaking by presenting proposed reforms as unthinkable. To present women's rights policy as politically illegitimate, conservative activists may invoke the same politically valid subjacent concepts used by women's activists. In democratic Niger, conservative activists appealed to people's understandings of democracy and fairness to contest women's rights policy proposals. In addition to connecting the policy proposal at hand to other political concepts, conservative activists may deploy salient symbols and construct causal stories through the media and by enacting public rituals. When successful, conservative activists paint a picture of mass opposition to reform. At the extreme, conservative mobilization may make a proposed reform a taboo subject, even among women's activists.

Niger is not the only country where the demands of women's activists are met with organized resistance. Scholars have noted that backlash against women's activism occurs in other parts of Africa. In Mali, women who attended the United Nations World Conference on Women in Beijing in 1995 found that other Malians viewed them as "Westernized," "feminist," and disconnected from Malian realities.[28] An expert on Islam and women's studies in northern Nigeria writes, "Many question [Gender and Development] programs on principle, viewing them as illegitimate because they are 'Western.' In line with this, Muslim women activists, including myself, may be branded Western agents, funded by foreign powers to undermine Islam."[29] In Uganda, a lecturer lamented, "I would say that the idea of feminism was not part and parcel of the Uganda thing, it is something that has been brought in."[30]

Nor is conservative mobilization against women's rights reform unique to Africa. Writing about the former Soviet Union, scholars find that "feminism is not just controversial; it is stigmatized."[31] Women's activists in Canada, the United Kingdom, and the United States have also encountered backlash from other women's leaders, political parties, and conservative organizations.[32] Thus, another contribution of this book is its focus on why states sometimes respond to the demands of conservative religious activists when there is concerted women's mobilization.

Let me be clear that the line between women's activism and conservative activism is porous.[33] In some instances, women's activists and conservative activists may form a common front, coming together to lobby policymakers for reform. Religious activists do not always mobilize against the adoption of women's rights policy. A religious community may become internally divided over women's issues, with some supporting women's rights reform and others opposing reform. At times religious activists are neutral, neither opposing nor supporting the adoption of women's rights policy. These shifts reflect the fact that women's activists and religious activists are not silos but dynamic, interactive entities.

I have thus far focused on how women's activists and conservative activists influence women's rights policymaking. The third claim that this book advances is that the national-level political context in which women's rights debates occur is important. Here I will discuss how the domestic political context matters.

States are not unitary actors. While scholars tend to view African politics as ruled by "big men," African states are composed of multiple actors, and significant negotiation may take place among them.[34] In democratic states, entities other than the executive branch ostensibly have the power to modify and reject proposed legislation. In moving between authoritarian and democratic rule, Niger oscillated between having no elected parliament, a relatively dependent parliament, and a relatively autonomous parliament. These changes affected women's rights policymaking. This is because a relatively autonomous parliament is a veto player, an actor whose approval is required to change the status quo.[35] In the chapters that follow, I show that in the case of the gender quota law and in the case of the Maputo Protocol, a relatively autonomous parliament modified or rejected women's policy proposals. In contexts where parliaments have such powers, the backing of the president, though important, is not always sufficient for the adoption of women's rights policy.

Parliament is an unusual state actor to make a center of focus. Scholars of African politics generally expect parliaments to play a minimal role in policymaking. African parliaments typically follow British or French models, in which the parliament's primary function is to debate, question, and affirm government-directed policy.[36] The implication is that the locus of policymaking lies in the ministries, not in parliament. "Instead, the action is elsewhere," as two analysts of Senegal's National Assembly write, in providing constituency services and seeking out donor funding to help advance their districts' economic development.[37] In Africa's illiberal democracies, moreover, power is highly centralized in the presidency such that the parliament operates like a rubber stamp.[38] I present case studies from an African liberal democracy where parliament can and does intervene in policy debates.

In addition to varying in terms of parliamentary autonomy, the political context varies in the degree to which religious authorities wield political influence. Church-state relations may in one time period be separate and antagonistic and characterized by assertive or extreme secularism.[39] In political contexts where church and state are assertively separated, religious authorities have less say over policymaking. Well-known examples of countries with a strict separation of church and state are France since the late nineteenth century, Tunisia under Habib Bourguiba's presidency, and Turkey during Mustafa Kemal Atatürk's reign. At the other end of the spectrum, church-state relations may be fused. Where church and state are closely intertwined, religious authorities have greater powers over policymaking. Iran since its 1979 revolution is a prime example of a religious state.

Most states fall in the middle of the spectrum between assertive secularism and strict clericalism. In these contexts, religious authority is public but partial. The United States and Senegal are examples of these passive secularist states. Where the state is neither pro-church nor anti-church, religious authorities do not have complete control over policymaking. Yet religious authorities are seen as legitimate players on the political field; their input on policy proposals may be sought and respected. Thus, policymaking may become stalled when women's activists and conservative religious activists clash over reform.

The Nigérien state partially and uneasily relies on religious authorities to carry out some of the state's day-to-day tasks. Courts are allowed to apply a combination of so-called customary and Islamic law to resolve disputes over marriage, divorce, and inheritance. The state has maintained close ties with Muslim leaders through the AIN, whose central headquarters serves as a semi-official court and civil registry through which Nigériens can register marriages, formalize divorces, and seek resolutions in matters of inheritance. Nigérien presidents regularly invite AIN's leaders to officiate religious-state holidays and seek the blessing of religious leaders such as Cheick Kiota and Mama Kiota of the Niassene *Tijaniyya* Muslim congregation—arguably the largest religious order in the country.

At the same time, Niger is officially a secular state. Successive constitutions emphasize the separation of the state from religion in Niger.[40] Unlike Nigeria to the south, where states in the northern part of the country have expanded the use of so-called Islamic law, most Nigériens are not interested in seeing their country turn into an Islamic state.[41] The *Tijaniyya* leadership does not call for the integration of Islam into politics, nor do Niger's Muslim politicians. Nigériens are aware of the extension of Islamic law across northern Nigeria and have close cultural and economic ties with their neighbors. The discourse of political Islam and the hardliner religious organizations of northern Nigeria has spread to Niger, but those calling for an Islamic state remain in the minority.[42]

This ambiguous position between extreme secularism and extreme clericalism is, according to political scientist Abdourahmane Idrissa, "a central element which defines the contemporary Nigerien context."[43] I contend that this dual stance influences women's rights policymaking. With the state's partial reliance on the church, religious authorities, including conservative religious activists, become informal veto players. Furthermore, once hardened, partial power-sharing arrangements between state and church become institutions in and of themselves, having long-lasting effects on how citizens and the state conceive what is thinkable and unthinkable.[44] Mounira Charrad has made a similar observation for authoritarian Algeria, where the postindependence state formed partial alliances with traditional and religious elites and subsequently struggled for decades to reform its family law.[45] I show that partial alliances between church and state resulted in protracted women's rights policymaking in a Muslim-majority democracy when conservative activists mobilized against reform.

In sum, women's mobilization, conservative mobilization, and the domestic political context in which actors vie for influence are important for understanding how women's rights policies are made. As political scientist Margaret Levi writes, "Policies are the outcome of an exchange between the ruler and the various groups who compose the polity."[46] How states seek to regulate the lives of women and men are not the direct outcome of so-called religious doctrine—a commonplace argument that I address next.

The Conventional Wisdom

By examining women's rights policy adoption in a predominantly Muslim country, this book demonstrates that the relationship between Islam and gender equality is not as simple as some claim.

The 9/11 attacks in the United States renewed interest in Muslim women. U.S. policymakers argued that "saving" Muslim women would help prevent future attacks.[47] Within this context, a 2002 study by a political scientist argued that "Muslim societies are distinct" in their "treatment and status of women and girls," which ultimately hinders democratization.[48] Two other political scientists, Ronald Inglehart and Pippa Norris, published in 2003 a major study on attitudes toward gender equality in seventy countries. Inglehart and Norris found that Muslims tend to hold the most conservative attitudes about gender equality, more so than their Catholic, Protestant, Jewish, Hindu, and Buddhist counterparts. This finding led the authors to conclude that "an Islamic religious heritage is one of the most powerful barriers to the rising tide of gender equality."[49]

These post-9/11 studies are not the first to attribute women's subordination on the Islamic faith. In the 1980s and 1990s, researchers argued that Catholic countries were more conservative on issues of gender equality and thus had lower levels of women's political representation.[50] Other studies found that the percentage of a population that is Muslim negatively correlates with the percentage of women in parliament, and that Muslim-majority countries tend to grant women suffrage later than do non-Muslim-majority countries.[51]

There are four reasons, however, to be skeptical toward claims that Islam is a worse religion for women than are others. One cause for skepticism has to do with sample selection bias, which occurs when analysts use nonrandom samples of information to make generalizations about a larger population. This kind of bias threatens the external and internal validity of one's study.[52] Scholars and others commit sample selection bias when they extrapolate findings from predominantly Muslim countries in the Middle East to the rest of the Muslim world. Muslim-majority societies in the Middle East are not representative of all Muslim societies. As Alfred Stepan and Graeme Robertson argue, predominantly Muslim countries in the Middle East have distinctive histories of authoritarian rule, high military spending, interstate conflict, and great power patronage that make them exceptional and not representative of Muslim-majority countries.[53] Correspondingly, some studies find that the status of women in Arab Muslim countries is significantly lower than that of other predominantly Muslim countries.[54] Yet others still confound a world region with a world religion. For example, a 1997 study on women's rights around the world finds that "in practice, dominant interpretations of the Qur'an inhibit or constrain women's ability to achieve political and economic equality."[55] This claim, however, is based on information from the Middle East and North Africa, whereas the largest Muslim publics live outside the region, in countries such as Indonesia, Nigeria, and Pakistan.

Studies that rely on public opinion data to understand the relationship between Islam and women's rights further suffer from sample selection bias because individuals in Muslim-majority countries are less frequently surveyed than are individuals in other kinds of countries. Between 1981 and the end of 2009, less than 14 percent of Muslim-majority countries were polled by the World Values Survey (on which Inglehart and Norris rely). In contrast, the World Values Survey reached more than 35 percent of non-Muslim-majority countries. I do not fault the World Values Survey for its relative lack of coverage of Muslim countries. The financial resources necessary for conducting large-scale surveys are significant. The surveys reach out to "ordinary" people, which elite-focused studies ignore, and they go to the most populous countries in the world. Yet the existing survey evidence from which scholars discern a negative relationship between Islam and women's rights does not adequately represent the spectrum of Muslim-majority countries in the world.

A second reason to question the conventional wisdom on Islam and women's rights has to do with spurious correlation. Michael Ross argues that it is not Islam that hurts women but natural gas and oil production.[56] Natural resource dependence, according to Ross, generates negative externalities for women in two ways: oil and mineral extraction tends to result in the employment of male workers over female workers, and it crowds out other industries that tend to employ women, such as textiles manufacturing. In oil- and mineral-rich countries, then, women are pushed into working in the informal economy, where they are more dispersed than are women who work in factories. As a result, women in oil- and mineral-rich countries have fewer opportunities to collectively mobilize. Norris's response to Ross's study maintains, "Patriarchal cultures in Arab states . . . have enduring historical roots that predate the discovery and production of oil."[57] Yet as discussed above, Arab countries are not representative of all predominantly Muslim countries.

Third, the conventional thinking about women's rights and Islam homogenizes and reifies Muslims, whereas in reality, the practice of Islam is diverse and dynamic. For instance, Inglehart and Norris assert, "Divorce is an important issue, especially in a few Catholic and many Muslim societies, where women have limited or no legal rights to dissolve the marriage."[58] Yet in Muslim-majority societies such as those in Indonesia, Malaysia, and across West Africa that follow the Maliki school of Islamic legal thought, women have legal rights to seek divorce.[59] According to court records of divorce cases in 1979, the divorce rate in northern Nigeria, which makes up one of the largest groups of Muslims in sub-Saharan Africa, was three times the divorce rate in the United States. Luigi Solivetti goes so far as to note that divorce "is a distinctive feature of Hausa society."[60] In Barbara Cooper's study of marriage in urban and rural Maradi, out of 212 marriages undertaken by 105 women, 51 percent ended in divorce.[61] Studies of the use of colonial courts in what is now known as Mali find that Muslim women sought out divorce in the courts more often than did men.[62]

To provide another illustration, some may see veiling and wife seclusion as indicators of women's low status. Arlene MacLeod's study of working-class women in Cairo, however, finds that wearing a veil can both empower women and perpetuate gender ideologies.[63] If religious practices carry multiple and at times contradictory meanings for women, then it makes it difficult to rank "low" and "high" women's status by world religion. Scholars have found that women's participation in the formal economy varies widely across predominantly Muslim countries.[64] Abdullahi An-Na'im, a scholar of Islam and human rights, finds that opinions about gender norms differ among Sufi variants of Islam in Africa.[65]

Opinions about gender equality can change.[66] The sentiment that men make better political leaders in African countries may have roots not in Islamic doctrine but in colonial government decisions to favor only male "traditional" leaders. Judith Van Allen observes that the decline of Igbo women's political power was a consequence of British colonial rule. Her analysis of "the Victorian view of women and politics which produced the expectation that men would be active in politics, but women would not" turns political culture assertions about "traditional" societies on their head.[67] Colonial policy is just one of many factors, such as precolonial shifts in power relations related to new forms of trade, that may lead to a decline of female leaders.[68] The idea that men should have more right to employment and university education is not unfamiliar to those who are knowledgeable about the ways in which colonial governments excluded women from wage labor and formal education opportunities.[69]

Finally, the conventional thinking about Islam and women's rights does not explain variation in women's rights outcomes across Africa. Figure 1 plots the percentage of the population that is Muslim against the percentage of women in parliament in fifty-three African countries as of the end of 2012. If Muslims were particularly anti–women's rights, then one would expect countries at the right end of the figure to have lower percentages of women in parliament. The evidence, however, does not support the conventional wisdom: there is no statistically significant difference in women's numerical representation between African countries with higher percentages of Muslims and African countries with lower percentages of Muslims.

Nor does the Islamic barrier hypothesis explain trends in the adoption of gender quotas in Africa. Gender quotas have a major impact on the percentage of women elected to public office around the world.[70] If countries with an Islamic heritage had lower levels of support for gender equality, then one would expect countries with high percentages of Muslims to be less likely to adopt gender quotas. As of December 31, 2009, political parties or governments in thirteen out of nineteen Muslim-majority African countries adopted

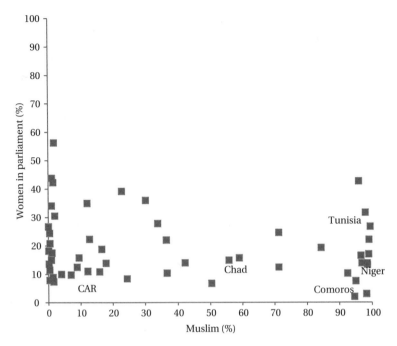

Figure 1. Women's numerical representation in parliament in Africa, 2012

Note: N=53 countries. The figure does not include South Sudan. The figure refers to unicameral or lower house parliaments as of December 31, 2012. See Inter-Parliamentary Union (IPU), "Women in National Parliaments, Situation as of 31 December 2012"; Pew Forum on Religion and Public Life, *Mapping the Global Muslim Population*, 29–31. Data on women in parliament in Ghana and Guinea come from IPU, "PARLINE Database on National Parliaments."

gender quotas for national legislative posts. In contrast, political parties or governments in slightly more than half of thirty-three non-Muslim-majority African countries adopted quotas.

I find that Muslim-majority African countries have been no slower to adopt gender quotas. Indeed, some of the earliest adopters of gender quotas were predominantly Muslim countries. One of the first African countries to adopt a law mandating a gender quota was Egypt (95 percent Muslim) in 1979.[71] One of the first major political parties to adopt a voluntary gender quota was in Senegal (96 percent Muslim) in 1982.[72] Perhaps Muslim-majority countries adopt gender quotas to overcome the public's bias against women candidates. If Muslim voters oppose having women in office, then why would parties and governments adopt quotas and risk losing votes? A more detailed understanding of the politics of women's rights in Muslim-majority countries is necessary.

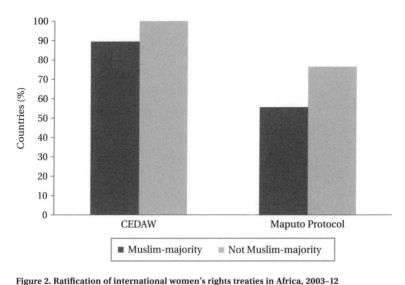

Figure 2. Ratification of international women's rights treaties in Africa, 2003–12

Note: N=53 countries for CEDAW. N=52 countries for the Maputo Protocol. The figure does not include South Sudan. The Maputo Protocol columns do not include Morocco because Morocco was not a member of the AU between 2003 and 2012. See UN Treaty Collection (TC), "Convention on the Elimination of All Forms of Discrimination against Women"; African Union, "List of Countries . . ."; Pew Forum on Religion and Public Life, *Mapping the Global Muslim Population,* 29–31.

Whether a country is predominantly Muslim does not explain differences in the commitment of African countries to international women's rights treaties. Figure 2 shows the percentage of Muslim-majority and non-Muslim-majority countries that ratified CEDAW and the Protocol to the African Charter on Human and Peoples' Rights on the Rights of Women in Africa (the Maputo Protocol) by the end of 2012. One hundred percent of non-Muslim-majority countries ratified CEDAW (34 out of 34), and 89 percent of Muslim-majority countries ratified CEDAW (17 out of 19), a difference that is not statistically significant using Fisher's exact test. Slightly more than 76 percent of predominantly Christian or religiously mixed countries ratified the Maputo Protocol (26 out of 34), and 55.6 percent of predominantly Muslim countries ratified the Maputo Protocol (10 out of 18)—a difference that is also not statistically significant using Fisher's exact test.

Two African countries that have not ratified CEDAW are Somalia and Sudan, which are predominantly Muslim (98.5 and 71 percent, respectively). This could lend support to the conventional wisdom that predominantly Muslim countries are more wary of promoting women's rights. Yet one still needs to explain why the majority of predominantly Muslim countries in Africa, such as Algeria, Egypt, Mali, and Senegal, have ratified CEDAW. It is also true that many Muslim-majority African countries issued reservations to CEDAW, more so than did Christian-majority or religiously mixed African countries.[73] More than a third of Muslim-majority countries issued reservations on CEDAW (7 out of 19).[74] In contrast, slightly more than 8 percent of non-Muslim countries issued reservations (3 out of 36). However, one is still left with the challenge of explaining differences among predominantly Muslim countries. Guinea, Mali, and Senegal, for instance, did not place reservations on CEDAW.

Religiosity does not help explain patterns in the ratification of women's rights treaties. Take, for instance, African countries in which 80 to 85 percent of survey respondents said that religion was somewhat or very important in their lives. Among these countries, the number of years it took to ratify CEDAW varied from one year (Cape Verde) to seventeen years (Botswana). Now take African countries in which more than 95 percent of survey respondents reported that religion was somewhat or very important in their lives. Liberia, which is highly religious, ratified CEDAW in five years. Lesotho, which is also highly religious, took sixteen years to ratify the convention. These patterns across Africa show that Islam cannot explain whether and how soon countries commit to promoting women's rights in Africa. As Sondra Hale, a critic of "overprivileging Islam," asserts, "Islam does not and cannot explain the condition of women."[75]

Studies that posit a link between Islam and women's rights do not make it clear how the predominance of one religion would eventually result in women's rights policy adoption or rejection. For all the attention that analysts give to women in Muslim-majority countries, we lack an adequate theoretical understanding of how states adopt women's rights policies and why attempts at reform sometimes fail.

Additional and Alternative Explanations for Women's Rights Policymaking

Other factors may help explain why states adopt women's rights policy when they do. These potential influences include the international context, the ideology of the leader or political party in power, and the attributes of the proposed policy. I show that although these are important, they do not fully explain Niger's record of policy adoption and rejection.

The international context can influence women's rights policy adoption in many ways. For one, states that care about their international reputation may be more likely to adopt women's rights policies when the adoption of the policy has become an international norm. Two scholars, Christine Wotipka and Francisco Ramirez, analyzed the ratification of CEDAW in 142 countries between 1979 and 1999.[76] In their findings, they show that states paid attention to what others did. As more states in the world (or in the region) ratified CEDAW, slower-moving states were more likely to follow suit. In the absence of an international norm, states may not see an issue as important enough to address. Jennifer Chan-Tiberghien contends that Japan did not adopt policies to protect minority groups until the 2000s because the international community did not pay much attention to minority rights until 2001.[77] Similarly, Japan's leaders only began to address issues of birth control, sexual harassment, and domestic violence after the 1995 United Nations Conference on Women in Beijing.

Indeed, as I will show in this book, in Niger, leaders were attuned to the international discourse surrounding women's rights. For the most part, Nigérien leaders did not like having their country ranked at the bottom of any list, whether it be in terms of wealth or women's representation. Women's activists compared Niger with other countries and invoked global trends to argue for policy change. At the same time, conservative activists in Niger challenged the idea that their country was behind the rest of the world and saw Niger's ostensibly low status as a thinly veiled critique of the fact that the country is predominantly Muslim.

Second, states may be more likely to adopt women's rights policy when their international donors support the change; that is, the international context may provide material incentives for states to enact women's rights policy.[78] President Paul Biya of Cameroon, for instance, adopted women's rights policies in part to attract foreign aid to fuel domestic patronage.[79] Another study finds that countries that receive higher levels of foreign aid are faster to adopt gender quotas.[80] Other studies, however, do not find a correlation between foreign aid and other women's rights outcomes.[81] This book shows that women's rights policymaking can be stalled even when international donors lobby for policy change.

Third, states may be more likely to adopt women's rights policies when local activists connect with activists from other countries. Transnational advocacy networks (TANs) have been shown to influence human rights outcomes around the world, as well as the adoption of gender quota laws.[82] The scholarship on TANs, however, does not adequately explain what happens when countermovements emerge. Nor does the scholarship fully address the possibility that TAN activity may inspire countermobilization.[83] The dominant models of TAN effectiveness assume that there are only two major actors—the state and pro-rights activists—whereas this book presents a three-actor framework.[84]

The last remaining way in which the international context might influence women's rights policymaking is through international law. Through an incremental process of "judicial policymaking," the European Court of Justice (ECJ) expanded the protection of women's pregnancy and maternity leave policy in the European Union's member states.[85] A coalition of international and Nigérien lawyers used the Economic Community of West African States (ECOWAS) Court of Justice to enforce Niger's 2003 antislavery law. The Court of Justice fined the Nigérien state for not meeting its obligations to a woman who was a slave, Hadijatou Mani.[86] The ruling is now binding for ECOWAS's fifteen member states. A significant body of research suggests that states that ratify CEDAW adopt more women's rights policies than states that do not, and it appears that women's living conditions improve more in countries that have ratified CEDAW than in countries that have not.[87] In a study of more than 132 countries, ratifying CEDAW decreased the gender gap in education and increased the likelihood that a state would adopt policies allowing greater access to contraception.[88]

The ideology of the country's leader or party in power might influence women's rights policymaking. For example, Habib Bourguiba of Muslim-majority Tunisia was ideologically committed to changing gender relations in his country. (In his will, Bourguiba asked that his mausoleum be inscribed with the words, "Supreme Combatant, Father of the Tunisian Nation, and Liberator of Tunisian Women.")[89] Under Bourguiba's rule, the government passed sweeping family law reform in 1956 that included the abolishment of polygamy. Thirty years earlier, Mustafa Kemal Atatürk of Turkey enacted a series of reforms based on an ideological commitment to secularizing the country. Women's movements in western Europe were more successful when the party in power leaned to the left, and leftist parties have done a better job of recruiting female candidates to run for office than have non-leftist parties.[90] Since the 1970s, Democrats in national and state legislatures in the United States have been more likely to propose and vote in favor of women-friendly legislation than have Republicans.[91]

On the other hand, left-leaning leaders and political parties can and do fall short of promises to promote equality between women and men. Having a left-leaning party in power did not influence whether states adopted women-friendly employment and child-care policies in France, the Netherlands, Sweden, or the United States.[92] The Provisional National Defense Council in

Ghana under Jerry Rawlings was a leftist party, but it also suppressed autonomous women's mobilization.[93] In South Africa, the left-of-center African National Congress has increasingly disappointed feminist activists.[94]

Last, the attributes of the proposed reform might affect its adoption. Policy proposals that touch on so-called doctrinal issues may be met with more controversy and slower adoption than proposals that do not.[95] A limitation with this explanation, however, is whether one can determine a priori which issues are doctrinal and which ones are not, because religious texts like the Bible and the Qur'an cover an extraordinarily wide variety of issues, from business to education to reproductive health. Omnibus reforms may be more difficult to pass than single-issue reforms.[96] The thinking here is that the more articles and issues addressed in a reform, the higher the chances that someone will find something to object to. The proposed and rejected 1994 family law reform in Niger was an omnibus policy containing more than nine hundred articles. Yet similarly large pieces of family law legislation have been adopted in other predominantly Muslim countries, such as Morocco, Senegal, and Tunisia. In this book, I analyze the politics behind two omnibus women's rights treaties: one that was ratified and one that was rejected. A final way of thinking about policy attributes and whether they influence policy adoption is to examine the perceived impact of the reform on gender relations. Gender role change policies, which would potentially make women less dependent on men, may be more difficult to pass than role equity policies, which simply extend rights to women. That is, one might expect women's rights reforms to pass more easily when they do not challenge existing gender norms.[97]

Why Niger?

This book's central arguments were developed by comparing cases of women's rights policy adoption and rejection within a single country, the Republic of Niger.[98] Niger's debates over women's rights merit wider attention because they defy two conventional wisdoms. One, addressed earlier, is that having a long history of Islam hinders the advancement of gender equality. Empirically, Niger challenges the Islamic barrier hypothesis because it adopted policies to promote women's political representation and access to family planning. The other conventional wisdom is that poor countries do the bidding of their international donors. In terms of per capita gross domestic product, Niger is one of the poorest countries in the world, taking in a significant amount of international aid. Yet Niger has resisted appeals from international donors, including the World Bank, to reform its family laws.

YEARS	REGIME	REPUBLIC	PRESIDENT
1960-74	Authoritarian	First Republic	Hamani Diori
1974-87	Authoritarian	Régime d'exception	Seyni Kountché
1987-89	Authoritarian	Régime d'exception	Ali Saibou
1989-91	Authoritarian	Second Republic	Ali Saibou
1991-93	Transitional		Ali Saibou
1993-96	Democratic	Third Republic	Mahamane Ousmane
1996	Transitional		Ibrahim Baré Maïnassara
1996-99	Authoritarian	Fourth Republic	Ibrahim Baré Maïnassara
1999	Transitional		Daouda Malam Wanké
1999-2009	Democratic	Fifth Republic	Mamadou Tandja
2009	Transitional		Mamadou Tandja
2009-10	Authoritarian	Sixth Republic	Mamadou Tandja
2010-11	Transitional		Salou Djibo
2011-	Democratic	Seventh Republic	Mahamadou Issoufou

Figure 3. Regimes, republics, and rulers in Niger, 1960-2012

Niger's experimentation with authoritarian, transitional, and democratic rule provides additional insight into the question of when states adopt women's rights policies. Between 1993 and 2011, Niger witnessed three successful military coups d'état, three competitive presidential elections, and at least one period of authoritarian rule (see Figure 3). Did debates over women's rights take a notably different turn in democratic contexts than in authoritarian contexts? It is useful for readers unfamiliar with Niger to first have an overview of Niger's political history.

Niger gained independence from France on August 1, 1960. Between 1960 and 1989, three authoritarian governments ruled Niger. Niger's first president, Hamani Diori, oversaw the elimination of all opposition parties. Diori was deposed in a military coup in 1974. His successor, Lieutenant Colonel Seyni Kountché, enacted a period of *régime d'exception*, which banned political parties in general and dissolved the national parliament. When Kountché died of a brain tumor in 1987, Colonel Ali Saibou became Niger's third president. Saibou ushered in a period of *décrispation*, in which political prisoners were freed and noncompetitive presidential elections were held.

The stories presented in this book pick up in the early 1990s. Shortly after coming to power, Ali Saibou conceded that authoritarian rule was no longer viable in Niger. In 1991, under Saibou's authorization, Niger's leading politicians and intellectuals held a national conference (following the example of Benin, Niger's neighbor to the south). Participants at the conference promulgated a new constitution that established a semipresidential, democratic regime. Mahamane Ousmane, an economist and statistician from Zinder, won the 1993 presidential election by forming a coalition with other opposition parties.

Political infighting resulted in government deadlock until 1996, when the military overthrew Ousmane in a bloodless coup. Colonel Ibrahim Baré Maïnassara, an orchestrator of the military takeover, headed the political transition and ran for president in a race plagued by fraud and boycotts from the opposition. Between 1996 and Baré's unexpected death in 1999, Niger was judged by most comparative standards to be an autocracy.[99] Under General Daouda Malam Wanké, relatively free and fair presidential and legislative elections were held in 1999. The 1999 transfer of power from a transitional to a competitively elected government marked a return to democracy in Niger until 2010, when President Mamadou Tandja dissolved the Constitutional Court and the National Assembly and organized a controversial constitutional referendum in August 2009 so that he could run for a third term. In the midst of massive demonstrations both against and for Tandja, the military invaded the presidential palace and arrested Tandja in February 2010. Yet another transitional government organized free and fair presidential and parliamentary elections in 2011.

Methods

I focus on four proposed women's rights reforms in the book. They are the ratification of CEDAW (which occurred in 1999), the adoption of a gender quota (which occurred in 2000), the reform of family law (which was repeatedly rejected), and the ratification of the Maputo Protocol (which was repeatedly rejected). This comparative case method allows me to make analytical generalizations about the causal mechanisms of policy adoption.[100]

Of the at least forty-one women-friendly policies that Niger considered between 1960 and 2008, I selected these four for several reasons (see Figure 4).[101] As previously indicated, it is important to examine the politics behind policies

ISSUE	YEARS	WOMEN'S ACTIVISTS	CONSERVATIVE ACTIVISTS	INTERNATIONAL COMMUNITY	FORMAL VETO PLAYERS	OUTCOME
Family law	1960–2011	Mobilized	Mobilized	Mobilized	Executive cabinet	Rejected
Gender quota law	1999–2001	Mobilized	Not mobilized	Not mobilized	Executive cabinet, National Assembly	Adopted with amendments
CEDAW	1994–99	Mobilized	Mobilized	Mobilized	Executive cabinet	Ratified with reservations
Maputo Protocol	2002–11	Mobilized	Mobilized	Mobilized	Executive cabinet, National Assembly	Ratification rejected

Figure 4. Women's rights reforms examined in the book

that were rejected as well as those that were adopted. Family law reform, arguably the most contentious women's rights issue in democratic Niger, was repeatedly brought up, debated, and abandoned. By contrast, the adoption of a gender quota law is, for many women's activists, a relative success story. CEDAW and the Maputo Protocol are both omnibus treaties, yet they met different outcomes; given that previous studies suggest that omnibus policy proposals are more difficult to adopt than single-issue proposals, I wanted to understand why one omnibus policy would be adopted and not another. Women mobilized for all four reforms, and conservative activists mobilized for three of the four; their varying degrees of success help me tease out whether and how activism influences policy adoption and non-adoption.

Earlier, I outlined the general expectation that international trends and donors influence low-income countries. Across these policies and over time, I examine the different kinds and levels of involvement of international norms and actors on policymaking. International actors supported the adoption of family law reform, the ratification of CEDAW, and the Maputo Protocol, yet Niger adopted only one of these proposed reforms. The international community, as I show later in this book, was only minimally or indirectly involved in lobbying for the adoption of the gender quota law (though the international community mobilized to help implement the quota after its adoption).

To identify the conditions under which states adopt women's rights policy, I conducted 14 months of fieldwork between 2006 and the beginning of 2013 in Niger.[102] I interviewed 133 people, some multiple times over the course of several years. By the end of my fieldwork, I had spoken with 36 women's activists, 29 religious activists, 27 bureaucrats and judges, 9 ministers, 21 parliamentarians, and 14 representatives of the international community.[103] Seventy-one interviewees were women, and 62 were men. I gathered primary sources, such as declarations and pamphlets produced by women's and conservative associations, draft legislation, recordings of parliamentary debates, parliamentary committee reports, and stories from the state-backed *Le Sahel* and the independent *Le Républicain* (among other newspapers). Some of the book's arguments crystallized in moments of personal observation or conversation. I attended religious ceremonies, women's day parades, conferences, and workshops organized by the Ministry of Social Development, and when possible, I watched the evening television news. (For more on how I gathered evidence, see the Research Methods appendix.)

The modus operandi in doing the fieldwork was to retrace as many steps of the policymaking process as possible: When was policy change first proposed in and outside the state, and by whom? Who supported the proposed policy in and outside the state? What resources did activists have at their disposal, and what tactics did they employ to influence policymaking? When did countermobilization emerge in and outside the state, and by whom? What resources did conservative activists have at their disposal, and what tactics did they employ to influence policymaking? At what stages can a proposed policy be stalled or rejected? Who has the power to restart the process and to adopt policy? What formal and informal rules do policymakers follow? In other words, I undertook a microlevel investigation into women's rights policymaking.

The majority of interviews took place in Niamey, where much of the bargaining over national-level women's rights reform occurred. Niamey is a trilingual city, where it is not uncommon to hear French, Hausa, and Zarma in a single conversation. Many of the interviews were conducted in French, in which I am proficient. To not exclude non-Francophone Nigériens from my investigations, I asked friends or research assistants to accompany me and interpret for Hausaphones and Zarmaphones into French or English. To understand whether and how women's and religious activists mobilized for or against women's rights policy outside Niamey, I interviewed women's activists, religious activists, bureaucrats, and "ordinary" people in the towns of Dosso, Maradi, and Zinder and in the village of Kiota.

Most Muslims in Niger are Sunni, yet there is great diversity among the faithful. Some Muslims adhere to a Sufi Sunni order, particularly the *Qadiriyya* (whose origins can be traced to Mauritania) or the *Tijaniyya* (whose origins can be traced to Morocco). Others follow the *Wahhabi* or *Salafi* movements (whose origins can be traced to Saudi Arabia and whose ideas flow from northern Nigeria). I tried to ensure that the interviewees covered a range of orders.

When friends and colleagues in the United States and Niger learn about my research, they are sometimes intrigued not by the study itself but by the person doing the study. I am a Korean American female Buddhist who visited Niger while I was in my late twenties and early thirties, unmarried, and childless. Although I presented myself as a U.S.-based researcher with a business card from an American university, it is likely that some of my interviewees either saw me as a Korean studying in the United States or incorrectly assumed that I was Chinese, which also happens in the United States. At times, older interviewees referred to me as *ma fille;* it is quite possible that our conversations would have gone in a different direction had I been older, been married, and had children. Still, interviewees spoke rather openly with me about what I considered taboo topics based on my own upbringing. In particular, conservative religious men and women spoke frankly to me about sex, which surprised me. Some friends suggested my status as a foreign researcher may have made it easier to gain access to higher-level ministry and political party officials, though the ease of obtaining interviews and documents highly varied across ministries.

Ultimately, I sought to understand women's rights politics in Niger as, to use Chandra Talpade Mohanty's words, a feminist in solidarity rather than a feminist tourist or feminist explorer.[104] Feminists in solidarity, for Mohanty, seek to narrow the distance and identify points of commonality among women while recognizing differences in political context and priorities. Thus, as I sifted through the small mountain of materials I had gathered in Niger, I compared women's rights debates in Niger with what scholars have learned about women's rights debates in the United States and in other countries. At the same time, I tried to appreciate the particularities of the time and place I was studying.

Defining Women's Rights Policy

Women's rights reforms are reforms, decrees, or laws made in the name of improving women's lives. This definition follows Christina Wolbrecht's work on women's rights policies as policies that "concern women *as women.*"[105] Gender equality policies are similar to women's rights policies. Note, however, that the former seeks to address women's status vis-à-vis mens, whereas the latter may maintain women's position in society relative to men's. For instance, a state subsidy to allow women to take paid maternity leave may seek to help women as women; it may also reify inequities in men's and women's work at home. A gender equality policy would provide parental leave for men and women to encourage a more equitable share of involvement in child rearing. I found in my interviews that many women's activists did not like to frame policies as *feminist* because of the negative connotations surrounding the word in the 1990s and 2000s.[106] Thus, in this book, I prefer to use *women's rights* or *women-friendly policy.*

I do not assume that women's rights policy adoption will automatically and uniformly improve women's lives. Policies adopted in the name of promoting women's rights may be used in ways that oppress women, including women minorities. For example, in the late 1990s, the Peruvian government enacted a mass sterilization campaign targeting poor, rural, and indigenous women by using a global feminist discourse to hide its population control agenda, with the support of feminist activists.[107] Nor do I assume that women's rights policy is the only type of policy that affects women's lives. Other policy areas, such as education, health, immigration, security, and welfare, may have a direct impact on the protection or violation of women's rights.

Plan of the Book

The book offers an analytic framework for understanding the adoption, and rejection, of women's rights policies. The framework focuses on the mobilization of social groups and the national-level political context. Chapter 1 situates Niger in a historical lens. The book then develops the central claims about mobilization and political context in chapters 2, 3, 4, and the conclusion.

Chapter 2 analyzes Niger's most controversial women's issue: family law reform. Women's activists in and outside the state helped put the issue of women's rights in marriage, divorce, and inheritance on the national agenda. Yet in spite of repeated demands (and the encouragement of international donors), Niger did not overhaul its laws governing marriage, divorce, and inheritance. Conservative activists, in the wake of a national debate over the issue of secularism, opposed family law reform on the grounds that it was anti-Muslim and pro-secularist. Making the proposed reform unthinkable, conservative activists publicly cursed three proponents of the reform in the early 1990s and burned a draft family law bill in the early 2010s. These public rituals intimidated women's activists and policymakers alike into abandoning the family law project.

In chapter 3, I examine the politics behind the first legal gender quota to be adopted by a Muslim-majority democracy. Niger's quota mandates that at least 10 percent of elected positions (e.g., parliamentary seats) and at least 25 percent of ministerial posts and promotions in public administration go to each sex. Niger adopted a quota through a combination of women's mobilization, a lack of countermobilization, and a political context in which the National Assembly had relative autonomy. Women's activists in and outside the state helped put the issue of women's representation on the national agenda and helped make affirmative action thinkable. A veto player, parliament, vigorously debated over the gender quota, ultimately arriving at a compromise that weakened a key component of the bill.

Chapter 4 compares Niger's ratification of CEDAW with the nonratification of the Maputo Protocol. Concerted women's mobilization, divided conservative mobilization, and the absence of an autonomous National Assembly help us understand the ratification of CEDAW. Divided women's mobilization, concerted conservative mobilization, and the relative autonomy of the National Assembly help us understand the nonratification of the Maputo Protocol.

The conclusion summarizes the book's main findings. Although the book is about women and politics in an African country, it carries broader implications for the study of Muslim women's agency, women's movements, and international women's rights, which I discuss here. Finally, I identify where the scholarship on women and politics ought to go next.

1 A FRENCH COLONIAL LEGACY

The Making of Niger's Legal System

Native justice applies in all matters of local customs, insofar as they are not contrary to the principles of French civilization.

—**DECREE OF 1903, ARTICLE 75** (ROBERTS, "CUSTOM AND MUSLIM
FAMILY LAW IN THE NATIVE COURTS OF THE FRENCH SOUDAN," 89)

Native courts will judge applying either Malikite rites . . . or by applying local traditions in regions where Muslim influence is not yet strong. Such application will be mostly in civil matters, property, obligations, contracts, marriage, affiliation, child custody, inheritance.

—**GOVERNOR-GENERAL OF FRENCH WEST AFRICA ERNEST ROUME,
1904** (ROBERTS, "CUSTOM AND MUSLIM FAMILY LAW IN THE NATIVE
COURTS OF THE FRENCH SOUDAN," 90N18)

The jurisdictions apply the customs of the parties:
1. In cases concerning . . . personal status, family, marriage, divorce, parentage, inheritance, gifts, and wills;
2. In those regarding property or property ownership and the rights arising therein.

—**RÉPUBLIQUE DU NIGER, LAW OF 1962, ARTICLE 51**
(TRIAUD "L'ISLAM ET L'ÉTAT," 20)

I BEGIN THIS BOOK BY EXPLORING how history has shaped the legal system of Niger. More to the point, I examine how French colonial rule influenced the contemporary state's regulation of marriage, divorce, and inheritance. According to its constitution, Niger is a secular state; yet in reality, the line between state and religion is often blurred. Nowhere is the distinction between state and religion more ambiguous than in the regulation of the family unit. To negotiate, contract, or dispute a marriage or divorce, or an inheritance of goods and property, the state allows Nigériens to consult religious and traditional authorities: village-level traditional chiefs; marabouts (Muslim teachers or healers); *qadis* (Muslim judges) in a sultan's court; regional-level traditional chiefs; and, in some cases, the quasi-state body—the Association Islamique du Niger (AIN). Official civil registries and state courts constitute but a sliver of a larger legal complex.

Beyond sanctioning the operation of traditional and religious institutions, the state uses traditional and religious authorities in official state courts to address family-related disputes. Judges on issues of family are required to "apply the customs of the parties," as noted above. If, however, the parties are Muslim, local customs are replaced by Islamic law. Because state judges are not trained in interpreting Islamic jurisprudence, judges are to rely on the counsel of official *assesseurs* (judicial advisers, or nonpresiding judges): chiefs, marabouts, or *qadis,* who apply their interpretation of Islamic law in matters pertaining to family.

Why does the state allow and use religious and traditional authorities to adjudicate family disputes? These practices did not appear out of thin air. The state's approach to regulating the family unit is modeled principally on French colonial policy. The colonial era was a "critical juncture," to use Ruth and David Collier's term, a "period of significant change, which typically occurs in distinct ways in different countries (or in other units of analysis) and which is hypothesized to produce distinct legacies."[1] I focus on three significant developments in the colonial period that subsequently influenced the structure of Niger's postcolonial legal system. First, in creating a colonial state, French authorities formed partial alliances with religious and traditional elites. Second, the colonial state invented customary-cum-Islamic law. In doing so, the state dichotomized French-based civil law and (in its words) customary law, and within the realm of customary law, it favored putative Islamic law over other possible modes of dispute resolution. Third, the colonial period saw the crowding out of women from official positions of power.

I deliberately focus on the state's relations with societal authorities rather than on relations between ethnic groups, as has been prevalent in the study of African politics in the United States. As Jean-François Bayart writes, "In Africa ethnicity is almost never absent from politics, yet at the same time it does not provide its basic fabric."[2] In Niger, it is not uncommon to hear scholars and ordinary people talk about interethnic competition between Zarmas in the west and Hausas in the center and east. Yet some of this competition stems from the colonial period.[3] In reality, ethnicity is highly malleable in

Niger, such that a Nigérien may be seen as belonging to one ethnic group in one context, and another ethnic group in another context.[4] In subsequent chapters, then, I pay less attention to ethnicity as a salient feature of women's rights politics and focus instead on mobilized groups.

Before sketching the antecedent to French colonial rule, let me clarify that animist, religious, and traditional authorities are not mutually exclusive or monolithic groups. One may simultaneously have multiple identities and move in and out of these categories over time. For instance, President Seyni Kountché was a high-ranking military officer who came from a royal family, and a Muslim known for being a spirit medium. Within groups, moreover, significant debate can arise over women's rights, as I show in subsequent chapters. Nevertheless, elites have vested interests and vie for influence as a group.

Late Precolonial Niger: Not One but Many Polities, 1880s

This chapter seeks to explain why Niger proclaims to be secular but partially relies on religious authorities and so-called Islamic law to regulate family matters. Although the French colonial period was critical in making this contradiction possible, in this section I highlight two points about Niger in the late nineteenth century that help explain why colonial rulers turned to traditional and religious elites to govern the territory. First, not one but many polities dotted the area known today as Niger on the eve of colonization. Second, in the largest precolonial polities, sultans depended on a coterie of elites, including royal women, lower-ranking chiefs, marabouts, traders, and warlords.[5] I limit my elaboration of these two points to the late nineteenth century, as power configurations shifted considerably over the long precolonial period.[6]

To gain a sense of the diversity of polities prior to colonization, let us examine the political map when France began its military excursion into what we today know as Niger. At the end of the nineteenth century, one would have encountered the following: (1) a loose confederacy of societies controlled by warlords (*wangari,* in Zarma) in the southwest, with Dosso as one of its centers;[7] (2) villages spread across the northwest, which sometimes paid tribute to Tuareg confederacies; (3) a sultanate of Tuareg families based in Agadez;[8] (4) the sultanate of Tessaoua toward the east; (5) war between rival groups in Ader, north of Tessaoua, in the region known today as Tahoua;[9] (6) the precolonial states of Maradi and Tibiri to the east, which had split off from the Sokoto Caliphate in northern Nigeria;[10] (7) the sultanate of

Damagaram, based in Zinder; and (8) Mangari, a part of the Bornu Empire, in the far east, near modern-day Diffa.[11] This list of precolonial polities is not exhaustive, merely suggesting the vast mosaic of political entities the French encountered.

Among precolonial Niger's diverse polities were large centralized states, which varied in their stability, reliance on slave labor, rules of succession, rulers' attitudes toward Islam, and relations with neighboring states.[12] Yet these centralized states had in common access to weapons, a system of taxation, involvement in trade, and an organized court life. French colonial authorities would eventually adapt some of the practices of these precolonial states. Damagaram (ca. 1812–1906) was arguably Niger's largest and most centralized state in the late precolonial period, and it is where the French initially and tentatively tried to establish the center of a colonial state.

Damagaram's alliances with elites enabled its army to maintain the state's autonomy from neighboring empires. To the east lay the empire of Bornu, and to the south, the Sokoto Caliphate. At the apex of Damagaram's army and administration was a sultan (*sarki,* in Hausa) who, according to historian Roberta Ann Dunbar, enjoyed "overriding authority and power."[13] An observer writing in 1851 estimated that Damagaram's army could marshal approximately two thousand cavalry and ten thousand bowmen to raid villages for slaves and goods, and more than five thousand cavalry and thirty thousand bowmen for a full campaign of war.[14] Slaves constituted the state's primary factor of production. As a point of comparison, an estimated 3,142 people lived in Niamey, Niger's current capital, in 1926.[15] Part of Damagaram's military success stemmed from the state's alliances with Tuareg and Arab traders and warlords, who provided cannon and soldiers in exchange for preferential tax treatment.[16]

The sultanate of Damagaram developed a regularized system of taxation that relied on intermediaries to serve as tax collectors. Male cultivators paid a personal tax *(karo)* of 5,500 cowries three times a year.[17] During periods of low rainfall, the sultanate levied an additional tax *(bude rumbu)* on millet. The state also imposed taxes on marriage, inheritance, and the Feast of Tabaski *(kurdin raguna),* and enacted numerous fines, including 4,000 cowries for girls who bore children out of wedlock. The Damagaram's power, however, was not absolute. Tax evasion was an issue for the sultanate. As Dunbar finds, "Middlemen absorbed much of the taxes, so that the Sarki was forced to seek other means of income."[18] When trading routes connecting modern-day Nigeria to modern-day Algeria shifted in the middle of the nineteenth

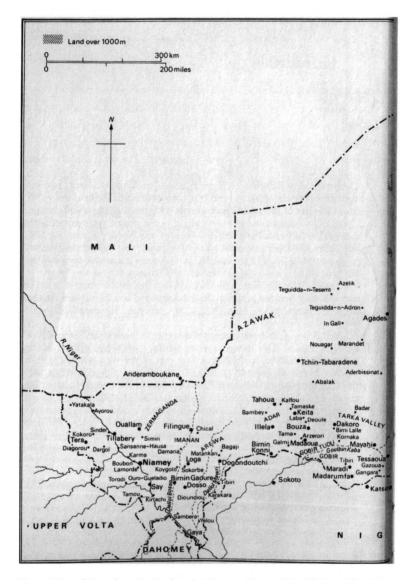

Figure 5. Map of Niger, from Finn Fuglestad, *A History of Niger, 1850–1960*, Copyright 1983 Cambridge University Press, reprinted with the permission of Cambridge University Press.

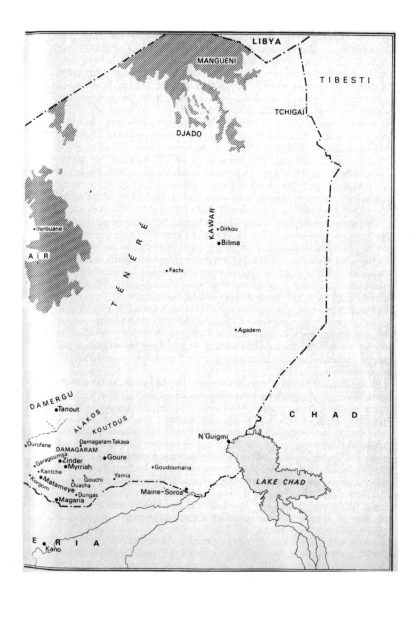

century from Katsina to Kano, the capital of Damagaram became an important stopping point between Kano and economic centers farther north.[19] Damagaram also served as a post in the East–West trade between Senegal and the Red Sea, becoming "the largest and most important trade center in Niger."[20] While currying the favor of traders by waiving their personal income tax and providing them with physical security, the sultanate benefited by levying taxes on the trade of salt, slaves, weapons, sugar, and textiles.[21]

A coterie of Muslim religious authorities sat with the sultan of Damagaram at his court, including an imam who led Friday prayers and a *qadi*.[22] These court officials helped the sultan serve, in the words of Dunbar, as the "overseer of the spiritual health of the state."[23] Marabouts were also an important part of court life. The sultan asked them to pray for success before a raid, and if the raid was successful, he gave at least one-tenth of the spoils to them. Illuminating the hierarchical nature of the sultanate, if the army captured a hundred slaves, fifteen would go to the head Imam, twelve to the head judge, and a smaller number to other titled marabouts.

In sum, no one central state ruled all of precolonial Niger. Many types of polities jockeyed for autonomy and control, from the relatively acephalous societies of western Niger to the hierarchical state of Damagaram. Yet even in the most centralized states, sultans depended on a variety of elites—chiefs, marabouts, traders, and warlords—to help run the state. French colonial administrators would seek to dominate but also rely on this array of societal elites.

Colonial Niger: Struggles in State Building, 1890s–1950s

This section identifies three developments during the critical juncture of French colonial rule that help explain contemporary family law in Niger. First, the colonial state did not crush local authorities; rather, it permitted them to thrive as long as they fell in line with the colony's economic and security interests (employing the oft-used expression *public order*). To help build a colonial state, French authorities formed uneasy partial alliances with religious and traditional elites. Thus, rather than undermining religious and traditional authorities, colonial rulers conferred a degree of political legitimacy to them and, in some cases, created new chieftaincies. Second, the colonial state invented customary law, favoring (in its words) Islamic law over other modes of dispute resolution. Third, the colonial period privileged men over women in according official positions of power over family matters.

France's conquest of Niger's diverse precolonial polities was, in the words of historian Kimba Idrissa, "extremely slow and long."[24] In 1899, the French, after fighting the queen of Lougou's army, killed the sultan of Damagaram and created the Territoire Militaire du Zinder. Violent challenges to French invaders, however, meant that a civilian-led Colonie du Niger was only established in 1922.[25] Across western Niger, revolts arose between 1902 and 1906, including the well-known 1905–6 anti-colonial uprising in Kobkitanda.[26] Back in the east, the French fought Tuareg insurgents in Kanem in 1902. In 1911, the French renamed the area the Territoire Militaire du Niger, officially joining Senegal, the coastal colonies, and French Sudan (Mali) as part of the Afrique Occidentale Française (AOF, French West Africa) in 1912. The French fought Tuareg insurgents in Kanem again between 1915 and 1918. Even after 1922, and until the end of World War II, military administrators ruled over the subdivision of Agadez in the north due to repeated insurrections in the region.[27]

Further illustrating the protracted nature of France's conquest of Niger, colonial authorities struggled to establish a permanent capital.[28] In 1901, the French established Zinder as a capital. In 1902, however, rebels from Kel Gress, Imuzurag, and Izkazkazen families recaptured the territory just north of Zinder. Shortly thereafter, in 1903, the French colonial government moved the capital to Niamey. Yet disagreement over the location of the political center continued among French administrators, with one camp preferring Niamey and the other preferring Zinder. In 1911, after French authorities saw several years of relative peace in the colony, the capital was relocated to Zinder. It would remain so until 1926, when the capital was moved, for the last time, to Niamey.[29]

Yet just as no one central state controlled all of precolonial Niger, no one centralized opposition movement emerged against colonial rule. Revolts against France's military were isolated to either a region or a set of villages. The French manipulated preexisting rivalries in their favor and formed alliances with elites who saw an opportunity to gain an upper hand over their local adversaries.

In its struggle to capture the territory, French rulers, in an ad hoc manner, used a combination of repression and co-optation to keep the colony intact. This approach stands in contrast to the French installation of direct rule in the Four Communes in Senegal. First and foremost, in the territory known today as Niger, colonial authorities sought to "amputate" the largest precolonial states into less threatening chieftaincies *(chefferie traditionnelle)*.[30] In

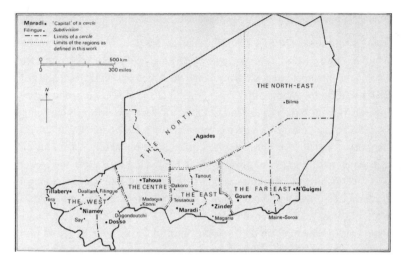

Figure 6. Administrative divisions of Niger before 1956, from Finn Fuglestad, *A History of Niger, 1850–1960,* Copyright 1983 Cambridge University Press, reprinted with the permission of Cambridge University Press.

the empire of Damagaram, the French created a separate canton of Gouré. Magaria, Kantche, and the Sossebaki became independent of the sultanate.[31] In Adar, the French considerably reduced the powers of ruling Tuareg families by favoring Hausa chiefs. The French took one-third of the canton of Maradi and made it the stand-alone canton of Madarumfa. Thus, colonial rulers sought to ensure that none of the precolonial polities dominated a single region or the country.

Furthermore, the French colonial state replaced uncooperative chiefs with ostensibly collaborative intermediaries. Sarki Ahmadu of Damagaram, who had ordered the execution of a French captain, was captured and killed.[32] The French replaced Sarki Ahmadu with Ahmadu II. In 1906, Ahmadu II plotted a revolt against the French with Mallam Yaro—a leading merchant and one-time French collaborator—but was found out, arrested, and exiled. The French also deposed the leader of Gobir in 1911, his replacement in 1912, the leader of Say in 1913, the leader of Myrriah in 1914, the leader of Maradi in 1922, and the sultan of Tessaoua and his lower-ranking chiefs in 1927.

French rulers, however, were still in want of a local administration, one that could tax peasants, implement a policy of forced labor, find soldiers to fight in French wars, and administer so-called justice. Colonial authorities attempted to co-opt preexisting forms of political organization. The chieftaincy, writes historian Kimba Idrissa, was "heavily used to help establish the colonial system."[33] In Zinder, the power of Muslim scholars and rulers "tended to grow as the French found their own staff to be inadequate to meet the demands of administering a colony."[34] In the Maradi region, "local hierarchies were left in place," in the words of historian Barbara Cooper. Factors that could disturb local power relations, such as Christian missionaries, were discouraged, and the aristocratic class "benefited from colonial rule while extracting as much as possible from the peasant classes who performed most of the agricultural labor upon which the economy was built."[35]

In western Niger, the French created chieftaincies where few had existed at the time of colonization.[36] According to noted scholar Jean-Pierre Olivier de Sardan, in the eighteenth and nineteenth centuries, no one ruler in western Niger was capable of controlling more than four or five villages for any significant period of time.[37] In the mid-1800s, Zarma, Mawri, and Dendi societies waged numerous wars against their Fulani rulers in the southwest region of Niger until 1866, at which point a "tenuous" confederacy was created.[38] "As the French found out, the *zermakoy* was at the end of the century still no more than an insignificant rustic princeling," writes historian Niger Finn Fuglestad. "This was true of *all* the chiefs of the West."[39]

Indeed, the canton of Niamey was an artificial creation. Its first *chef de canton* was a guide for a French expedition and had no aristocratic connections. In the region of Filingue, no one chief dominated the area. The French picked Gado Namalaya, a warlord, to head the newly created canton. In this position, Gado led extensive raids, increasing his wealth such that he was the "*de jure* and *de facto sarkin* Filingue, as he now called himself."[40] France's relationship with Awta, a warlord in the Dosso region, reveals one of the ways French rulers and their collaborators manipulated the chieftaincy. Awta had collaborated with French administrators in the early 1900s, and with French backing, he became Zarmakoy of Dosso in 1904.[41] France then temporarily extended Awta's territory to regions that Dosso had previously been unable to control: Sokorbe, Falwell, and Kiota, the seat of a different chief. For his and the French administrators' benefit, Awta collected taxes and organized "group labor" sessions, amounting to what Jean-Pierre Olivier de Sardan calls "despotic exploitation."[42]

To recapitulate, the French colonial state perpetuated, and in some instances invented, the institution of the chieftaincy. Yet at the same time, French rulers purposefully broke down larger political entities to minimize internal threats to colonial rule.

The Invention of Customary-cum-Islamic Law

Although French colonial officials worried that Muslim leaders would disrupt or seek to overthrow the state, colonial administrators promoted the use of Maliki legal principles, confounding so-called customary law with so-called Islamic law. The colonial state in Niger further delegated to chiefs, marabouts, and *qadis* the authority to regulate family disputes. By the end of colonial rule, customary law had become a moniker for Islamic law in the adjudication of family disputes.

A key factor in the invention of customary-cum-Islamic law was France's adoption of a decree in 1903 that established a legal system for the AOF, which included the territory of Niger. The decree created two legal jurisdictions: one covered French nationals and naturalized French African citizens *(citoyens)*; the other addressed non-citizens or subjects *(indigènes)*.[43] To regulate disputes over marriage, divorce, and inheritance for *citoyens,* the legal system applied the 1804 Napoleonic civil code. For subjects, colonial administrators were to apply "local customs." Thus, the 1903 decree created a legal binary between French law and customary law, between citizens and subjects.

Colonial administrators were faced with the decision of how to apply local customs. The overwhelming majority of Niger's inhabitants were categorized as subjects. In 1926, not one naturalized French citizen in the federation of French colonies was Nigérien.[44] By 1936, forty-two naturalized French citizens resided in the colony of Niger, but it is unclear whether the citizens were bureaucrats from other colonies working in Niger.[45] Facing the task of ruling over subjects, administrators preferred to rely on written texts, which promised to be simpler than relying on orally transmitted codes. As noted previously, the governor-general of the AOF, Ernest Roume, wrote to his local administrators in 1904 that local courts would apply "Malikite rites" in civil matters in which Muslims seemed to be the majority. Colonial administrators were encouraged to use such texts as the *Précis de législation musulmane de Sidi Kahlil* and the Seignette translation of Maliki legal principles.[46]

At this stage, it is useful to make a brief note about Islamic jurisprudence and terminology, around which there are many misconceptions. In classical Islamic legal theory, *shari'a* refers to God's will, which is perfect and immutable.[47] In seeking to understand God's will, one may make legal opinions, or apply *fiqh* (human understanding), which is produced by using human agency or effort, *ijtihad.* Thus, in classical Islamic jurisprudence, legal decisions are fallible, subject to debate, and likely to change. To confirm, revise, or create rulings to address new problems, classical legal scholars use analogy to older cases and also examine the scholarly consensus. Over time, dozens of schools of legal thought have been whittled down to four: Hanafi, Maliki, Shafi'i, and Hanbali, of which Maliki predominates in Francophone West Africa.

By recommending the use of a handful of texts, French colonial authorities narrowed down the field of Islamic jurisprudence considerably. French colonial administrators, however, were not the first to simplify classical Islamic jurisprudence into a more legible set of dictates. What is important here is that the colonial state—in Niger and other areas of AOF—chose to favor the use of written Islamic texts over alternative modes of dispute resolution, including a more open interpretation of Islamic jurisprudence and a legal framework acknowledging the complex interplay of Muslim and animist beliefs.[48] In essence, by privileging written texts, colonial officials glossed over the complicated ways in which multiple forms of belief informed people's everyday lives.

In addition to creating customary-cum-Islamic law, the colonial state conferred authority to chiefs, marabouts, and *qadis* to help resolve family-related disputes. Some of these religious and traditional authorities were paid by the colonial state, working as *assesseurs* in official courts. Barbara Cooper notes that in Maradi, *qadis* and an official from the *sarki's* traditional court (the Durbi, to represent animists) worked in both the *sarki's* court and colonial courts.[49] Richard Roberts finds that the preference for using Islamic law and Muslims as judicial advisers extended to areas where Muslims were the minority; a colonial administrator noted that in Bobo-Dioulasso (in present day Burkina Faso), "there are only Muslims on the native tribunals."[50]

Later, in the 1930s, administrators sought to codify local customs in Niger. Male informants, however, tended to give aristocratic men and senior wives more power over junior wives and concubines. The 1933 *coutumier juridique* on Hausas and Peuls, for instance, states that among Muslims, "when a woman betrays her husband with a lover both are condemned to death." Among animists, "the husband has the right, without taking his case to court, to kill his wife's lover."[51] Yet earlier reports of marriage practices in the region suggest that if a wife committed adultery, her husband could repudiate or physically punish her, or the wife could pay a fine and avoid a beating.[52]

In practice, the implementation of the 1903 decree and subsequent laws varied over time and space. Richard Roberts finds that initially in French Soudan (present-day Mali), women "quickly engaged and often used to their advantage" the courts to seek divorce.[53] In a court in Kayes, women initiated 45 percent of the 295 marital cases heard between 1907 and 1913, and in almost all of these cases, women asked for a divorce.[54] Some women cited assault and battery, and others argued that their husbands did not provide for them. Still others cited abandonment, in which case the women would not have to return bridewealth payments (given by the family of the groom to the family of the bride). In a court in Bamako in 1936, women instigated 227 out of 267 cases.[55] Women in Diezon, Ivory Coast, sought divorce to such a degree that the president of the court told a colonial-era researcher, "Without women, we would close the court!"[56] In Saint-Louis, Senegal, "decisions in cases of dowry, divorce, neglect, and inheritance dominate" the *tribunal musulman.*[57] Women seeking divorce constituted half of the civil cases in 1937 in Kindia, Guinea.[58] These opportunities for women, however, seemed to close over time.

By contrast, in Maradi before 1946, cases were handled not by a civilian judge but by a military officer or colonial administrator.[59] The brutal military character of the colony overcast any sense that one could find justice in a colonial court. "The Hausa population came to fear and revile the arbitrary exactions derived through the *indigénat* and the colonial administrators who could enforce its penalties for quite minor offenses," writes Barbara Cooper.[60] Given the unpopularity of French colonial institutions in Maradi, women and men used other mechanisms to resolve disputes.[61] In some cases, intermediaries in the colonial courts abused their power against the local population. Emily Osborn notes that the French colonial government stripped Ousmane Fall—an interpreter working in the French Soudan—of his medals for forging colonial documents and hiring four employees to hear cases, collect fines and tributes, and pass down judgments in the name of the colonial state. Fall had also held a former female slave captive, and kidnapped and sold another woman into slavery following her husband's passing. Osborn concludes:

> The French succeeded in establishing the colonial state as a force to be reckoned with in the Soudan. Yet colonial symbols, personnel and instruments could be used for purposes that diverged significantly from official goals and policies. The ambiguity that surrounded French trappings of rule undermined efforts by the colonial state to organize a smooth running bureaucracy and to assert French authority consistently and reliably.[62]

Jean-Pierre Olivier de Sardan, writing about western Niger, reinforces the point that the legal system was a tool of domination: "It is indeed customary law that gave cover to a system of rent-seeking (that had for a long time been chiefs' main source of profit) . . ."[63]

French authorities occasionally tried to reform marriage practices. The 1939 Mandel Decree sought to reduce the prevalence of child marriage, setting the minimum age for marriage at fourteen for girls and sixteen for boys.[64] In 1951 the Jacquinot Decree allowed governors to set a maximum limit for bridewealth. The decree also forbade family members from interfering in the marriage choice of divorced or mature (over twenty-one) women. Finally, the Jacquinot Decree mandated that male citizens make a choice to enter into a monogamous or a polygamous marriage. In general, however, the state did not enforce the Mandel and Jacquinot decrees. A professor of comparative law, writing about Francophone Africa in 1969, states, "The official regulation of such law never really took hold."[65] Nigériens working for the colony were required to register births, marriages, and deaths, as were Nigériens seeking to claim land in Niamey. Yet only a minority of Nigériens went to the office of *état civil* to register life events. In Maradi, only twenty-one marriages were registered in 1956 at city hall.[66] To quote Mahamadou Arzika, "There can be no doubt that . . . the application of French civil law in Africa had little impact on people's daily lives."[67]

In sum, by the end of colonial rule, chiefs, marabouts, and *qadis* had the state-backed authority to help administer family law. The state not only sanctioned the use of customary law but encouraged the use of (in their words) Islamic law as the default.

The Gendered Effects of Colonial Rule

French colonial administrators and Nigérien intermediaries crowded women out of the official state realm.[68] Women were not chosen to hold French-sanctioned chieftaincies, nor were they selected to become judicial advisers. Men disproportionately received colonial schooling, later dominating the bench in postcolonial courts. Thus, French rulers gave male elites the authority to address marriage, divorce, and inheritance disputes.

I do not claim that relations between the sexes were equal before the arrival of the French military, but women did hold positions of political power in different precolonial polities. In Damagaram, for instance, women held a variety of titled positions. A female official *(magaram)* and her assistants collected taxes from women.[69] The sultan's wives also held titles, and although less is known about their role in the sultanate,[70] it is possible that they exerted some authority. Women served as court messengers-cum-negotiators *(jekadiya)* in Maradi and other areas of Hausaland, a position that retained its importance in colonial Niger.[71] Albeit in a significantly different context, Heidi Nast argues that palace concubines in the city-state of Kano (south of Zinder) oversaw the slave production of indigo-dyed cloth.[72] Yet, to my knowledge, the French did not officially confer chieftancies to women in either Maradi or Zinder. Similarly, in western Niger, the French similarly favored men over women when allocating official roles in the state. The French favored the male sarki of Arewa the chef de canton of present-day Dogondoutchi, overlooking Sarrounia, queen of Lougou.[73] Adeline Masquelier argues that the state's exclusion of female religious leaders in Dogondoutchi had enduring consequences: "The colonization of Arewa by the French and its subsequent integration into what would one day become the Republic of Niger introduced new relations of power and production, new levels of transactions, and new forms of authority."[74]

In terms of education, the colony of Niger's schooling system was paltry compared to that of the coastal colonies of Dahomey and Senegal. Colonial authorities in Niger worried that schools would become a site of anticolonial mobilization and discouraged missionaries from establishing primary schools in the territory.[75] Thus, in the 1910s, the colonial education system in Niger was all but nonexistent. A regional school in the neighboring colony of French Soudan provided schooling for children of royal families. Other parents refused to send their children away from home for French-based schooling.[76] Niger's first regional school was established in Zinder in 1913. By 1922, eighteen schools operated in the territory of Niger (the number of schools fluctuated between twelve and eighteen between 1912 and 1922). But "the growth [in the number of schools] was extremely slow," writes Mahaman Tidjani Alou, and at times the schools only ran for two months at a time.[77] In 1922, fewer than 700 children attended school out of a population of approximately 1,740,000. At the time, the total number of children who attended school in the AOF was 28,200.

Within this context of limited opportunities to receive a French-based education, boys' education was privileged over that of girls. This is important because of the colony's preference for hiring French speakers who formed a small class of évolués (French-educated elites) and would later fill administrative posts in independent Niger. In Dogondoutchi in the 1950s, relatively few girls attended mission schools; of those, most were likely the daughters of non-Nigérien Africans from Dahomey and other colonies.[78] In 1961, a government report stated that nearly twenty-eight thousand Nigériens were enrolled in preschool, primary school, or secondary school, or were on study-abroad scholarships. Of those, approximately eight thousand were girls, and of the one hundred scholarship recipients, none were women.[79]

Over thirty-eight years of colonial rule, French colonial rulers did not create a centralized, autonomous state in Niger. Their use of corporal punishment, application of forced labor, and unrelenting taxation resulted in famines and waves of outmigration.[80] Even though they implemented a stringent system of taxation, French administrators were unable to fully control the peanut, livestock, fabric, and kola trade along the 1,600-kilometer commercial frontier between Niger and Nigeria.[81] To keep the colony viable, then, French administrators pursued a dialectical policy of domination and dependence. Colonial authorities dismantled the largest states, which meant that at independence, no one region or group dominated Niger. Authorities relied on multiple types of intermediaries to control the territory: male chiefs and marabouts, and a new group, évolués. Colonial rule conferred authority over family law to male chiefs and marabouts, and invented customary-cum-Islamic law as the default law for matters relating to the family. Lastly, whereas women in precolonial Niger held positions of political power, colonial rulers chose men over women to join the administration and reap some of the rewards of colonial rule.

Independent Niger: Uneasy Alliances, 1940s–1960s

As nationalist movements swept across Africa in the 1940s and 1950s, Nigérien elites formed uneasy alliances such that when Niger became independent in 1960, political power was splintered among évolués, chiefs, and marabouts. Starting in the 1940s, France permitted the formation of political parties in its colonies and allowed some Nigériens to vote for their own representatives to the French national assembly and Niger's own territorial assembly. The Parti Progressiste Nigérien (PPN) was created in this context. Concerned about PPN's seemingly left-wing tendencies, the governor of Niger, Jean Toby, encouraged chiefs and PPN dissidents to form a separate political party, the somewhat ironically named Union Nigérienne des Indépendants et Sympathisants (UNIS, Union of Independents and Sympathizers).[82] In 1951, UNIS won a sufficient number of votes in the legislative elections to unseat PPN's Hamani Diori from the French assembly.

In 1957, another political party emerged, under Djibo Bakary. The Mouvement Socialiste Africain (MSA, later Sawaba party) united members of the socialist Union Démocratique Nigérienne and the Bloc Nigérien d'Action. Sawaba included évolués as well as Zarma aristocrats—most notably Issoufou Saidou Djermakoye, a French-educated son of the Zarmakoy of Dosso who previously belonged to PPN and UNIS.[83] Bakary also built alliances with merchants, marabouts, and members of the *Tijaniyya* congregation.[84] The union between Bakary and chiefs, however, was "eminently fragile."[85] Bakary's alliance split over the 1958 referendum on France's new constitution, which contained a proposal to dissolve the AOF and replace it with a French Community composed of non-independent African republics. A no vote would have meant a call by Africans for independence and a breaking of ties with France.[86] Bakary urged Nigériens to vote no, while chiefs were encouraged by the French to favor a yes vote.[87] As a result, the chiefs joined other elites (including the PPN) who also supported the French proposal.

Upon independence, Niger's rulers—facing a divided elite—adopted the colonial state's dual stance toward custom-cum-religion. In line with the French constitution, the 1960 constitution proclaims: "The State of Niger shall be an indivisible, secular, democratic, and social Republic."[88] The state also maintained the colonial use of so-called customary law in matters of marriage, divorce, and inheritance. In 1962, Hamani Diori's government adopted a law establishing the organization and jurisdictions of Niger, cited at the beginning of this chapter. Article 51 of the March 16, 1962 law stipulates that the "customs of the parties" shall be applied in matters of marriage, divorce, and inheritance, among other areas of law. Designated *assesseurs* would provide advice to the courts on the parties' customs.

Following the model set by the French colonial state, Niger's legal system applied Islamic law as a stand in for "custom." In 1979, the attorney general of the *Cour d'État* wrote in legal journal, "Although no reference was made to Islamic law, which governs more than 90 percent of Niger's population, it is this law, in fact, that is applied in the vast majority of cases that fall outside the realm of written law." The attorney general further remarked that Nigériens swear on the Qu'ran to resolve land disputes, and that the some judges in official state courts were even using the Qu'ranic oath in criminal cases. This led the attorney general to conclude, "Ultimately, it is Islamic law that is under the cloak of custom, influencing the judge's decision and being applied . . . we are in the domain of Islamic law, which the legislator did not see fit to legitimize given the principle of the secular state."[89]

Conclusion

In contemporary Niger, chiefs, marabouts, and *qadis* wield significant state-sanctioned authority over family matters. Why these religious and traditional authorities enjoy influence over family law stems from history. In precolonial

Niger, no one central polity extended its reach across the territory. French colonial rulers, with limited resources, had to find ways to build a state. To manage the task, colonial rulers formed power-sharing arrangements with a specific set of societal elites. In particular, French colonial policy consolidated rather than undermined the power of male religious and traditional authorities to regulate matters of marriage, divorce, and inheritance. The colonial state also conferred political legitimacy to the use of (in their words) Islamic law over other forms of dispute resolution in matters pertaining to the family unit.

By the time Niger gained independence in 1960, the state's reliance on societal elites and customary-cum-Islamic law had sunk in. Independence leaders maintained the French colonial state's dependence on chiefs and marabouts to resolve disputes related to the family. In 1962, President Diori's government designated "the customs of the parties" as the default law for handling family matters in official state courts. Yet, the constitution declared Niger to be a secular state. To make sense of debates over women's rights in the family, then, it is necessary to understand the partial integration of the religious and traditional into the colonial and postcolonial state in Niger. Attuned to this existing power structure, we can next examine how activists tried to influence the state on issues of women's rights in the family. We will see that Niger's contentious and seemingly interminable debate over family law reform is a distinct legacy of French colonial rule.

2 THE PUZZLE OF NON-ADOPTION

Why Niger Has No Family Code

ON A MAIN AVENUE THAT HEADS NORTH from an army training grounds and past the headquarters of the country's major political parties, hundreds of men and women gathered in February 2011 at the behest of the Association pour la Culture et l'Orientation Islamique (ACOI) at a public square, Place Toumo. The meeting's organizers took out a duplicate of a draft bill on marriage, divorce, and inheritance, the *Statut Personnel du Niger*. Calling the document "satanic," the conservative activists burned the copy of the draft bill in front of television news crews.[1] The next month, on March 4, Minister of the Interior Ousmane Cissé met with representatives of Islamic associations and announced that the government would abandon its plans to adopt the *Statut Personnel*.[2]

The 2011 controversy is the latest in a long string of attempts to revise Niger's laws on marriage, divorce, and inheritance. Concerned about the rights of women to divorce as well as child custody, women in state-controlled associations helped put the issue of family law reform on the national political agenda during the authoritarian era. In the democratic transition of the early 1990s, women in autonomous women's associations, the Ministry of Social Development, and parliament brought the issue of family law reform to the public spotlight. Yet in the same democratic transition, conservative activists helped put the issue of Niger's official status as a secular state on the national agenda and subsequently framed the proposed family law reform as an anti-Muslim, pro-secularist plot. Conservatives opposed the proposed code, invoking such concepts as national identity and democracy, and they further made its adoption unthinkable by issuing a curse and calling the code the work of Satan. In the 2000s, women's activists and conservative activists came together to lobby for reform, but the government was unresponsive to their calls.

Numerous scholars have commented on the family code controversy of the early 1990s, highlighting the strength of religious countermobilization,[3] problems in the content of the draft reform,[4] and divisions within the pro-code lobby.[5] Others have stated the truism that family law reform has not been adopted because it is not in the interest of the country's rulers to do so.[6] There remains a need to explain why policymakers would care about conservative religious actors in the first place, and why, when religious activists mobilized in favor of family law reform, policymakers were also unresponsive to them. To answer these questions, I draw on the previous chapter's argument that colonial authorities constructed a passive secularist state—one that proclaimed to be secular yet in practice partially relied on religious and traditional authorities. In a political context in which the state partially relies on religious authorities for legitimacy and to carry out some of the state's day-to-day tasks, conservative religious activists may help block family law reform.

The rest of this chapter takes the reader through three periods of women's rights policy rejection. In the first, from the 1960s through the 1980s, authoritarian rulers—partly in response to women's mobilization—assembled committees to draft a family code, but state-controlled women's associations had relatively little bargaining power to pressure rulers to do more. In the second period, between 1991 and 1994, democratization facilitated the rise of a relatively autonomous women's coalition, which lobbied the government to send a family code bill to the National Assembly. At the same time, democratization facilitated the rise of relatively autonomous religious associations, which formed an anti-code coalition. In the third period, the mostly democratic 2000s and early 2010s, women's activists learned to directly involve religious elites in advocating for change. Family law reform was underway until a faction of conservative religious activists mobilized yet again in 2011.

Family Law Debates in Authoritarian Niger, 1960–1989

Under authoritarian rule, women mobilized several times to reform the country's family laws. Women within the ruling party lobbied President Hamani Diori for new family legislation, as did members of the state-sponsored women's association during President Seyni Kountché's rule. Although women's activists put the issue of women's rights in the family on the national agenda, their autonomy from, and influence on, the state was limited. In the meantime, a state-sponsored religious authority emerged, further blurring the lines between religion and state.

Women's Mobilization

Women's activists were among the first to call for family law reform in Niger. In the midst of independence, the Union des Femmes du Niger (UFN) called for changes in family law. The UFN was created in 1958 as a women's wing of the Parti Progressiste Nigérien–Rassemblement Démocratique Africain (PPN-RDA). The UFN asked President Hamani Diori to adopt legislation that would improve women's rights to child custody and to curb men's ability to unilaterally divorce their wives in an act of repudiation *(répudiation)*.[7]

Instead of satisfying the UFN's wishes, Diori's government, in a 1962 law, retained the colonial-era system of relying on so-called customary law for matters relating to marriage, divorce, and inheritance. More precisely, Articles 51 and 52 declared that on family matters, the courts would apply the "customs of the parties" unless the decision would violate the principles of public order and individual liberty.[8] Following French colonial practices, the postcolonial state appointed *assesseurs* to advise judges on local customs, but in practice, *assesseurs* and judges used so-called Islamic law as a stand-in for customary law in matters pertaining to the family.

The UFN's inability to influence Diori and his government was partly due to its lack of autonomy from the one-party state. In fact, the UFN served as a tool for mobilizing women for the party, including conscripting women to work for the state. A former UFN member told historian Barbara Cooper that "they took *all* the women who weren't married . . . and they had to work in a big field down in the valley, a government field."[9] Although the UFN had its own president and secretary-general, its patron was First Lady Aissa Diori, whose commitment to promoting women's rights was debatable. Financial resources for the UFN's activities came directly from the PPN-RDA, further limiting the association's autonomy.[10] The organization disbanded in 1974, when Diori was removed from power in a military coup d'état.

This is not to say that women in the UFN were agentless puppets. Some of its members later became leaders in civil society and members of the cabinet in democratic Niger. One member, Fatouma Zara Sabo, later became the state's director of the Office on the Advancement of Women, served as president of CONGAFEN, and was appointed minister of civil service and labor.[11] Daughters of women in the UFN also became politically active. To illustrate, Hadiza Noma Kaka, a minister of professional training and employment in the early 2010s, is the daughter of a former UFN member. Nigérien women were also active in other areas of civic life: as leaders of farming, credit, and insurance cooperatives; possession cults; and Qur'anic schools.[12]

Following the 1974 coup and at the request of several women, Seyni Kountché—Niger's second president—created an organization to succeed the UFN. Subsequent to a March 13, 1975 ordinance, the Association des Femmes du Niger (AFN) was created on September 21, 1975.[13] The AFN was originally intended to mobilize women for the state, particularly for development projects. Akin to the UFN, a woman who was a member of the AFN in Dogondoutchi in the 1980s recalled to me, "They said you have to work. They made plots of land for the women. We farmed. . . . We weren't given ownership [of the association]. It wasn't independent, but it's normal, it was the beginning."[14] The president of the AFN's Zinder branch told me of its start, "The mayor of the urban community of Zinder, he made an announcement to all the women of Zinder. He had them meet at city hall. We created a local office. He said to not stay at home. . . . All the information came from city hall."[15]

Although it received direction from above, the AFN provided a space for women to meet and organize at the grassroots level. The president of AFN-Zinder said, "We went into the neighborhoods. Before, there were twenty-three neighborhoods, twenty-eight peripheral villages. I went right to the grassroots, saw the villagers. . . . we did a lot of outreach."[16] AFN offices ran preschools; organized public education campaigns on topics such as hygiene; and opened women's community centers (*foyers féminines*), where girls and young women could learn how to cook and embroider. Several of the women I interviewed who belonged to the AFN in the 1980s noted that participating in the organization was fun. "It was for amusing ourselves," said the Dogondoutchi member.[17] AFN-Zinder's president recalled, "We talked, we laughed, we sang, we danced."[18]

At the national level, the AFN became the most vocal and persistent supporter of family law reform during Kountché's rule. At its first congress in May 1977, women enthusiastically supported the idea of reform.[19] In March 1983, during a national discussion on health, the AFN launched an appeal for "the drafting of a family code adapted to our socio-cultural context."[20] The AFN's fourth congress, in 1984, was held around the theme of the legal status of women in Niger. At the meeting, members again discussed the issue of family law, specifically raising concerns about repudiation, child custody, inheritance, and women's access to land.[21] One woman, a member since 1976 and a member of the executive bureau, said:

After the congress, we approached the president. It was he who authorized the creation of [the AFN]. . . . We explained to him the necessity. Nigérien women, none of their rights are recognized. They suffer. Yet they do everything. . . . And when there is a divorce, they don't have the right to keep the child.[22]

In 1985, the same year as the United Nations Third World Conference on Women in Nairobi, the AFN formally asked Kountché to revisit the issue of family law reform.[23]

Women in the AFN sought to represent the interests of women through a "purely Nigérien" family code.[24] A key question, however, was what kinds of changes Nigérien women wanted. Members of the organization debated about whether polygyny should be banned, and whether they wanted a gendered social order in which men and women complemented each other *(complementarité)* or one in which men and women were equals *(égalité)*.[25] To help resolve these debates and hear for themselves what reforms people wanted, they conducted focus groups with men and women in Niamey.[26] Through these focus groups, the AFN found that men and women alike supported the idea that both parties should consent to marry, a minimum marriage age of seventeen for girls and twenty-one for boys, setting a maximum amount for bridewealth, making divorce more difficult to obtain, and the notion that following a divorce, men should respect a period of delay before remarrying (which women were required to do). The AFN also found that women wanted equal grounds for divorce in the case of adultery, better access to child support, a chance to win child custody, and an option for monogamy and community property.[27]

At the same time, women in the AFN, which included Christians and Muslims, were interested in learning more about Islam. The AFN's office in a Niamey neighborhood hired a female *conseillère islamique* (Islamic adviser) to help women "learn more about the Qur'an and perfect their religious practices . . . but also to learn their rights and roles in Islamic society."[28] The AFN's branches in Niamey and Zinder invited marabouts from the Association Islamique du Niger to give sermons on Islam.[29] Yet the women's organization, created by the state to be a secular entity, steered clear of using religion to buttress its appeals for family law reform. Another statist entity would be delegated with the task of managing the country's religious affairs.

The Rise of a State-Sanctioned Religious Authority

Before creating the AFN, Kountché's government established on September 13, 1974, the Association Islamique du Niger (AIN).[30] The AIN was initially installed to help clamp down on extremist marabouts, not unlike the French colonial state, which maintained fact sheets *(fiche de renseignements)* on marabouts. Under the authoritarian regime, Muslim preachers who appeared threatening to the "public order" were imprisoned or exiled to Nigeria. Although it did not wield complete control over the country's religious leaders, the AIN issued authorizations to preach, reviewed preachers' sermons, and censured lectures that were deemed too critical of the regime or the state-sponsored religious body. AIN members further served as *assesseurs* in official courts, advising judges on customary-cum-Islamic family law.[31] In some cases, local branches of the AIN elected the imam of the town's main Friday mosque, an important position at the local level.[32] Further, the body helped coordinate pilgrimages to Mecca, disburse international Muslim aid for the construction of mosques throughout the country, and represent the state to foreign donors from the Middle East and Muslim-faith NGOs.

Perpetuating the ambiguous relationship between religion and state inherited from French colonial rule, the AIN established its own semiofficial system of Islamic courts in which AIN officials hear disagreements over marriage, divorce, and inheritance.[33] During my fieldwork in Niger, I often heard women say that the qadis at AIN's headquarters at the Grand Mosque were sympathetic to women. As the secretary-general of the AIN, Cheick Dotia Boubacar, told Aïcha, "For 75 percent of the couples who come here, it's because of the men's wrongdoing, they do not fulfill their obligations as husbands."[34] People would tell me that qadis were generous toward women, giving recompense that went above and beyond what was required in Islamic law, which is why women would go to the AIN if their ex-husbands did not pay child support, as recommended by Maliki guidelines. Indeed, both men and women seemed to prefer to visit AIN's headquarters to the official state courts—AIN's semiofficial legal process appeared more legible to ordinary Nigériens. Led by erudite men such as then president Cheick Oumarou Ismael, the system seemed less corrupt than that of the official state courts.

Upon the urging of fellow doctoral students and researchers in Niamey, I visited AIN's headquarters and was struck by the amount of paperwork that its staff produced and kept on file. Though marriages and divorces are supposed to be registered with a state-run vitals records office, I saw that AIN's offices are a site where Nigériens record life events. Their papers look official—they are dated, signed, and stamped by a *qadi* or an assistant. Indeed, when a jurist (and women's rights activist) explained to *Haské* that repudiation is not legal but that one can go to a "customary judge" who will make an ordinance to confirm the act, she was most likely referring to the AIN.[35] In 2007, AIN's headquarters at the Grand Mosque declared 797 divorces. In 2009, that figure increased to 913.[36] (The state-backed *Le Sahel* also makes a point of publishing end-of-the-year statistics for AIN, but not for any of the state-run courts or civil registries.) Although I could not obtain the number of divorces declared at state-run offices for the entire city, Commune II in Niamey declared a total of 108 divorces in 2007 (of which 87 involved repudiation).[37] This suggests that AIN's level of activity is at least commensurate to that of official state institutions in the regulation of the family unit.

AIN—through its everyday state-sanctioned work of authorizing, giving and reviewing sermons, and hearing disputes over divorce and inheritance— became a state-sanctioned arbiter of family disputes. As scholars of Niger have remarked, the AIN "gradually took on the appearance of being Niger's established church" and effectively "institutionalized the partnership between politics and religion," eventually becoming "one of the pillars of the regime."[38] This meant that the Nigérien state was not under the control of one "big man." Rather, the state was composed of multiple actors, with their own identities and interests.

Bargaining within an Authoritarian State

President Kountché's government, having created the AFN and the AIN to serve its own purposes, found itself dealing with their claims upon the state. Following the creation of the AFN, the government formed an ad hoc interministerial committee in 1976 to discuss family law reform. The committee had four members including a representative of the AFN and was coordinated by the Ministry of Justice.[39] The group examined Mali's Code du Mariage et de la Tutelle and conducted study tours in Mali, Mauritania, and Senegal.[40]

By 1977, the committee disbanded without finalizing a draft code. Roberta Ann Dunbar reports that Kountché suspended the committee's work because of "political opposition," though it is unclear who constituted the opposition and exactly what was being opposed.[41] The Ministry of Justice told a member of the AFN that absenteeism was the reason the committee fell apart.[42] The AFN member partly blamed top officials who aired doubts that the committee could draft a code, at least one that reflected all the various practices and customs of the country.[43] According to a Ministry of Social Development official who worked on the family code in the 1990s, the committee had reached an impasse concerning whether to adopt the Malian model, which did not address the issue of inheritance.[44]

In January 1987, the Ministry of Justice created another committee to compile a draft family code. Like the previous one, the team of judges, lawyers, and Minister of Justice Abba Moussa Issoufou studied the family codes of other predominantly Muslim countries. The members examined family codes from Algeria, Senegal, and Tunisia, with Senegal and Tunisia representing different models of regulating the family. Senegal's family code was relatively accommodating of Islamic law (e.g., polygyny is allowed), whereas Tunisia's family code sought to override it (e.g., polygyny is banned).

After some hesitation, the government decided that the draft reform would address the issue of inheritance, thus making the task one of adopting a full omnibus family code. The government established yet another committee, this one composed of jurists, government officials, and representatives from the AFN, the Association des Femmes Juristes du Niger (AFJN), and the AIN. Although, according to an officer in the Islamic body, the AIN did not overtly oppose the idea of creating a family code in the 1970s or 1980s, both the AFN and AIN debated whether to use French-based family law or Islamic law as the default option.[45] Members of the AIN argued that Islamic law should be default except for the minority of non-Muslims in the country. That is, upon the death of a Muslim, Islamic law should be applied regardless of whether there were written instructions to that effect. Others argued that in a secular state, Islamic law should not be the default. As Leonardo Villalón writes, "This seemingly rather minor point became the single most controversial component of the draft code, resurfacing as a symbolic point of contention when changed circumstances allowed the opposition to renew its attack on the code."[46] In the final draft, French-based civil law was chosen to be the default on issues of inheritance.

The committee's work was put on hold after Kountché died of a brain tumor in 1987. Two years later, in 1989, Kountché's replacement, Ali Saibou, restarted the effort to create a family code. An office in the Ministry of Social Development was charged with drafting a code in collaboration with other ministries.[47] A few months later, Aïssata Moumouni, the minister of social development, told the state newspaper *Le Sahel*, "Modern law will be applied to everyone," and Islamic law could be applied if requested.[48] In 1990, it appeared that the draft family code was underway.[49]

To take a step back, scholars of women's movements contend that mobilization helps push leaders into adopting women's rights policy. Given the pressure, albeit circumscribed, from both the UFN and the AFN, why did Diori's and Kountché's governments not adopt a family code? From a perspective that emphasizes the endurance of institutions, it makes sense that Diori and Kountché did not revamp the country's family laws. As outlined in the previous chapter, colonial rulers struggled to create a centralized bureaucracy.

Under French rule, relatively few Nigériens became colonial administrators; instead, the colonial state brought in bureaucrats from neighboring Benin and Burkina Faso. Many of these "foreign" African bureaucrats left Niger after independence. Thus, each postindependence government "quickly established a connection to local aristocracies to establish its domination," integrating the chieftaincy into an alliance with French-educated *évolués*.[50]

Mounira Charrad similarly argues that historical institutions affect the trajectory of family law reform in North Africa.[51] Charrad compares the adoption of family codes in postindependence Tunisia, Morocco, and Algeria. All three countries gained independence around the same time, yet it took five months in Tunisia, less than two years in Morocco, and twenty-two years in Algeria to adopt a family code. Tunisia (99.5 percent Muslim) banned polygamy in its Code of Personal Status in 1956, a significant departure from preexisting law.[52] In Morocco (99 percent Muslim), the conservative Code of Personal Status of 1957–58 permits polygamy. Algeria (98 percent Muslim) also adopted a conservative Family Code.

Charrad argues that the relationship between the state and societal elites explains differences in the timing and content of family law. These relationships are affected by, among other things, the extent to which tribes were used to fight against French colonial rule and the level of bureaucratic centralization that developed during the precolonial and colonial eras. Tunisian independence leaders did not need tribal authorities to fight for independence and inherited a highly centralized state. Algerian elites, like elites in Niger, formed uneasy alliances with one another, and the state was partially bureaucratized. In this context, authoritarian rulers are constrained by their relations with societal elites.

Thus, it is important to note that chiefs were, in the words of William Miles, "indispensible in resolving low-level conflicts which might otherwise overwhelm meager police and judicial resources."[53] Chiefs also collected taxes for the state. Diori placed a number of chiefs in ministerial positions and on the PPN's executive board.[54] In a context of political uncertainty and the Sawaba threat, Diori relied on traditional institutions and authorities. In one speech, a member of Kountché's government asked *chefs de canton, chefs de province,* and sultans to be "the eyes and ears of the government."[55] Chiefs and marabouts were able to profit from their positions of authority, and a number of them amassed considerable economic power that could be used to help the state. In the droughts of 1984–86, for example, the emir of Daura provided relief aid to his region, and the prefect of Zinder held a ceremony to honor his contribution.[56]

To bolster their legitimacy and a sense of national identity, Diori and Kountché put a public face to their Muslim faith. Both attended public prayers for the major holidays and went on a pilgrimage to Mecca. Kountché courted the Organization of the Islamic Conference (OIC), Kuwait, and Saudi Arabia for development aid. With funds from Libya, Kountché oversaw the construction of the Grand Mosque in Niamey, the largest in the country.[57] In his speeches, Kountché referred to Muslim principles to create a sense of national unity. For instance, in 1981, Kountché proclaimed, "All Muslims, despite their variation in color and language, are one community. They follow the same path and are of one culture."[58] Conservative activists would later adopt this discourse of one religion, one culture in the midst of the democratic transition.

It would be incorrect, however, to say that the relationships between rulers, marabouts, and chiefs were smooth, unchanging, or consistent. Diori and Kountché harbored reservations about the chieftaincy. According to analysts of Niger, Diori, who was not of aristocratic origin, distrusted chiefs.[59] Part of this distrust stemmed from the preindependence period, when French colonial rulers coaxed chiefs to side with Diori's rival, Djibo Bakary. It was not until 1958 that a number of chiefs switched sides and joined Diori's party. Kountché, too, was wary of the chieftaincy. Starting in 1981, Kountché made it easier for the government to name and remove chiefs directly, in contrast to the previous policy, which allowed chiefs to be elected by the population or an electoral college.[60] Nevertheless, Diori's and Kountché's administrations relied on chiefs and marabouts to police, tax, and resolve disputes on behalf of the state. The 1962 law formalized this power-sharing agreement.

Comparing Niger to other authoritarian states in the region that adopted controversial family law reform, we see that Niger's leaders had less autonomy from societal elites than did some of their peers. In the Ivory Coast, the legislative body in 1964 adopted a civil code that abolished bridewealth, banned polygamy, set a minimum age of marriage at eighteen for women and twenty-one for men, and recognized children born out of wedlock.[61] President Félix Houphouët-Boigny enjoyed the support of the majority of Ivorians, particularly as the country's economy grew in the 1980s. In 1983, the National Assembly passed a bill that limited the husband's authority in the household and restored women's individual property rights, "but not without vehement opposition from many MPs," as Jeanne Maddox Toungara writes.[62] Houphouët-Boigny had direct control over the selection of members of parliament.

In contrast, Kountché struggled to control his own ruling coalition. In 1975, Souna Sido Sani—minister and vice president of the ruling Conseil Militaire Suprême (CMS)—was arrested for trying to take over the government in collaboration with Djibo Bakary. In the following year, on March 15, 1976, three members of the government led an unsuccessful coup attempt. Seven years later, on October 6, 1983, Amadou Oumarou (known as Bonkano)—the head of the presidential guard and Kountché's confidant—led another unsuccessful coup attempt against Kountché. By the end of his rule, only one individual from Kountché's first governing council remained.[63]

Kountché also struggled to maintain control over the country's main economic resources, which consisted of groundnuts (the country's chief export in the first four years of his rule) and uranium (the country's chief export for the remainder of his rule). Kountché depended on peasant producers and wholesalers in the central and eastern regions of Niger for groundnut revenue. Once uranium receipts surpassed that of groundnuts, Kountché's government experienced a period of relative wealth, but in the mid-1980s, the price of uranium plummeted, and so did the state's coffers.

To recapitulate, starting in the 1960s, both UFN and AFN members asked Niger's leaders to improve women's rights in the family. Although these organizations' dependence on the state constrained their lobbying for the adoption of a family code, a code was finally drafted by the end of the 1980s. The transition to democracy, in events unforeseen, would create new opportunities as well as challenges in women's activists' fight for family law reform.

Family Law Debates in Democratizing Niger, 1991–94

In the midst of economic decline, student protests, the end of the Cold War, and democratization in the region, President Ali Saibou announced in 1990 that Niger would hold a National Conference. Starting in July 1991, the National Conference, inspired by that of Benin, brought together civil society leaders, union organizers, and politicians to hammer out a new framework for democracy. In November, a transitional government under Prime Minister Amadou Cheiffou was established, as was a temporary parliament, the Haut Conseil de la République (HCR). Voters approved the adoption of a new constitution in December 1992, and Niger's first multiparty legislative and presidential elections in thirty years were held in February and March 1993.[64]

Women's Mobilization

Women in and outside the state helped put the issue of family law reform on the national agenda during the democratic transition. These activists included women from new and relatively autonomous women's associations. In contrast to the AFN, the associations were not created for or funded by the state. Most prominent in the fight for family law reform was the Rassemblement Démocratique des Femmes du Niger (RDFN). Led by sociologist Mariama Gamatié Bayard, the RDFN was created in 1992 to defend and promote women's rights, and it made the adoption of a family code a key priority.[65] The AFJN, mentioned earlier, was officially created in 1991 and also supported the family law project. Women inside the state mobilized for the adoption of a family code. During the time of the caretaker government, Minister of Social Development Aïssata Bagnan Fall vocally supported the family code project. The ministry adopted a national policy agenda for the advancement of women *(Politique de Promotion de la Femme au Niger)* in January 1993, which, among other things, called for the adoption of a family code.[66] Bagnan Fall's replacement, Minister Mariama Ali, was appointed in April 1993. Ali was a member of RDFN and also sought the passage of a family code. In the National Assembly, Aïchatou Foumakoye (CDS-Zinder)—a female member of parliament (MP) as well as a founding member of RDFN—put the issue of family law reform on the National Assembly's agenda. In March 1994, Foumakoye requested Minister Ali to come before the legislature. The following month, on the floor of the National Assembly, Foumakoye asked Minister Ali about, among other women's and children's issues, the status of the draft code.[67] (MPs may invite a minister to come before the assembly and may also write to the ministries for information.)

In advocating for a family code, women in civil society and the state advanced several arguments. For one, activists asserted that family law reform would help women enjoy their rights, particularly in issues relating to divorce and child custody. Talking about the code, Habsatou Liman Tinguiri—director of the Ministry of Social Development's Office on the Condition of Women—told *Haské* in 1991, "In truth, the Nigérien woman needs more rights."[68] Bayard, in a 1993 interview with *Le Républicain,* had this to say:

> We in RDFN, we have not been involved in drafting the bill. But what is sure, we know the broad outlines of the code, and we will continue to fight for this code to be adopted. For us, the family code is not an end in and of itself. It is a way, a tool to put in the hands of the Nigérien woman.[69]

In the same year, Minister Bagnan Fall told the women's magazine *Amina,* "Know that what the family code proposes is nothing more nor less than to redress the injustice and discrimination that women and children are victims of in Niger."[70]

Second and related, supporters argued that family law reform would improve the efficiency of the judicial system. Supporters lamented that Niger had not one but three types of law to regulate family matters: French-based civil law (if requested), customary law (the de jure default), and Islamic law (the de facto default). This multiplicity of laws, contended pro-code advocates, created opportunities for abuse and resulted in arbitrary rulings. As Tinguiri said, "This can lead to all kinds of interpretations, with everyone having the right to choose what is advantageous to them. In this case, the code will homogenize these 'matters.'"[71] The multiplicity of family laws was a particular concern for judges and lawyers. Islamic law, according to some of the code's proponents, is written but not respected. "The law is manipulated," said one law professor to me. "There are three types of law, and people choose what is favorable to them. Even Islam, which gives women rights; they don't apply what Islam says. Without a code, there is no legal order."[72] Customary law, according to the proponents, is more unwieldy, for it is not even written. "Certainly, customs have the advantage of being adaptable to the circumstances," said the 1993 preamble to the abridged draft of the family code, "but [customary law] remains imprecise and creates insecurity for those seeking justice. . . . Each judge makes a decision based on oral information and has no means for verification."[73]

Third and to a lesser extent, women's activists argued that the family code would help promote democracy. The director of the Office on the Condition of Women said to *Haské*, "At a time when we are talking about democracy, about freedom, the code is arriving at just the right moment to ensure fairness and justice."[74] To quote Bayard's 1993 interview with *Amina*, "With respect to family life, there must be a framework that is consistent with the new democratic values that we laud in Niger."[75] Relatively few documents, however, invoked the concept of democracy to justify the need for a family code.

Comparing women's activism for the family code in the early 1990s to that of the authoritarian period, pro-code advocates made significant gains during the democratic transition. The Socio-Cultural Committee of the National Conference recommended the dissemination of a draft family code and its adoption to the transitional government. To this end, the secretary-general of the Ministry of Social Affairs told two researchers in 1991 that a national debate on the draft code would take place before sending it forward for a national referendum or to the National Assembly.[76] In January 1992, the transitional government released a 118-page draft family code containing 906 articles. Due to disagreements within the transitional government and the HCR over the draft code, however, the government did not adopt it.[77]

In May 1993, after President Mahamane Ousmane took office, Bayard told *Le Républicain*, "We will continue to fight for the code's adoption."[78] Prime Minister Issoufou announced in a declaration of the government's agenda that the government was making the family code a priority and planned to send a bill on the family code to parliament.[79] In November, Ali's ministry created a committee to organize a public outreach campaign on the draft family code.[80] The ministry issued an abridged version of the code in French, Hausa, Zarma, and Arabic, making thousands of copies to disseminate as part of the campaign.[81] In February and May 1994, the committee held training workshops on popularizing the draft code in Dosso, Kollo, and Maradi. In early May, the committee met with President Ousmane, and at one of the workshops, a spokesperson for Ousmane conveyed the president's support for the project.[82] A special edition of *Le Sahel* on the draft family code was underway, theatrical pieces were being developed, and stickers and T-shirts were being made—all to promote the draft family code. The campaign was to begin June 6, and the prospect of the family code's adoption looked bright.

Countermobilization

Women's activists are not necessarily the only ones who care about how states regulate men's and women's lives. Conservative activists mobilized repeatedly over the draft family code—the first time concerning the framing of the new constitution in 1992; the second time in May 1993, following Bayard's interview and the prime minister's speech; and the third time in May 1994, before the planned public outreach campaign on the draft family code. Conservatives had an important ally inside the state: the Association Islamique du Niger, which continued to perform state functions in democratizing Niger. Activists put the issue of secularism on the national agenda and tied it to the draft family code. Painting public opinion as opposed to the code, they deployed causal narratives about Niger's identity and democracy. Through public rituals, anti-code activists essentialized Islamic jurisprudence as did colonial and postcolonial rulers, but this time advancing an absolutist argument that one was either for Islam or against it. The campaign against the family code culminated in the issuing of a curse against three women's activists.

Just as democratization enabled the rise of new women's associations, it also enabled the rise of new, relatively autonomous Islamic associations.[83] Of these, four in particular mobilized against the family code. The Association Nigérienne pour l'Appel et la Solidarité Islamique (ANASI), with no official ties to any one congregation, was officially created in 1991. The Association pour le Rayonnement de la Culture Islamique (ARCI) was created in 1992 to promote Sufism and had ties to the *Tijaniyya* congregation.[84] Influenced by the Izala reform movement was the Association pour la Diffusion de l'Islam au Niger (ADINI Islam), officially created in 1993. The fourth anti-code organization was the Association des Étudiants Musulmans de l'Université de Niamey (AEMUN), also founded in 1993.

The four autonomous Islamic associations formed an alliance with the statist AIN to oppose the draft family code. Following the prime minister's speech, ADINI Islam, AIN, ANASI, ANAUSI (a splinter group from ANASI), and ARCI released a joint declaration on the code and sent a letter to newly elected President Ousmane, both of which appeared in May 1993 in the state-run newspaper, *Le Sahel*. The activists said that the draft family code "ought to take its inspiration from the Qur'an, the Sunna . . . and why not modern law, otherwise known as positive law, as long as it does not contradict religion. To concoct and apply any text thought otherwise would be to impose an unholy family code."[85] The associations objected to the use of French-based civil law as the default in inheritance—the issue that divided the 1987 committee.

A year later, when the government announced that it was organizing a public awareness campaign on the draft family code, the anti-code coalition issued another press release, calling on Nigériens to attend a special meeting on May 20 at the main mosque of the Grand Marché.[86] At the meeting, activists declared that 603 of the 906 articles of the draft bill were "radically anti-Islamic" and "an insult to the Muslim faith."[87] According to the anti-code coalition, marabouts who did not oppose the proposed reform supported "forces of evil." Supplanting the Ministry of Social Development's plans to visit the major regions of the country for its outreach campaign, the anti-code coalition split into three groups and traveled to Agadez, Diffa, Dosso, Maradi, Tahoua, Tillaberi, and Zinder. In each town, anti-code activists met with marabouts to convince them of the evils of the proposed reform and gave sermons denouncing the draft family code.[88]

Conservative women also mobilized against the draft family code. Women's sections of ADINI Islam, AEMUN, ANASI, and ARCI gathered "thousands" of women on June 4, 1994, at the mosque of the Grand Marché.[89] The conservative women issued their own press release. It declared:

> We reject the draft family code and any other text that seeks to be a substitute for Divine Law. We ask our believing sisters to pray to Almighty Allah that he destroy

the wind of subversion and blasphemy blowing across our country that seeks to suppress or even destroy Islam.[90]

Conservative women felt empowered in the democratizing context to oppose the family code. Unlike the authoritarian period, when the AIN and the state censored religious speech, Nigériens had relative freedom to practice religion and speak publicly against state projects. As one female member of ANASI—a post office administrator who protested against the draft—affirmed, "We weren't afraid. We had to denounce this document."[91]

To make sense of why men and women mobilized against the draft family code, I first want to dispel some misconceptions that the reader may have about the conservative activists. Rather than being uneducated, poor, and based in remote areas of Niger, leaders of the anti-code associations were generally well-educated, middle class, and based in Niamey. Three leaders of the conservative Muslim women's movement, moreover, held middle-ranking positions in the state's civil service. Another conservative female leader was a small business owner; when I was in Niger, she ran a highly successful pharmacy.

It is also important to take a step back and note that before they agitated against the draft family code, conservative activists mobilized over the framing of the constitution for the Third Republic. The draft constitution, like that of previous ones, designated Niger as a secular state *(état laïc)*.[92] Before the constitutional referendum, AIN, ANASI, ANAUSI, and ARCI submitted a memorandum to the president of the HCR asking that "due regard be given to rights in Islam and of Muslims."[93] Part of the memo states the following:[94]

Memorandum from Muslims Addressed to the Haut Conseil de la République

. . . We, elected and appointed representatives of the Muslim community of Niger, bring to your kind attention the following demands:

1. The removal pure and simple of the word *laïcité* from fundamental texts.
2. The inclusion of "In the name of God the Most Forgiving, the Merciful" at the beginning of the Constitution.
3. An affirmation of Niger's Islamic identity and its belonging to the Islamic Community.
4. The inclusion of Islam's role in the creation and consolidation of national unity and its contribution to the creation of the national culture.
5. The commitment of the Nigérien people to the ideals of Muslim humanism and to the civilizational values contained in the Qur'an and the Sunnah.
6. The establishment of Islamic education in [state] schools.

7. That the President of the Republic, the Prime Minister, the President of the National Assembly, and the President of the Supreme Court belong to the Islamic faith.

This discussion was new, for to my knowledge, AIN's leadership under Kountché never publicly questioned Niger's official status as a secular state. The democratic opening, then, provided a space for challenging the status quo. As a concession to the activists, the transitional government replaced the word *laïc* with *non confessionnel,* but the other demands were ignored. Unhappy with this compromise, the associations called for a boycott of the constitutional referendum. Although voter turnout was significantly lower than that of the 1989 constitutional referendum, the constitution was approved by 89.8 percent of voters in December 1992.[95]

In putting the issue of secularism on the national agenda, conservative activists advanced a story of Niger as a homogeneous Muslim society, a country with an "Islamic identity." Islam, according to the AIN and its allies, created and consolidated "national unity" and constituted the heart of its "national culture." This narrative of Niger as a historically and uniformly Muslim society was not accepted by all. The president of the Union pour la Démocratie et la Progrès (UDP) party said to *Le Républicain,* "Only four Islamic associations" wrote the memorandum, whereas there are "at least five hundred" associations, unions, and political parties in Niger.[96] Representatives of the Catholic Church and the Evangelical Church of Niger wrote to *Le Démocrate,* stating that religion "does not need political power."[97] A writer for *Le Démocrate* derided those who many in the press called *intégristes,* calling their ideas a "danger" and a "menace." "If the country cedes to these first set of demands," the writer continues, "tomorrow they will demand that the country be proclaimed an Islamic republic."[98] In a response to *Le Démocrate,* the coalition of conservative associations accused the newspaper of being the "policemen of the American new world order in Niger."[99]

Following their circumscribed victory over the constitution, conservative activists took the issue of secularism and drew it into a debate over the draft family code.[100] Conservatives equated secularism with France, and France with cultural imperialism and discrimination against Muslims. For instance, the president of the AIN told the Islamist journal *L'Avenir,* "This code is nothing other than a copy conforming to the French code. . . . France wants to pit misguided citizens against other citizens to destroy a strong religion: Islam."[101] The family code, in the words of conservative activists, was an "unholy text," a "satanic work" perpetuated by an "anti-Islamic lobby."[102]

In the process of opposing French neocolonialism and constructing a national identity based on religion, conservatives perpetuated a simplified understanding of Islam, not unlike colonial and postcolonial leaders. Rather than present Islamic jurisprudence in the classical legal tradition, that is, as subject to debate and change, conservatives essentialized Islamic jurisprudence as a fixed set of dictates. For instance, the anti-code lobby declared in May 1994 that 603 out of 906 articles "are against Islamic legislation."[103] A women's activist told *Le Républicain* in June 1994, "Just three months ago, I could chat with female members of the Islamic associations about the importance of the project for women and children. . . . today, this is not possible because of this cliché—the Qur'an is our law and it is set in stone."[104] In reality, Niger's Muslims belong to a variety of congregations and do not practice Islam in the same way.

Conservative activists in Niger constructed what Tamir Moustafa calls "dueling binaries"—between international human rights law and Islamic law, between secularism and religion, and between what is foreign and what is national.[105] Moustafa points out that these legal binaries are not natural or inevitable. Similar to Niger, British colonial authorities in Malaysia invented and institutionalized difference by creating a dual-track legal system, with one set of laws and courts applying Islamic law, and another set of laws and courts applying English law. Liberal and conservative activists in postcolonial Malaysia reinscribed this binary between rights-based law and Islamic law to advance their own agendas. Through the design of the legal system, the agency of activists, and the media (which give the activists attention), the belief in the incompatibility between rights-based law and Islamic law can become deeply ingrained.

In addition to invoking the politically valid subjacent concepts of secularism and national identity, conservatives—more so than women's activists— invoked democracy. Leaders of the anti-code coalition argued that because the majority of Niger is Muslim and because democracy entails majority rule, then the family code of a democratic country ought to reflect (in their words) Muslim values. Opposed to the idea that in matters of inheritance, Nigériens would be required to ask in advance for the application of Islamic law, the anti-code coalition wrote to President Ousmane: "No Nigérien text should marginalize Muslims in favor of a miniscule number of non-Muslims."[106] A female member of ANASI said she denounced the code because it "crushed the majority," since Muslims constituted the "overwhelming majority" of Nigériens.[107] Similarly, a male member of ANASI told me that by making secular law the default inheritance law, "the majority became the exception."[108] By requiring Muslims to opt-in to Islamic law, "Muslims will be strangers in Niger."[109]

Conservatives, then, perpetuated the idea that Muslims constitute the majority to oppose the draft family code. Activists stated that Niger was anywhere from 95 percent to 100 percent Muslim. In 1997, a representative of ADINI Islam wrote a letter to *Le Républicain* that combined the concepts of secularism, national identity, and democracy to oppose the code: "The real calamity that threatens our country, it's the secular anti-Islamists who refuse to take Islamic values into consideration in a country that is 98.7 percent Muslim and are imposing Western culture in an authoritarian manner."[110]

Still, Nigériens debated precisely who constituted the majority. Some argued that women and young people made up the majority of the country and that, correspondingly, the family code ought to meet the needs of women and the youth. A student wrote to *Le Républicain* about the family code in 1993:

> Since we live in a democracy, majority rule undoubtedly triumphs. And God knows, it is important that the majority seeks things (including law) to change. This majority consists of women who make up 52 percent of the population, young people who make up 70 percent of the population, and finally all the Muslims, Christians, and animists who want in their hearts and minds the development of our country.[111]

A philosophy teacher also wrote a letter to *Le Républicain* questioning the idea that 99 percent of Niger is Muslim: "I wonder, when, where, and by whom these statistics have been created."[112] A politician wrote to the same newspaper, "They say 90 percent are Muslim. That's absolutely false. The night of Maoulid [a Muslim holiday], after having crisscrossed the city of Niamey, I saw that there were more people in bars, night clubs, and tea drinking groups etc. than in the mosques."[113]

Nigériens also debated whether the draft code was designed by foreign imperialists or whether the conservatives were foreign imperialists. The same philosophy teacher wrote, "The fundamental objective of this international work, through the creation of international Islamic wings, is to control all the countries where there are Muslims, and ultimately to create a vast entity completely committed to the cause of a limited number of Arab powers." Similarly, the student previously quoted wrote, "Westerners don't have the monopoly on cultural imperialism."

Mobilization against the family code reached a critical point when a Muslim preacher went on the radio and invoked a curse against Mariama Bayard Gamatié (head of the RDFN), the president of the AFJN (who was working for the Ministry of Justice), and the president of another women's association.[114] The curse, and its attendant sermons demonizing the proposed reform, made the family code's adoption unthinkable. *Le Républicain,* referring indirectly to the curse, reported that members of the committee organizing the public outreach campaign "have been threatened" and that "such intimidation hangs suspended above their heads like the sword of Damocles."[115] In response, the public outreach committee wrote to the prime minister on June 7, 1994, lamenting the "total silence of the government" against the "deformation of texts, insults, threats against certain associations."[116] The committee asked why the Ministry of Interior, charged with overseeing the country's associations, did not clamp down on the hardliners among the conservative activists, and urged the prime minister to "act quickly to save our democracy."

Although not everyone believes that curses cause intended harm, curses are sometimes used to gain leverage over one's opponents. As *Africa Confidential* reported upon Kountché's passing in 1987, "Many blame Kountche's long illness and recent death on a curse laid on him by Bonkano [his former confidant]."[117] One scholar noted that in a village he was studying, rumors circulated that a candidate for the town's traditional chief would put a Qur'anic curse on those who voted for his opponent.[118] The threat of a curse may also be used in religious media to discourage so-called bad behavior. In 1999, a call-in radio show in Niamey advised women to allow their husbands into their bed; if not, the women would "be cursed by the angels until dawn, and a curse of an angel is extremely serious."[119] A Muslim self-help tape I bought at Radio Bonferey in Niamey instructed female listeners to not make their husbands suffer; otherwise, they would encourage the wrath and curse of God.[120]

Since the 1994 controversy, few of the original female proponents have spoken publicly in favor of family law reform. One of the targets of the curse said, "I tried to forget everything. I told myself to work on this no more if women were not ready to fight for it. . . . I became amnesiac."[121] Nearly twenty years after the issuing of the curse, women's activists brought up the curse in their conversations with me. The following interview excerpt with a women's activist is illustrative:

AJK: What do you remember about the family code debate? Did you talk about it with your friends?

Aïcha: When the debates over the family code started, I did discuss it with others. I heard the woman who was the leader of RDFN received threats from religious leaders, that if she didn't stop, then she would be cursed. Those were the beliefs or superstitions. The religious leaders threatened the government. They said that nobody will back you.[122]

A member of CONGAFEN—a devout Muslim—said in another interview that she did not believe in the power of the 1994 curse, but she thought it important to mention that the women who were targeted were doing well today. She pointed out that Bayard ran for president, that AFJN's president became president of the Cour des Comptes, and that the third is a director of human resources at a major telecommunications company.[123] These conversations indicate the currency that such public rituals have in Nigérien politics.

Holly McCammon's magisterial study of women's mobilization for the right to serve on juries in the United States contends that women's activists are more effective when they strategically adapt to the broader political context and to their opponents.[124] In the early 1990s, women's activists struggled to strategically adapt to the mobilization against the family code. Both in and outside the state, women's activists were slow to respond to conservative mobilization. For instance, the committee in charge of the draft code's public education campaign did not write to the prime minister until June 7, 1994, after the project was declared moribund. Moreover, in its public letter, the committee did not address whether Islamic law should be the default for matters of inheritance. Yet as the committee and others point out, the government also fell silent after the curse was issued. How does one strategically adapt to a curse? We will see in the next major section that women's activists did try to adapt in the 2000s.

Bargaining in a Time of Crisis

On May 30, 1994, President Ousmane released a declaration on the family code. Ousmane began his statement noting that Niger is a social and democratic republic. In this context, according to the president, "Whether it is the family code or other texts to adopt, they must have the approval of the population. Therefore, a text whose provisions have not been accepted by the people, of course, we cannot adopt it ourselves."[125] After Ousmane's declaration, work on the family code came to a halt, thus concluding the family code debate of the early 1990s.

The times of the draft family code debate under Ousmane were politically turbulent. The February 1993 parliamentary elections resulted in a fragmented legislature. The previous regime's ruling party, the Mouvement National pour la Société du Développement (MNSD), won twenty-nine of eighty-three seats. The coalition of parties that Ousmane belonged to, the Alliance des Forces du Changement (AFC), held the majority. After several postponements, a second round of presidential elections was held. Mahamane Ousmane was elected with 54.4 percent of the vote. After the election, social unrest struck the country's second and third largest towns, Maradi and Zinder. Conservative marabouts preached that the lack of rains that year was divine punishment for allowing girls to wear skirts and pants. In the name of protecting the country from so-called loose women, rioters in Zinder burned down the AFN's headquarters.[126]

In 1994, political strife at the national level continued. In early March, rumors spread of an aborted coup attempt.[127] In April, three opposition parties sent a letter to Ousmane threatening to create a parallel government.[128] Anti-government demonstrations in Niamey resulted in one death, and twenty-four people were wounded. The leaders of the MNSD and two other opposition parties were arrested after the protest. Two members of the government were taken hostage in eastern Niger; the kidnappers demanded the release of MNSD's leader, Mamadou Tandja.[129] The rate of inflation increased from .43 percent in 1993 to 40.6 percent in 1994. A government study found that Niger's economic crisis was worse in 1994 than it had been in 1989, when Ali Saibou's government was in crisis.[130] In September 1994, Prime Minister Mahamadou Issoufou resigned, and the ruling coalition broke apart. In this context of particularly fragmented state power, conservative religious activists mobilized, and the family code was shelved.

Family Law Debates in Democratic Niger, 2000–2011

The events of 1994 stunned the women's activists who lobbied for the family code. For several years, few of its proponents talked about the code in public. As one scholar, Fatimata Mounkaïla, wrote in 2001, "The draft family code . . . has caused such an uproar that no one dares mention it for fear of being publicly scorned."[131] Yet while some preferred to forget about the family code, a new set of women's activists emerged in the 2000s ready to take on the issue. These activists, reflecting on the failed attempt to pass family law reform in 1994, saw that religious authorities had significant bargaining power with the state and thus decided to reach out to religious activists. The activist who said that she tried to "forget everything" about family law reform said in 2008, "It's coming back. We have learned a lot."[132] Women's activists and religious activists, including those who opposed the family code, arrived at a consensus on how the state ought to regulate marriage and divorce, until a faction of conservative hardliners mobilized against reform in 2011.

Following the 1994 family code controversy, a new umbrella group, the Coordination des Organisations Non Gouvernementales et Associations Féminines Nigériennes (CONGAFEN), became a primary engine in civil society for women's rights policymaking. Officially created on July 3, 1995, CONGAFEN's provenance was inspired by a workshop in Sherbrooke, Canada, attended by Aïchatou Mindaoudou (a PhD in law from the Sorbonne who was appointed minister of social development in February 1995) and Mariama Keita (Niger's first female journalist). Seeing examples of networks from other countries, Mindaoudou and Keita were inspired to create a coalition of women's organizations in Niger.[133] At the start, CONGAFEN's network brought together more than thirty women's NGOs and associations. By 2010, that number had grown to more than fifty.

Initially, CONGAFEN avoided mobilizing on the issue of family law reform. Over time, however, the organization became increasingly open to talking about women's rights in the family. Women's activists in particular learned to involve Muslim leaders and associations in their advocacy. In February 2001, for instance, CONGAFEN, Christian associations, and Islamic associations co-organized a workshop on the theme Nigérien Women and Family Rights. The workshop included speakers from conservative Islamic associations that had opposed the family code in the 1990s. Conservative women also attended the workshop, including Haoua Nargoungou, a leader of ANASI's women's section.[134]

Taking interest in women's rights in the family further, a member association of CONGAFEN, the Union pour la Promotion de la Femme Nigérienne (UPFN), helped organize Niger's first nationwide study on repudiation. The UPFN was created in 1992 "to combat all forms of discrimination and violence against women and children and to defend the rights of women and children."[135] UPFN's president was inspired to work on the issue of repudiation while studying Arabic as an adult at a *makaranta* (Qur'anic school).[136] The president consulted her Arabic teacher about doing a project on repudiation and then visited the president of the AIN, who gave his support to the idea. With AIN's backing, researchers interviewed more than a thousand women who had been unilaterally divorced across six regions in 2001.

After the study was complete, Muslim leaders, traditional chiefs, judges, and women's activists met to review the results of the study in September 2001. They agreed that repudiation should be curbed and that, more generally, people did not understand how to apply Islamic jurisprudence. The recommendations from their meeting reflected this consensus:

> Considering that most marriages are made according to Islamic rules,
> Considering that divorce in Islam has specific procedures,
> Considering that the current practice of separating couples takes the form of repudiation, even though the term repudiation does not exist in Islam,
> Considering the magnitude of the phenomenon,
> The workshop recommends:
> —The removal of the the term repudiation,
> —In cases of divorce, the strict observance of the procedures according to Islam,
> —For clerics to conduct a broad awareness campaign . . . ,
> —For the State to make rules to legislate repudiation according to Islam . . . ,
> —To NGOs and associations the organization of training sessions on divorce procedures in Islam.[137]

A committee of clerics, traditional chiefs, women's associations, judges, and lawyers was established to draft a bill on repudiation.

The drafting committee met at the Association des Chefs Traditionnels du Niger's (ACTN) headquarters in Niamey starting in May 2003 to study written sources on marriage and divorce under Islamic law.[138] In September, work on a first draft of a proposed bill, titled the *Loi Réglementant le Mariage et le Divorce,* was complete. To polish the draft, Muslim cleric Cheick Boureima Abdou Daouda and former minister of justice Soli Abdourahmane reviewed the proposed reform together. The draft bill, with 175 articles, was approved in a plenary session of judges, jurists, professors, clerics, and representatives of women's and religious associations in July 2005.

As can be seen in the preceding recommendations, women's activists and other attendees adopted the AIN's and conservative activists' stance that the majority of the country follows Islamic precepts, which involve "specific procedures" that require "strict observance." While the draft *Loi Réglementant le Mariage et le Divorce* did not directly cite hadiths or the Qur'an, the committee gave a copy of the Qur'an to each subcommittee.[139] The drafting team drew on additional religiously-derived texts, such as *Droits et devoirs de la femme en Islam, La vie familiale,* and *La Risala.* To codify Islamic jurisprudence for a secular state, the committee sought out documents at the Supreme Court (none were obtained); Abdou Moumouni University; the Franco-Arab high school; the Grand Marché; and the embassies of Saudi Arabia, Morocco, and Egypt (none were obtained), among other places.

If women's activists learned to engage with Muslim leaders and associations, they also learned to distance the draft law on marriage and divorce as far away from the failed family code project as possible. Women's activists and their religious compatriots decided to focus solely on the regulation of marriage and divorce and not address the particularly thorny issue of inheritance. Recall that women's activists, jurists, and the AIN struggled over what type of law ought to be the default on matters of inheritance. In narrowing the reform down to the issue of marriage and divorce, women's and religious activists also wanted to increase the chances that it would be implemented. "We looked at Senegal's family code," one member of the ACTN and committee member told me. "It exists only on paper. It isn't followed. . . . We have to be realistic."[140]

The committee gave the proposed draft bill to the Ministry of Justice with the hopes that the ministry would then present the bill before the executive cabinet, which would then submit it to the National Assembly for adoption. (The majority of laws in Niger are proposed and drafted in the ministries.) The president of the UPFN deposited the draft bill at the ministry in January 2006. Upon receiving it, Minister Maty praised the women's and religious coalition for its ability "to reach consensus on a set of conclusions and recommendations that can prevent tragedies related to divorce and estate settlement experienced by society in general, and women and children in particular."[141] The minister promised to send the bill to "the national authorities."[142]

The draft bill, however, did not advance. With no news of progress, the president of the UPFN visited the Ministry of Justice in January 2007 to ask about the bill. She was told that there was no money to put together a commission to study the draft law. That fall, UPFN's president tried a different tactic and met with the female minister of social development, who was widely known for being a strong women's rights advocate. The president, however, was referred back to the Ministry of Justice. As a judge who helped draft the proposed bill told me, "We sense reticence [from the government] and do not know why."[143]

Given the support of women's activists and conservative activists, why did the Ministry of Justice and the Ministry of Social Development not advance the draft bill on marriage and divorce? Perhaps the government feared backlash against the draft law. Yet conservative activists who opposed the family code backed the draft bill. As a male member of ANASI told me, "If the bill got to the National Assembly, if they understood it, they would accept it. It would be acceptable to the *grands marabouts*. It resolves all problems concerning marriage. It's very important."[144] Some interviewees speculated that the government was waiting for international funding to create an ad hoc committee, seeking the per diem that came with participating in a donor-funded activity.

Perhaps officials in the Ministry of Justice wanted to avoid advancing a bill that was explicitly based on religious texts. In the eyes of ministry officials, the bill may have crossed the fragile line that the state towed between secular normative law and Muslim-inflected practice. The state's dual stance, inherited from the French colonial state, proved to be resilient, even in the face of united women's and religious mobilization. With the draft *Loi Réglementant le Mariage et le Divorce* stuck in the Ministry of Justice, relatively little movement took place over family law reform in the late 2000s.

Bargains Fall Apart

Fifty years after the UFN first raised the issue of women's rights in the family, the issue of family law reform returned yet again after President Mamadou Tandja was ousted from power in February 2010. Soldiers led by Djibo Salou and calling themselves the Conseil Suprême pour la Restauration de la Démocratie (CSRD) set up a transitional government. The transitional government sanctioned new work on family law reform, to be overseen by Sanady Tchimaden Hadattan—a career civil servant—who served as the transitional government's minister of population, the advancement of women, and the protection of children. Instead of pursuing a piecemeal legislation like the proposed *Loi Réglementant le Mariage et le Divorce,* the transitional government instead pursued the adoption of an omnibus reform. But like women's activists in the 2000s, the government sought to distance the proposed reform from the family code and thus named the draft legislation the *Statut Personnel du Niger.*

Like that of previous ministers, Minister Hadattan sought to take a "participative approach," which would respect the country's religious denominations and customs.[145] A local consultancy group, Cabinet Horizon, was contracted to write a first draft.[146] The group, similar to that of previous drafting committees, used the family laws of other Muslim-majority countries in the region as a guide, specifically those of Morocco, Tunisia, and Senegal. By September 2010, the consultancy group completed the first draft, containing 539 articles.

The Ministry of Justice helped assemble a committee *(comité d'ethique)* to revise the draft and conduct a nationwide review. The committee included members of civil society: Cheick Khalid Moctar (of the AIN, president of the committee), the president of the AFJN, the secretary-general of the ACTN, and the president of the Association Nigérienne pour la Défense des Droits de l'Homme (ANDDH). It also included the president of the Conseil Islamique, two representatives of the Ministry of Justice, the minister of population and her staff, and a representative from the prime minister's office.[147] The committee took two months to revise the draft.

After finalizing a second draft, the committee spent approximately four days in each of the country's eight major regions: Agadez, Diffa, Dosso, Maradi, Niamey, Tahoua, Tillaberi, and Zinder.[148] Before arriving in each regional capital, the committee sent around documents concerning the bill. Representatives of different Muslim sects, Muslim women, and Christians were invited to give feedback on the draft *Statut Personnel*. The committee also invited chiefs, other members of civil society, and government officials to the meeting. At the start of each encounter, Moctar and a judge gave a summary of the draft bill, which was then followed by open debate. According to a representative of the Ministry of Population, the more "difficult" of the eight regions were Maradi, Tillaberi, Zinder, and Niamey. Yet according to a committee member, at the end of every encounter, attendees encouraged the transitional government to quickly adopt the bill.[149]

Problems arose in January 2011, when the committee organized a national workshop to make a final set of amendments before submitting the *Statut Personnel* to the executive cabinet. Approximately one thousand people met at the Palais du Congrès in Niamey to discuss the draft. A minority of religious activists, however, said that they had not been invited to comment on the draft text. This minority contended that the authors of the draft bill did not know Islamic law. (According to some interviewees, the draft was approved at the Palais. According to others, disagreement arose during the national workshop itself.) Then, other groups began protesting against the reform. A coalition of Islamic associations called the Collectif des Associations Islamiques du Niger (CASIN) announced at the Lazaret mosque in Niamey that it opposed the draft *Statut Personnel*.[150] CASIN also denounced the state for modifying the draft bill without letting them know.[151] CASIN exhorted the two presidential candidates who advanced to the second round, Mahamadou Issoufou and Seyni Oumarou: to "the full extent possible . . . do not make any bargains for this satanic draft." On February 20, 2011, the ACOI held a public meeting during which they denounced the draft as "satanic" and burned a copy of the draft bill. Later, in March, the AIN declared that it opposed the adoption of the *Statut Personnel*.

The transitional government responded quickly to the protests. On February 28, representatives of Islamic associations met with Prime Minister Mahamadou Danda to discuss the *Statut Personnel*. On March 5, Minister of the Interior Ousmane Cissé, speaking on behalf of Djibo Salou and Danda, told Islamic associations that the transitional government had no intention of adopting the draft bill.[152] The second round of presidential elections took place on March 12, 2011.

Several points are worth raising here. The first is that conservative activists used similar tactics against the draft *Statut Personnel* to those they had used against the family code. Opponents vilified the draft text as "satanic." They enacted public rituals, such as public prayers, creating fear among pro-reform actors. Presenting Islamic law as a clearly defined set of rules, conservatives argued that the proposed bill went against "Islamic legislation," specifically taking umbrage at Articles 11, 17, 18, 112, 113, 235, and so on.[153] Echoing the language of the 1994 anti–family code activists, a representative of the AIN, Abdoulaye Moussa, noted, "Of 530 articles in this text, fifty-nine go against Islamic precepts."[154] According to the organizers of one of the protests, the draft bill was likely to "pervert Islam and cause the disintegration of the family."[155] Conservatives further painted the draft bill as an anti-religious feminist text. In the same news article, Abdoulaye Moussa said, "The principal problem with this text is that it reflects the concerns of frustrated feminists." Similarly, CASIN argued, "Family values are sacred and should not be neglected or mixed up with pagan and feminist principles."[156] Last, conservative activists invoked the democracy-is-majority-rule argument, claiming a population "more than 90 percent Muslim" or "more than 99 percent Muslim" as a reason for opposing reform.[157]

The second point concerns a division that arose among Muslim leaders—a division that may have hampered the advancement of the *Statut Personnel*. Whereas some religious authorities supported the promulgation of the text (such as Moctar), others did not. Moreover the AIN at the time was going through significant internal division over who would be the new president of the association. Some marabouts wanted Cheick Khalid—the father of Moctar—to be the next president. Others favored Cheick Djabir Ismael, the son of the recently deceased AIN president Oumarou Ismael. In a contested internal election, Djabir Ismael was selected to be the next president. It is possible that rivalry within the AIN affected moderate Muslim leaders' ability to push for the passage of the *Statut Personnel*.[158]

Third, in the debates over the *Statut Personnel*, women in the AFJN and the Ministry of Population worked on the reform, but compared to the conservative activists, women's activists were silent. Bayard, the activist who fought for the family code in the early 1990s, was rumored to have attended the debate at the Palais de Congrès, but she was quiet. I did not find evidence of any declarations or protests made by women's civil society associations in support of the draft reform. Perhaps the news media gave more attention to conservatives because of their provocative statements and tactics. Women's activists, however, had strong connections with the news media, particularly the state-run Office de Radiodiffusion Télévision du Niger. If women's activists had wanted to speak publicly in favor of the reform, ostensibly they would have been able to. In private, women's activists certainly had strong opinions about the proposed reform and its troubled trajectory.

Looking back, we see that once a proposed reform is made unthinkable, it becomes all the more difficult for subsequent proposals to pass. Conservative activists continued to vilify the family code. Following the contested ratification of CEDAW, conservative activists wrote a letter of opposition to the president at the time: "By ratifying . . . you have done the 'dirty work' that nobody has wanted since the National Conference. This document is the twin sister of the draft family code that Muslims fiercely criticized."[159] Indeed, news articles on the mobilization against the *Statut Personnel* referred to proposed reform, in the language of its opponents, as the *code de la famille*.[160]

In the democratic transition and in democratic Niger, autonomous women's and Islamic associations debated over the family code. Women's activists edged family law reform forward, whereas conservative Islamic associations made reform unthinkable. In a context in which the state is fragmented and partially dependent on religious authorities, proposals to reform family law were repeatedly rejected. The state-sanctioned practice of relying on customary-cum-Islamic law, marabouts, and traditional chiefs to regulate family matters remained unscathed.

Additional and Alternative Explanations

This chapter suggests that Niger's lack of family law reform is best understood through the lens of political contestation among women's activists, conservative activists, and state actors in a political context in which the state partially relies on religious and traditional authorities. There are helpful additional and alternative interpretations, but they do not supersede this book's focus on activists and the political context.

International Influence

The influence of international norms, donors, and laws was important but it was indirect and, at times, its effects on the family code debate were contradictory. At the international level, activists in the 1960s helped create an international norm that women had rights within the family. Women working for the UN Commission on the Status of Women (CSW), for instance, helped insert a clause in the 1948 UN Universal Declaration on Human Rights stating that men and women "of full age" are entitled to "equal rights as to marriage, during marriage, and at its dissolution."[161] Concerned that the declaration did not go far enough in protecting women's rights in the family, the CSW drafted the Convention on Consent to Marriage, Minimum Age for Marriage, and Registration of Marriages, which the UN adopted in 1962.[162] The convention requires that both parties give their consent to marry and recommends that governments pass laws establishing a minimum age of marriage. The issue of women's rights in the family was consistently raised at UN World Conferences on Women in 1975, 1985, and 1995.

Niger's leaders had knowledge that there was a growing international norm on women's rights in the family. Diori's government ratified the Convention on Consent to Marriage on December 1, 1964. For the first World Conference on Women in 1975 in Mexico City, Kountché's government created a preparatory committee, whose final report recommended that the government draft a family code.[163] In Mexico City, delegates adopted a World Plan of Action that urged governments to work with women's organizations on women's issues.[164] Less than three months after the adoption of the Plan of Action, Kountché's government created the AFN. According to a member of the 1987 family code committee, Kountché's government restarted efforts to draft a code partly as a response to the 1985 Third World Conference on Women in Nairobi.[165]

Prominent Nigérien scholars were also engaged with international legal discourse on family law. In the throes of independence across Africa, law professors in Europe and the United States argued that newly independent countries needed to unify their laws. Calling for "legal modernization" at such forums as the London Conference on the Future of Law in Africa in 1959 and 1960, legal experts saw legal pluralism as confusing and inefficient.[166] These scholars further worried that maintaining a plurality of ethnic and religious laws would undermine national unity. Additionally, they argued that local authorities used customary laws in ways that discriminated against women.[167] As Denis Cowen wrote in 1962, "Family law, succession and the status of women must inevitably attract the attention of the law reformer."[168] Illustrating a position held by many legal experts, Antony Allott, a scholar of African law at the School of Oriental and African Studies, wrote that a reformed legal system could be an "instrument of social change."[169] Similarly, Nigérien judges called on their governments to replace colonial legal systems with omnibus codes in the name of nation building, development, and improving women's lives.

International donors provided money and training to the women's associations and state institutions that advocated for the family code. For instance, in the 1980s, the United Nations Children's Fund (UNICEF) and the United Nations Development Fund for Women (UNIFEM) financially supported the AFN. Fondation Hanns Seidel, a private foundation based in Germany, provided trainings for members of the AFN for development projects. The Canadian International Development Agency (CIDA) trained staff in the Department on the Advancement of Women—the state body that was created to support the AFN—and paid for a technical adviser to assist the body.[170] CIDA also provided funding to CONGAFEN in 2007.[171]

Donors also helped finance the drafting of a family code. In 1983, for instance, the United Nations Development Program allocated $250,000 to the United Nations Population Fund (UNFPA) to hire an international expert and administrative staff and pay for office equipment and training seminars; these resources were intended to help the state draft a family code.[172] In 1994, Issoufou's government secured funding from UNFPA for a draft family code public outreach campaign, which was eventually abandoned. Coopération Suisse, Oxfam NOVIB, OXFAM Quebec, UNICEF, and UNFPA helped fund the 2001 national study on repudiation. The U.S.-based Academy for Educational Development (AED), Coopération Suisse, Oxfam NOVIB, and OXFAM Quebec provided money for the working group that drafted the proposed bill on marriage and divorce in 2003. UNFPA helped fund the 2005 workshop that finalized the draft bill, which Minister of Justice Elhadji Moussa Maty attended. Between 2004 and 2010, the African Development Bank's African Development Fund (ADF) gave approximately 4 million U.S. dollars to the state to address issues of gender inequality, including the drafting of a family code.[173]

The World Bank has been an important donor in the reform effort. In the early 1990s, a series of working papers written for the World Bank argued that so-called legal modernization in Africa would advance gender equality, which would promote economic development.[174] The World Bank has also sought to promote the protection of women's rights in the name of population health (which is not disconnected from the term population control). In 2007, the World Bank agreed to give the Republic of Niger a grant of $10 million to administer a Multi-Sector Demographic Project on population health. One of the grant's areas of focus was "women's autonomy and couple's empowerment," which, among other things, aimed to "trigger legal reforms, including measures aimed at raising the minimum age at first marriage."[175] During the 2010 to 2011 transition, the World Bank also provided technical support for the drafting of the *Statut Personnel,* among other draft legislation.[176] In addition, the World Bank supported the day-to-day functioning of the Ministry of Social Development between 1992 and 1998 and between 2007 and 2013.[177]

Perhaps Diori's and Kountché's governments would have adopted a family code had Niger ratified CEDAW. Countries that ratify CEDAW are required to submit periodic reports to the UN Committee on the Elimination of Discrimination against Women. Diori and Kountché's governments might have felt pressure to show that they were making progress on protecting women's rights in the family by adopting a family code. Niger, however, did ratify CEDAW in 1999, and subsequent governments have yet to adopt family law reform. It is true that Niger ratified CEDAW with reservations on Article 2, paragraphs (d) and (f); Article 5, paragraph (a); Article 15, paragraph 4; Article 16, paragraph 1 (c), (e), and (g); and Article 29, paragraph 1. These reservations declare that Niger will not necessarily "take all appropriate measures, including legislation, to modify or abolish existing laws, regulations, customs and practices which constitute discrimination against women," as mandated by Article 2 (f). Yet in declaring their opposition to family law reform, conservative activists rarely invoked the reservations on CEDAW, nor did state actors use the reservations to justify their inaction.

I want to make two points about these international contributions. The first is that the non-adoption of family law reform demonstrates that international donors do not always dictate policy, even in low-income countries such as Niger. International donors made their preferences clear; they unreservedly supported family law reform. Yet the government, constrained by the political context and the demands of mobilized groups, did not reform family law. A key point is that local actors were at least partly responsible for directing international aid to legal reform. According to my sources, it was the Nigérien government that asked international donors for help to promulgate a family code and a *Statut Personnel,* rather than donors laying down which reforms to pursue.

Second, the impact of international factors is not only indirect but it can also be contradictory. Conservative activists can depict international norms and support for those norms as anti-Muslim or anti-Nigérien. International organizations and networks can also provide inspiration to conservative activists at home. In the 1980s, Kountché's government deepened the country's connections with the Organization of the Islamic Conference and Muslim-majority states, namely Libya. These diplomatic moves helped construct Niger's identity as a predominantly Muslim country, which conservative activists later used to contest the proposed family code in the early 1990s. Conservative religious mobilization in northern Nigeria also influenced conservative activism in Niger. One of the most vocal anti–family code associations in the early 1990s, ADINI Islam, was an extension of the Sunni orthodox Izala movement, which originated in northern Nigeria. We need to account for how Nigérien decision makers mediated these multifaceted international impulses.

In sum, international activists, academics, and donors created a favorable environment for the adoption of a family code. Connected to the world outside their borders, Nigérien actors picked up ideas about family law that were circulating globally. However, while international donors backed the adoption of a new set of family laws, activists and state actors operating in a particular domestic context debated and ultimately affected the trajectory of family law reform.

Ideology of the Leader or Party in Power

Another helpful but incomplete explanation for Niger's lack of a family code emphasizes the ideology of the country's leader or ruling political party. Comparing Niger with other countries in West and North Africa, it appears that the ideology of the country's leader or party in power helps us understand the content of family law reform. Houphouët-Boigny of the Ivory Coast was ideologically pro-French and pro-modernization when he promulgated a unified, French-based civil code in 1964. Ideologically committed to "liberating women," Bourguiba's government in Tunisia passed a family code that banned polygamy in 1956. By contrast, Niger's leaders, whether autocratic or democratically elected, have never espoused strong ideological commitments to promoting women's rights. Although from the socialist Parti Nigérien pour la Démocratie et le Socialisme, President Mahamadou Issoufou—elected in 2011—has yet to broach family law reform as a key priority.

Although a leader's or party's ideology may tell us about the content of reform, it does not necessarily tell us when reform might occur. Upon closer inspection, leaders in the Ivory Coast and Tunisia adopted family codes at moments when the state exerted significant control over potential challengers to reform. Houphouët-Boigny in the 1960s held de facto control over the national parliament. By the time Bourguiba came to power in Tunisia, state authority had been centralized in the capital, and the state was relatively autonomous of so-called traditional leaders.[178] Ideological commitment to women's rights alone is not enough for the adoption of women's rights reforms. One must examine whether leaders and parties in power are autonomous of other elite actors and able to make the laws that they prefer.

Policy Attributes

A final alternative approach to understanding policy non-adoption focuses on the policy's attributes. Scholars surmise that omnibus reforms offer more chances that someone will object to the reform.[179] Additionally, they suggest that policies that concern the family lend themselves to controversy. By any measure, Niger's draft family code from the early 1990s was large, standing at more than nine hundred articles. On March 2, 1993, just before the end of the transitional government's reign, Niger adopted a rural code *(Code Rural)*—an omnibus reform on the complicated issue of land tenure—but it was shorter, with only 153 articles.[180] Other countries in the region, however, have adopted omnibus family law reforms. Benin, for instance, adopted a family code in the early 2000s that contained more than a thousand articles.

Was the content of Niger's draft family code particularly radical in altering gender relations? Comparing Niger's draft code with Mali's 1962 *Code du Mariage et de la Tutelle* and Senegal's 1972 family code, there is little to suggest that Niger's proposed reform bucked regional trends.[181] Mali's code sets the minimum age of marriage at eighteen for men and fifteen for women (Article 4), and Senegal's code sets the minimum age at twenty for men and sixteen for women (Article 108). The proposed reform that Niger discussed in the early 1990s falls between Mali's and Senegal's, setting the minimum age of marriage at eighteen for men and sixteen for women (Article 16).

Nor was Niger's draft family code particularly radical on the issue of polygyny. Mali's and Senegal's family laws establish polygyny as the default form of marriage (Articles 7 and 8 of Mali's code, Article 134 of Senegal's code). Niger's proposed code from the early 1990s states that men can choose between monogamous and polygamous marriage (Article 114). Furthermore, Niger's draft code, word for word, follows that of Mali's on forced marriage. Both documents state, "The marriage agreement is not allowed through any kind of force." The content of Niger's proposed family code was not particularly unusual for the region.

Conclusion

Spanning fifty years, this chapter examined Niger's multiple attempts to create a more women-friendly set of family laws in Niger. Women's activists in and outside the state repeatedly mobilized for reform, putting family law on the national political agenda in every decade since independence. Conservative religious activists, however, mobilized against the family code in the 1990s and the *Statut Personnel* in the 2000s. Making family law reform unthinkable, opponents organized public prayers against reform, issued a curse against women's leaders, and burned a draft bill. Policymakers bowed to the conservative activists' demands and abandoned attempts to reform family law.

Continuing north on the main avenue from Place Toumo, where conservative activists burned the draft *Statut Personnel du Niger,* one encounters Niger's largest mosque. With regularity, the president of the country, the prime minister, and the head of parliament arrive in their motorcades at the Grand Mosque to celebrate Tabaski and the beginning and end of Ramadan. What's more, political leaders come to the mosque to participate in other religious ceremonies. In particular, Niger's leading politicians sometimes call on religious authorities and all Nigériens to pray for rain. (More than 80 percent of Niger's labor force farm or herd, and approximately 40 percent of the country's GDP comes from agriculture, so the timing and abundance of rain is of vital importance.)[182] This is not a new practice. In 1974, three months after coming to power, the Conseil Militaire Suprême asked Nigériens to spend a day praying for a good rainy season.[183] Neither strictly secular nor strictly clerical, Niger is a democracy where religious acts carry meaning and power.

3 BARGAINING FOR WOMEN'S REPRESENTATION

The Adoption of a Gender Quota

AT A LITTLE BEFORE ONE IN THE AFTERNOON on February 18, 2010, President Mamadou Tandja was at his weekly cabinet meeting at the presidential palace. Tandja and the ministers sat in the usual conference room at a long table, with the president sitting under a framed portrait of himself, and the Nigérien flag in orange, white, and green on a stand on the white tablecloth in front of him. They were preoccupied with the task of reviewing who would be promoted in the ministries. Just as the high-ranking officials were counting the number of women on a proposed list of promotions, gunshots rang from outside the room. A band of soldiers took control of the palace. Tandja was deposed that day in a military coup d'état.[1]

Why was President Tandja, in what would be his last moments in office, fastidiously tallying up the number of women being considered for promotion? Much of the attention to women's numerical representation in Niger can be traced to its gender quota. Approximately ten years earlier, on June 7, 2000, President Tandja signed the Law Instituting the Quota System for Elective Office, in the Government, and in the Administration of the State (hereafter, "gender quota law").[2] In doing so, Niger became one of the first Muslim-majority democracies in the world, let alone in West Africa, to adopt a gender-based affirmative action law for elected positions in politics. Niger's gender quota law requires that no less than 10 percent of elected offices and no less than 25 percent of cabinet appointments and promotions in public administration be filled by either sex. The quota has since been enforced for the most highly coveted positions in politics: between 1970 and 2011, the presence of women in parliament increased from 0 percent to more than 13 percent, and the presence of women in the cabinet increased from 0 percent to more than 25 percent.[3]

This chapter investigates how Niger adopted a gender quota. In a favorable global context, Niger adopted its gender quota through the mobilization of women in and outside the state, who helped make women's underrepresentation a public problem. Women's activists made the adoption of a quota law thinkable by arguing that improving women's representation was democratic and that women were worthy candidates for positions of power. Conservative religious activists did not mobilize against the proposed gender quota; including more women in politics was thinkable to Islamists. The national political context also figured prominently. Flexing their veto power, a relatively autonomous National Assembly modified the quota bill and lowered the proposed minimum percentage for elected offices from 25 to 10 percent, much to the dismay of women's activists. Through this compromise, parliament passed the quota bill.

More broadly, Niger's adoption of the gender quota law illustrates the promises and challenges of promoting women's rights in a democracy. In democratic Niger, women's activists were better able to organize demonstrations, create independent associations, and network with parliamentarians to lobby for greater numbers of women in politics. Yet in the same democratic context, parliamentarians used their constitutional power to modify the gender quota bill. In opposing parts of the bill, moreover, parliamentarians invoked democracy more so than they invoked Islam and tradition. Thus, this chapter highlights the manifold ways in which democratic freedoms and institutions influence the passage of women's rights reforms in Muslim-majority countries.

The Scope of Women's Underrepresentation in Niger

Between 1960 and 1988, the presence of women in Niger's formal halls of power was close to nil. When there was a sitting parliament, no women were to be found occupying a seat, nor were there any female ministers.[4] The most prominent woman in politics during Hamani Diori's presidency (1960–74) was First Lady Aissa Diori. First Lady Diori, a mother of six, was the honorary president of the women's wing of the country's only legal political party, the Parti Progressiste Nigérien–Rassemblement Démocratique Africain (PPN-RDA).[5] First Lady Diori, however, also constructed and rented villas to the U.S. and French embassies at steep prices, and used state-owned land to grow and sell vegetables.[6] In the 1974 military coup, it was First Lady Diori who was shot and killed, allegedly with a gun in her hand, while her husband surrendered and survived.[7] President Seyni Kountché's government (1974–87) did not have as notorious a first lady as Aissa Diori, but it also excluded women from its highest ranks.

That is not to say that women were invisible, ignorant of, or uninterested in the public sphere in authoritarian Niger. Many women's activists in civil society in the 1990s worked for the state as nurses, midwives, journalists, and teachers in the 1960s, 1970s, and 1980s. Maiga Amsou Amadou, the first director of Niger's Department of the Advancement of Women, started her career as a state nurse.[8] Said to have escaped an early marriage due to the intervention of a school principal, her work in public health earned her the prestigious Chevalier de l'Ordre du Mérite and Croix d'Officier de l'Ordre du Mérite. Amadou later pursued her interests in health in democratic Niger as president of the Comité Nigérien sur les Pratiques Traditionnelles (CONIPRAT), a nongovernmental organization that fights against female genital mutilation. Salamatou Traoré, trained as a nurse and midwife, directed a maternity hospital in Niamey in the late 1980s. In the 1990s and 2000s, she became a champion of women's reproductive rights, particularly the rights of women with fistula. Mariama Keita, who served as the first president of CONGAFEN, democratic Niger's largest umbrella women's association, reported for the state's radio station under authoritarian rule in the 1970s. Michèle Claude Hadiza taught junior high in the 1970s and 1980s before advocating for women's rights in the Ministry of Social Development's Office on the Advancement of Women in democratic Niger. Hadiza also served as the third president of CONGAFEN.

In addition to working for the state, women shone in the public sphere as oral historians and praise singers.[9] Scholars such as Ousseina Alidou bring to life these public figures. Habsu Garba worked at a bank before becoming an "artistic icon" for the one-party state, greeting foreign presidents with her original songs and large musical troupe.[10] As a high school student, she had loved learning Qur'anic verses through song. Women, moreover, participated in politics at the community and regional levels as traditional or spiritual leaders (e.g., magajiya, iya, inna, maidaki), by taking part in state-organized youth organizations (samaria), and by volunteering with the Association des Femmes du Niger (AFN).[11] Women were not among the official, national elite during Niger's authoritarian era, but they were not absent from politics.

The number of women in formal political posts began to change under Ali Saibou (1987–93).[12] Five women won seats in Niger's ninety-three-seat National Assembly in the December 10, 1989, election. (The only political party that was allowed to participate in the election was the Mouvement National pour la Société du Développement [MNSD].) This marked the first time that women served as members of parliament (MPs). These first female representatives were Roukayatou Abdou Issaka (representing Mirriah), Bibata Adamou Dakaou (Kollo), Marie Lebihan (Maradi), Aïssata Karidjo Mounkaïla, a longtime secretary-general of the AFN (Niamey), and Hadizatou Diallo Souna (Niamey), who later became the first woman to head a political party, Parti Nigérien pour le Renforcement de la Démocratie (PNRD) Al-Fidjir. Together, they made up 5.4 percent of the National Assembly.

Although women made their way into the National Assembly in the late 1980s, the percentage of women in the National Assembly declined over the 1990s (see Figure 7). In Niger's first multiparty elections (1993), women won five out of eighty-three seats (6.0 percent). Aïssata Karidjo Mounkaïla was reelected. Fatouma Djibo Annou represented the MNSD. Haoua Barazé Zada and Binta Tankary represented the Alliance Nigérienne pour la Démocratie et le Progrès (ANDP) party, and Aïchatou Nana Foumakoye represented the Convention Démocratique et Sociale (CDS).[13] In the following 1995 elections, three women were elected (3.6 percent): Mounkaïla and Foumakoye were reelected, and Hawa Garba Wonkoye represented the ANDP. The number of women elected to the National Assembly then dropped to just one in the highly dis- puted 1996 elections (1.2 percent). Jeanette Schmidt Degener represented the Union Nationale des Indépendants pour le Renouveau Démocratique (UNIRD). In the relatively free and fair 1999 elections, only Aïssata Karidjo Mounkaila of the MNSD entered into the National Assembly.[14]

Following the adoption of the gender quota law, the percentage of women in the National Assembly jumped from 1.2 percent in 1999 to 12.4 percent in 2004, when fourteen women entered the newly expanded 113-seat assembly.[15] Eight women came from the MNSD, which won 47 seats. Three women came from the CDS, which won 22 seats. Two women represented the Parti Nigérien pour la Démocratie et le Socialisme (PNDS) (25 seats); one woman repre- sented the ANDP (5 seats); and no women represented the Rassemblement Social-Démocratique (RSD) (7 seats), the Rassemblement pour la Démocra- tie et le Progrès (RDP) (6 seats), or the Parti Social-Démocrate Nigérien (PSDN) (1 seat). The numerical representation of women in parliament continued to hover near or above 10 percent in the 2000s. In the 2011 elections, fifteen women won seats in the assembly (13.3 percent). The quota, as I will explain later in the chapter, helps account for the difference in the percentage of women in par- liament before and after 2000.

Like women in the National Assembly, women joined the executive cabi- net for the first time in the late 1980s. In 1989, Aïssata Moumouni became Niger's first woman minister as minister of social affairs and the status of

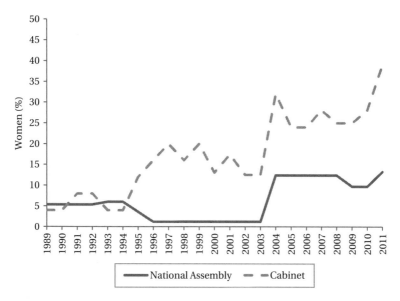

Figure 7. Women's numerical representation in Niger, 1989–2011

Note: The values for the National Assembly refer to the percentage of women as of December 31 of the year. See Chaïbou, *Répertoire biographique, Vol. 1 Les Parlementaires;* Inter-Parliamentary Union, "Niger: Election Archives"; Inter-Parliamentary Union, "Niger: Last Elections, 2011." The values for the cabinet include ambassadors and permanent representative to international organizations. See CIA, *Chiefs of State and Cabinet Members of Foreign Governments;* Hamani, *Les femmes et la politique au Niger.*

women. In an interview with the women's magazine *Aïcha,* Moumouni recalled her surprise at the appointment and her reluctance to accept the post. Her husband, Abdou Moumouni—a renowned physicist who was then president of the University of Niamey—encouraged her to accept the nomination.[16] Moumouni started her career as a high school math teacher in Niamey in 1964. She then became principal of the country's then only public high school for girls (*Lycée des jeunes filles,* now *Lycée Kassaï*). In 1985, Moumouni organized and taught night school for girls who had been expelled from school for becoming pregnant.[17] Her work was recognized with an appointment as secretary of public health and social welfare, in charge of social affairs and the status of women, which she held between 1987 and 1988.[18] After her first spell as minister, Moumouni continued to participate in politics at the national level as an adviser to Prime Minister Hama Amadou in 1995 and as minister of education from 1996 to 1999.[19]

Along with Aïssata Moumouni, thirty-two other women held cabinet posts between 1989 and 2010. Women have served as ministers of agriculture, commerce, communication, education, foreign affairs, labor, public health, small business, social welfare, tourism, and transportation. The presence of women in the cabinet increased from an average of 0.3 percent during Kountché's *régime d'exception* (1 of 377 ministers between 1974 and 1989) to an average of 3.9 percent during the Second Republic (2 of 51 ministers between 1989 and 1991). Women made up an average of 8.5 percent of the cabinet under the Third Republic (6 out of 70 ministers between 1993 and 1995). The figure dropped to an average of 5.2 percent in the Fourth Republic (5 of 96 ministers between 1996 and 1999). Starting in 2005, women occupied at least 24.0 percent of the cabinet and remained at this level during Mamadou Tandja's and Mahamadou Issoufou's presidencies. The gender quota law, as we will see later, helped make the ascent of women to the executive cabinet possible.

Gender Quotas: A Primer

Before going into the role of women's activism in bringing about Niger's gender quota, it is useful for the reader to become familiar with quota systems. A quota is a "rule of redistribution of a benefit or burden among at least two groups on the basis of a fixed percentage or share for each group."[20] Gender quotas specifically seek to redistribute benefits and burdens between men and women. Quotas can appear nearly anywhere: in university selection processes, company boardrooms, and politics—the focus of this chapter. Gender quotas for elected office are common; they have been adopted in more than a hundred countries, leading Karen Celis, Mona Lena Krook, and Petra Meier to call gender quotas "the most prevalent electoral reforms of recent years."[21]

Types of Gender Quotas

Gender quotas in politics appear in many forms.[22] The first and most common type is the voluntary party quota, or party quota for short. This is a situation in which a political party, of its own volition, redistributes roles or resources to encourage a more equal representation of men and women. In the United Kingdom, the Labour Party has used gender quotas since 1997.[23] In 2010, members of the Labour Party voted that a minimum 31.5 percent of the shadow cabinet should be women.[24] In Africa, political parties have voluntarily adopted gender quotas in at least fifteen countries: Algeria, Burkina Faso, Cameroon, Ethiopia, Ghana, Ivory Coast, Kenya, Mali, Morocco, Mozambique, Namibia, Senegal, South Africa, Tunisia, and Zimbabwe.[25]

A second type of gender quota is the legal quota, also known as a legislative candidate quota or mandatory party quota. Legal quotas require all parties to front a minimum percentage of female candidates. Argentina's legal gender quota, first adopted in 1991, requires that women make up at least 30 percent of party lists for national elections. In Africa, legal quotas have been adopted in at least twelve countries, including Niger: Angola, Burkina Faso, Djibouti, Guinea, Kenya, Libya, Mauritania, Morocco, Senegal, Togo, and Tunisia.[26]

A third type of quota is the reserved seat. Reserved seats are similar to legal quotas in that they are legally or constitutionally mandated. Reserved seats, however, are different from legal quotas in that the percentage of seats that go to women is regulated. In Africa, at least ten countries have or had reserved seats for women. Uganda's reserved seat system, which dates to 1987, reserved at least 112 seats for women out of a total of 385 seats in 2011.[27] Tanzania's system ensures that women occupy at least 20 percent of parliamentary seats. Rwanda introduced a 30 percent reserved seat system in 2003. Other countries that have (or had) reserved seats for women in Africa are Burundi, Egypt, Eritrea, Somalia, South Sudan, Sudan, and Zimbabwe.[28]

The last type of gender quota is the appointed quota. Here, the executive is allowed or required to appoint a minimum number of women to the parliament, the cabinet, or public administration. For example, Kenya's previous 1997 constitution allowed the president to appoint at least six women to parliament. In Swaziland, the king appoints twenty senators of the thirty-one-body senate. Of those twenty senators, the king is required to appoint at least eight women.[29]

Niger's Gender Quota

Not a country to simply copy what others have done, Niger's law calls for the use of multiple types of quotas. For the sake of simplicity, I will refer to Niger's quota as a legal quota, since it is mandated by law.

Niger's quota requires political parties to take gender into account when recruiting candidates to vie for office. More precisely, the law states, "During legislative and local elections, candidate lists presented by political parties, party coalitions, and groups of independents must include candidates of both sexes."[30] Niger uses a closed-list proportional representation (PR) electoral system composed of multimember districts. Political parties present a list of candidates for each multimember district. Under this type of system, the electorate votes for a party list. The number of seats a party wins in a district is proportional to the percentage of votes the party receives. If a party presents a list of candidates that does not include any women (or any men), then the Constitutional Court is required to reject that list.

One note needs to be made here concerning elections to Niger's parliament. Niger has a unicameral legislature, which, since 2004, contains 113 seats. One hundred five seats are filled through the PR electoral system. The remaining eight seats are filled through a majoritarian (also known as first-past-the-post, or majority-plurality) electoral system. These seats were created to encourage greater representation of minority groups (such as Arabs, Gourmantchés, and Toubous) that live in relatively remote areas in Niger (for example, Bilma and Torodi). These seats are often incorrectly referred to as Tuareg seats. For these eight special-constituency seats, the electorate votes for a candidate rather than for a party. Because the law refers to candidate lists, the quota applies to the 105 seats and not to the eight special seats in the National Assembly.

Niger's gender quota law further requires parties to take gender into account when selecting whom from their lists will win a seat in office. Specifically, the law says, "In announcing the final election results, the proportion of elected candidates of either sex must not be less than 10 percent."[31] To further clarify how this would be enforced, on February 28, 2001, President Tandja passed Decree No. 2001–056 on the application of the gender quota law.[32] The decree specifies that if a party wins three or more seats in a district, then the party must meet or exceed the 10 percent minimum quota. In other words, if a party wins three seats in a district, one seat must go to a woman if the other two seats go to men (and vice versa). If a party's seat allocation violates the gender quota law, then the proclamation of results can be challenged before the Constitutional Court.

Finally, Niger's gender quota law requires the executive branch to take gender into account when making appointments to the cabinet and giving promotions in public administration. The law stipulates, "When members of the cabinet and promotions in senior public service are announced, the proportion of either sex must not be less than 25 percent."[33] That is, when the president and prime minister finalize the composition of the cabinet, having taken into account the recommendations of the parties allied with the party of the president, they must ensure that at least a quarter of the cabinet is made up of women (or men). And when the executive cabinet meets to approve of promotions for high-ranking officials in public administration, the cabinet is required to ensure that the 25 percent minimum is respected. The 2001 decree further states that violations of the gender quota in appointments and promotions can be brought before the administrative chamber of the Supreme Court.[34]

Women's Mobilization for a Gender Quota

Women's mobilization in and outside the state is crucial to the story of how Niger adopted a legal gender quota. Activists helped make the absence of women from formal positions of power a public problem and gender quotas a thinkable solution. Although they at times struggled with internal divisions, women in civil society, the Ministry of Social Development, and the National Assembly formed a common front on the issue of gender quotas.

Naming, Blaming, and Claiming the Problem of Underrepresentation, 1991

Women's activists transformed the lack of women's political representation from a taken-for-granted fact into a public problem on May 13, 1991. On this day, thousands of women and men protested in the capital of Niamey against the exclusion of women from the Commission Nationale Préparatoire à la Conférence Nationale (CNPCN), the committee tasked to lead Niger's transition to democracy. President Saibou's government—under duress from student and union demonstrators, in a period of acute economic instability, and in a context of global and regional democratization—had initiated a political transition from one-party military rule to multiparty democratic rule in early 1991. The sixty-eight-member committee responsible for transitioning Niger from an autocratic regime to a democratic regime had one woman, Haoua Alio, who resigned from the CNPCN to join the protest.[35] Protesters, who included civil servants, high school students, teachers, union members, and members of the AFN, left their offices, schools, and homes to join the demonstration and carried signs saying, "Preparation for the National Conference without Women: Discrimination," "Reaffirming Our Determination to Defend Our Rights," and "Vive la Femme Nigérienne."[36]

Protest organizers drove around Niamey with loudspeakers, calling on women to march to the Ministry of Foreign Affairs, where the preparatory committee was meeting to discuss the National Conference. Police commissioner Barry Bibata, who happened to also be a women's rights activist and founding member of the AFJN, helped organize the march and ensured that the police would not disrupt the demonstration.[37] Inside the ministry, protesters blockaded the main conference room. "The women literally besieged the conference room in the Ministry of Foreign Affairs preventing everyone—CNPCN members, ministers, and guests—from entering the room, either by forming barricades or by booing at them," reported *Le Sahel.* The following day, women in the towns of Diffa and Zinder joined the protest hundreds of miles outside Niamey. Demonstrators carried signs that declared, "Down with Injustice," "Yes to Women's Participation in Nation-Building," and "Give Women All Their Rights," and presented their demands to the prefects of Diffa and Zinder.[38] The May 13 demonstration was Niger's largest postcolonial women's protest.

Protest leaders presented a list of demands to the leaders of the National Conference, reproduced here.[39]

Special Motion on the National Conference

—Considering that women make up more than 52 percent of the population of Niger;

—Considering the low representation of women in politics today;

—Considering the need to take into account the specific needs and aspirations of women in Niger;

—Considering that the rise of democracy requires the participation of all living forces in the Nation;

—Considering the crucial role that Nigérien women play in the country's development;

—Considering the importance of the National Conference to the future of our country;

—We, Nigérien women, demand the full and effective participation of women on the preparatory committee of the National Conference;

—Require the inclusion of women on all items of the agenda of the National Conference;

—Require the presence of women in all delegations that will participate at the National Conference.

Made in Niamey, May 13, 1991

Nigérien Women

The May 13 protest provides a textbook example of what sociologists of law William Felstiner, Richard Abel, and Austin Sarat call "naming, blaming, and claiming."[40] Naming is a crucial antecedent to social action. Without the perception that something is wrong, there is no impetus to change the status quo. In the first two items on the Special Motion, protesters named the injury: women are numerically dominant in Niger yet excluded from politics. The next two items on the Special Motion identify who and what is being injured: women who have "specific needs and aspirations" and democracy, which "requires the participation of all living forces." Although women had been marginalized from the formal political sphere for decades, it was in 1991 when Nigérien women finally put the issue of women's underrepresentation on the national political agenda.

Women's activists did more than identify an injury in the exclusion of women from the CNPCN. They found blame, or "attribut[ed] an injury to the fault of another individual or social entity," depicting the injury as something that somebody could remedy.[41] The protesters faulted the prime minister, to whom they read aloud the Special Motion. The protesters also placed blame on party leaders for excluding women from their delegations to the National Conference. "The responsibility," as Thérèse Keita, one of the protest leaders, said, "falls on the Government and the political parties who took the easy route to make up the CNPCN."[42] Pointing the finger to a specific set of actors, the protesters transformed the perceived wrong into a grievance.

Finally, protesters made specific claims, directing government officials toward a response. The claims are clearly stated in the last three items of the Special Motion. The demonstrators claimed the need for "the full and effective participation of women on the preparatory committee," sought the inclusion of women's interests on the agenda of the National Conference, and asked for representation on all the delegations to the National Conference. As Aïssata Bagnan Fall, one of the protest leaders, reiterated when meeting the prime minister, political party leaders, and union heads, "We are claiming our place."[43] Women protesters identified and articulated specific demands.

In naming, blaming, and claiming the problem of women's absence from formal politics, the May 13 protest was an important victory for women's activists in Niger. The leaders of the democratic transition compromised with the protesters. Four women were added to the CNPCN, increasing the total number of women on the CNPCN from one to five.[44] After the conclusion of the National Conference, a transitional government was established, and two women were appointed to the executive cabinet. Aïssata Bagnan Fall was made minister of social development, population, and the advancement of women, and Mariama Banakoye was made minister of public service and labor.[45] When Niger's first democratically elected government replaced the transitional government in 1993, another protester, Aïchatou Boulama Kané, became secretary of planning in the Ministry of Finance and Planning.[46] May 13 was made an official national holiday, the Journée Nationale de la Femme

Nigérienne.[47] Women's activists who participated in the march look on this day with gladness.[48] May 13 represented what Nigérien women could achieve if they were mobilized and unified.

Amid the euphoria of the May 13 demonstration, some women were skeptical about the male political leaders and whether they were truly committed to including women in positions of power. Thérèse Keita was particularly wary of the male politicians. Upon observing party leaders complain about having to include more women during one of the May 13 negotiations, Keita remarked to the room of men, "We are seeing here some very close-minded people who are not ready to make concessions. Tomorrow when you will be in power, you will continue to marginalize women."[49]

Renaming, Reblaming, and Reclaiming the Problem of Underrepresentation, 1991–99

As Thérèse Keita had predicted, women continued to be marginalized from positions of political power in the 1990s. Yet mobilization for a gender quota law did not happen immediately. It would take women's activists almost ten years of minimal progress, repeated experimentation, chance encounters abroad, and the installation of a transitional government before they would try to lobby for a gender quota law.

In spite of the gains made during the National Conference, women were excluded in party lists for legislative elections in the 1990s. Recall that Niger has a PR electoral system, in which a party assembles a list of candidates for each region. The electorate votes for the party's list, not for individual candidates. Based on the number of votes a party obtains in the region, the party selects which candidates will go to parliament. In the first multiparty elections (1993), the MNSD—the party that won the most seats—placed three women on its list of eighty-three candidates (3.0 percent). The socialist-leaning PNDS-Taraya did slightly better, putting five women on its list (6.4 percent). In 1999, the number of women on party lists declined: MNSD-Nassara and PNDS-Taraya each put two women on their lists of candidates.[50] Meanwhile, women were performing the grunt work of recruiting and organizing party members in the cities and countryside.[51] Women did fare better in making it into the parties' executive offices: 11.4 percent of CDS's executive party members were women in 1999, 16.8 percent of MNSD's in 1998, and 10.5 percent of PNDS's in 1995.[52] Yet women were not candidates.

In contrast to the women's activists in 1991 who were clear about whom to blame (the prime minister and the political parties), activists in the mid-1990s did not point the finger to specific politicians or political institutions, nor did they find fault with the country's laws. As noted by one participant at a 1999 workshop on women and decentralization organized by the European Union and the PANOS Institute, "Niger's laws do not discriminate between men and women."[53] Indeed, advocates and policymakers thought that Niger's laws against discrimination were better than those of other countries.[54] Instead, activists, "women's experts," and ministry officials blamed women for being too timid. "The ball is now in the woman's court, the woman who has the confidence to exercise her right to access political office," said a government document on the status of women in 1994.[55] Women were stricken with "shyness, fear of failure, and lack of confidence," said one so-called expert on women at the 1999 workshop on women and decentralization.[56] The Ministry of Social Development stated in a draft policy document that the lack of women in politics stems from "the unwillingness of women to assert themselves."[57]

Activists in and outside the state blamed the lack of women's representation on societal norms *(pesanteurs socioculturelles)*. The absence of women in politics stemmed from "discrimination," "family responsibilities," "lack of support," and "social pressures."[58] The remedy to the problem of women's underrepresentation was vague, placed as it was in the paternalistic teaching of women to be more self-confident, in public education campaigns to combat societal discrimination against women, and in pleas by party women to party leaders to put more women on their lists.[59]

To this point, women's activists in and outside the state did not immediately or vociferously claim the need for gender quotas. Once, in 1994, a 30 percent gender quota was proposed in a draft ministerial document, which shows that the government was aware of gender quotas early on—only three years after Argentina adopted its landmark quota law and one year *before* the United Nations Fourth World Conference on Women. The draft document suggested that the government "institute a minimum 30 percent quota for women in decision-making positions, such as those in public service."[60] It also suggested that the government "equally divide between men and women quotas given to Niger in international, regional, and subregional organizations."[61] The idea of using quotas, however, was dropped in the final version of the ministerial document. Instead of calling for quotas, the final document vaguely calls on the government to "increase the presence of women in decision-making positions, such as those in public service," and to "give men and women the same opportunities to represent Niger in international, regional, and subregional organizations."[62]

Nor did the government's national report in preparation for the 1995 World Conference on Women in Beijing mention gender quotas. Instead, to improve women's status, the report recommends the ratification of CEDAW, the adoption of family law reform, more education for women, and more mobilization among women.[63] In 1998, the government again called for more women in decision-making posts but without any mention of quotas.[64] If legal quotas were raised in the public sphere in the 1990s, it was by male researchers. In his book on women and politics in Niger, Abdou Hamani argued that women were not in parliament because women were not being put on party lists. Another study of Niger's political leaders mentioned that countries like Bangladesh and Nepal use reserved seats for women—information that was buried in an appendix on page 425 of a 465-page book.[65]

As women's numerical representation in bodies like the National Assembly hung in the balance, the women's movement split over issues unrelated to the gender quota. Several reasons are offered for why the women's movement lost its unity. One study suggests that multiparty politics resulted in the "fragmentation and weakening of independent associational life."[66] Although women's associations are officially "apolitical," the leader of the RDFN was said to have backed the socialist-leaning PNDS, whereas the AFN was linked with the behemoth MNSD.[67] Divisions within the women's movement intensified after Ibrahim Baré Maïnassara led a successful military coup in 1996. Some women's leaders backed the previous government, whereas others supported Baré: the president of the RDFN became Baré's spokesperson.[68]

Proposing a Thinkable Solution, 1999–2000

Seeing that they were dividing themselves into smaller and potentially less powerful groups, women's activists formed an umbrella women's association, CONGAFEN. In 1999, CONGAFEN asked a transitional parliament to include a gender quota in the new constitution and electoral code. Another military coup had taken place in April, and a transitional parliament, the Conseil Consultatif National (CCN), was set up in May to draft a new constitution for referendum and other laws, including those governing the conduct of elections. Ninety-two people were appointed to the transitional parliament, including past presidents, past presidents of the National Assembly, political party presidents, and past Supreme Court judges. In the transitional parliament were also representatives of the unions, human rights organizations, and religious organizations. The largest women's organizations (AFN,

CONGAFEN, Fédération Kassaï, RDFN) had representatives in the transitional parliament; CONGAFEN's president at the time was among them.

Before the legislative elections, CONGAFEN "grabbed the opportunity," in the words of its president at the time, to talk to the country's most powerful decision makers and public opinion leaders.[69] The president of CONGAFEN called for the adoption of a 30 percent legal gender quota, so that for every two men, there would be one woman in political and decision-making posts.[70] She had learned about gender quotas when she attended a meeting of the Commission on the Status of Women at the United Nations in New York City. This direct address to the consultative body marked an important departure from the routine awareness-raising campaigns and workshops that women's activists had previously organized.

Legislative elections took place in 1999, and no women were elected to the National Assembly. Despite CONGAFEN's proposal, the CCN did not insert a gender quota into the new electoral code. The proposed quota did not receive the support of the transitional president, Daouda Malam Wanké, or by other male members of the CCN. Some women opposed the idea. Women from other organizations and parties in the CCN did not speak up in favor of the gender quota in the standing committees or in the plenary session. Following the elections, the president of CONGAFEN told the CCN that the soon-to-be-installed parliament was a "parliament of shame" for leaving out their mothers, sisters, and daughters. This remark sparked a three-hour debate over women's representation. Some men in the CCN proposed increasing the number of MPs to include more women. The leaders of the CCN pointed out that it could not change the size of parliament just after the holding of elections. Following the debate, leaders of the MNSD removed one male MP and replaced him with a woman. On its last day, the CCN adopted a resolution that the Fifth Republic do everything to increase women's representation in positions of political power. Women's activists helped plant the idea of a gender quota, but its adoption into law would require buy-in from both women and men in the executive cabinet.

When a civilian government was reinstalled and Tandja elected president, women's activists fighting for greater numbers of women in politics found an important ally in Minister of Social Development Aïchatou Nana Foumakoye.[71] The granddaughter of a well-known Muslim judge, Foumakoye was born in 1952 in Magaria and taught French, history, and geography in the 1970s and 1980s.[72] When the door to multiparty politics opened in the early 1990s, Foumakoye joined CDS-Rahama. CDS's home base is in Zinder, close to Foumakoye's birthplace and where she attended school. Foumakoye was an active member of the party, serving as the secretary-general of the party's women's wing, the Association des Femmes Rahama (AFR).[73] In the first multiparty legislative elections in 1993, Foumakoye got on CDS's candidate list for the Zinder region, campaigned for her party and her candidacy, and was selected to become the first CDS woman in parliament. Once there, Foumakoye was elected by her fellow MPs to be the third vice president of the National Assembly, along with political heavyweights Sanoussi Jackou (first vice president) and Bazoum Mohamed (second vice president). She served until May 1994, when Hama Amadou took her place.[74] In 1995, she was reelected to the National Assembly.

In addition to being a loyal partisan of the CDS, Foumakoye was active in civil society. She was a founding member of the RDFN and served on its executive board. As shown in chapter 2, the RDFN was not any run-of-the-mill women's organization. A feminist association, the RDFN lobbied hard for family law reform in the early 1990s. Foumakoye also served on the board of Niger's leading human rights association, the Association Nigérienne pour la Défense des Droits de l'Homme (ANDDH), and presided over a women's nongovernmental organization, Biyan Bukata.[75] Thus, by the time she was named minister of social development in April 1999, Foumakoye had gained significant experience working with political party leaders, parliamentarians, and civil society, and had acquired a reputation for being forceful and speaking her mind. In Hausa, her colleagues and fellow parliamentarians called her *mace nda wandon karfé*, or in French, *la femme au pantalon de fer*—"the woman in the iron pants."[76]

Like women's activists in CONGAFEN, Foumakoye saw gender quotas as a way to address the lack of women in politics.[77] She had been inspired by the Inter-Parliamentary Union's (IPU) 1994 Plan of Action, which encouraged countries to adopt gender quotas.[78] Foumakoye approached Prime Minister Hama Amadou about revising the country's electoral code to include a gender quota. The prime minister suggested instead that the Ministry of Social Development draft a law apart from the electoral code. The ministry then drafted a bill, framing the quota as addressing both men's and women's representation, so as not to alienate male parliamentarians. "We made sure it said one of either sex, so that the men wouldn't complain," explains a longtime member of the AFN. "If 100 percent of the Assembly were women, 10 percent would have to go to men."[79] The bill emphasized that the quota would be a temporary fix for a structural problem that impeded women's full participation in Niger's new democracy.

When the quota bill was brought to the cabinet meeting for approval, some male ministers opposed it. Nevertheless, "with the support of the Prime Minister and the President of the Republic," said Foumakoye in an interview with *Aïcha,* "we were able to keep the quota at 25 percent for elected posts and nominated posts."[80] The timing was right, noted Foumakoye: "The leaders of the Fifth Republic were favorable to the advancement of women . . . and women had witnessed that they had fought for the restoration of democracy. They [the women] knew . . . that the moment had come."[81] Prime Minister Amadou, backed by President Tandja, said that the quota would be adopted.

By 1999, women in and outside the state renamed the problem of women's underrepresentation as undemocratic. Women's activists argued that the exclusion of women from politics went against democratic principles because women amounted to the majority of the electorate. In document after document—beginning with the first item in the Special Motion on the National Conference—women's activists noted that women made up 52 percent of Niger's population to contend that women's underrepresentation was undemocratic. Women had "electoral weight," wrote the minister of social development in a 1995 government document.[82] Later on, we will see that parliamentarians adopted this discourse in supporting the gender quota bill.

Furthermore, women's activists argued that women not only had an innate right but also deserved to hold positions of power. In the previously mentioned 1995 government document, the minister of social development wrote that women had the "primary role of mobilization in the political parties."[83] In the same document, activist Mariama Keita lamented that women were "a lemon to be squeezed and thrown away, when it comes to sharing political positions or even administrative and technical positions. They are merely forgotten."[84] This causal narrative, that party women were hardworking but systematically excluded, was not new. According to a study by the Ministry of Social Development, in Niger's one-party era, "women, while very active in different parts of the political party, did not participate in the running of the country."[85] As a former minister said, "Tandja believed that it was the women who really fought for him. That the women were behind his ascent to power."[86] Women did not constantly switch parties; they did not take part in *nomadisme politique.* Women were the "real workers" of the party, and the "voters one could count on."[87] In other words, women deserved to hold positions of political weight.

Activists argued that women had a proven record of serving successfully in the highest political positions dating back to precolonial Niger. Women's advocates in the Ministry of Social Development wrote about Queen Amina from the fifteenth century and Saraounia Mangou from the nineteenth century, yet "at the dawn of the 21st century, women are denied the chance to manage public affairs."[88] A woman from Niamey, Aïchatou Arifa, pointed out in a 1992 letter to *Haské* that men opposed the nomination of a woman to the head of a subprefecture, "yet there is Sarraounia Mangou, Queen Daoura, Queen Zinga, all these women."[89] We will see later that parliamentarians agreed that women were deserving candidates, a line of reasoning that can be traced back to women's mobilization for better representation.

At the National Assembly, the pro-quota coalition used several tactics to lobby for the bill's passage. The minister of social development and the director of the Office on the Advancement of Women visited two parliamentary committees to answer MPs' questions and further explain the merits of the quota.[90] Foumakoye targeted MPs in both the ruling coalition and the opposition and became known as "Madame Quota." The minister and the only woman in parliament also connected before the parliamentary debate, coming to an understanding that the female MP should represent women and defend the quota on the floor. Knowing that some MPs opposed the quota bill, Foumakoye notified women's organizations of the date on which the quota would be debated and asked them to come in great numbers to the National Assembly, hoping that the presence of women's activists would pressure the MPs into voting for the bill.[91] On the day of the vote, women's activists "came out in large numbers, massively, to support the debate, which they followed for many long hours right until the end."[92]

As we have seen, women's activists in civil society and in the Ministry of Social Development proposed, pushed for, and wrote a gender quota bill. President Tandja and Prime Minister Amadou supported the proposed legislation. Yet as one member of the pro-quota coalition recalled to me, moving the bill through the National Assembly was "quite a challenge."[93] The quota would eventually be adopted, but in a form that women's activists in and outside the Ministry of Social Development did not anticipate. It is now time to turn to the MPs who voted on the quota bill.

Bargaining over the Quota in the National Assembly

On May 5, 2000, Niger's parliamentarians met to discuss and vote on the quota bill. In an illiberal democracy or authoritarian context, one would expect the National Assembly to serve as an applause chamber and unquestioningly approve the quota bill. Yet Niger was experimenting with democracy, and if new democratic laws provided opportunities for women's activists to lobby for the gender quota, the constitution also provided a space for parliamentarians to question, modify, or even reject the gender quota bill.

The Legislative Process in Niger

In democratic Niger, the National Assembly's approval is required for most bills before they can become law.[94] Generally, there are two types of bills.[95] Government bills *(projets de loi)* are proposed by ministries (see Figure 8). Private member bills *(propositions de loi)* are proposed by MPs. In contrast to a U.S.-style Congress, in Niger, the vast majority of bills originate from the government; MPs, whether male or female, rarely propose new pieces of legislation.[96] In the case of government bills, bureaucrats in a ministry draft legislation that then goes to the minister, who then takes the bill to the cabinet. (Informally, the minister may discuss an idea for a bill with the prime minister or president to assess his or her level of support.) The executive cabinet reviews the bill, and if approved, the bill is sent to the National Assembly.

At the National Assembly, the Executive Office *(bureau de l'assemblée)* makes several key decisions. Along with the Office of Legislation, the Executive Office establishes a calendar for the debate and vote on government bills and private member bills. If a bill is put on the calendar, the main office decides whether and when to send the bill to parliamentary committees *(commissions)* and which committee will be the lead *(commission saisie au fond)*. The Executive Office then sends the bill to the committees.

Each parliamentary committee inspects the bill in a committee sitting.[97] For legislation proposed by the government, the committee reads a statement of purpose *(exposé des motifs)* submitted by the ministry that proposed the bill. The statement of purpose justifies the need for a new law. A minister or representative of the ministry can attend the committee sittings to answer questions and defend the proposal.[98] The committee discusses the contents and form of the bill and whether there is a need for any amendments. A member of the committee *(rapporteur)* synthesizes the discussion and includes the committee's proposed amendments into a report. The committee's report is then sent to the Executive Office of the National Assembly.

Following the calendar, the bill then arrives on the floor in a plenary session *(séance plénière)*, which the public is allowed to attend. The president of the National Assembly leads the session. In the first part *(débat)*, a representative of each committee, starting with the lead committee, makes a brief statement that includes the committee's suggested amendments to the bill. Once

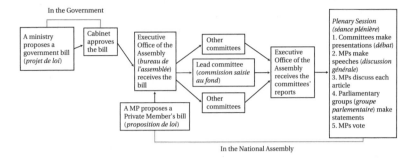

Figure 8. Stylized depiction of the legislative process in the National Assembly of Niger based on the Republic of Niger's 2000 version of the Règlement intérieur de l'Assemblée Nationale

all of the committees have summarized their reports, the floor is then opened for individual MPs to make statements about the bill *(discussion générale)*. Following the MPs' statements, a representative from the ministry that proposed the government bill may address the National Assembly to make one last appeal in favor of the bill. The assembly discusses each article to either approve or attach amendments, often referring to the lead committee's report. Before the assembly votes on whether to approve the bill, the chairperson of each major political party or coalition of parties (parliamentary group or *groupe parlementaire*) states the group's opinion on the bill.

Finally, MPs vote on the bill. MPs vote "aye" by raising their hand. Note that there is no roll call vote: the assembly does not record how each MP votes. An MP can vote on behalf of an absent MP by raising his or her other hand. If a recount is needed, votes are counted by asking MPs to stand. In the event that a second recount is needed, voting is done by secret ballot. If the bill passes with an absolute majority, the bill is transmitted to the Constitutional Court for review. If approved by the Constitutional Court, the president of the republic then signs the bill into law.

Disagreements Arise over the Quota

At the committee stage in the National Assembly, parliamentarians vigorously debated over the gender quota bill. Seven committees in the National Assembly examined the bill, and nearly all of them gave different recommendations. Two committees—the Committee on General Affairs and Institutions, and the Committee on Economic Affairs and Planning—accepted the quota bill as it stood, suggesting only cosmetic changes to the bill in their reports.[99] One committee, the Committee on Social and Cultural Affairs, opposed the very idea of instituting a gender quota.[100] The other committees fell in the middle, not happy with the government bill in its original form but not wanting to reject it. Even the three middle-ground committees proposed different amendments. The Finance Committee suggested that the quota for elected office be eliminated.[101] The two others suggested that the quota regulate the proportion of women and men on party lists, as opposed to the proportion of women and men who win seats.[102] The Defense and Security Committee proposed that the quota be lowered from 25 to 10 percent for both elected office and nominations.[103] This multitude of recommendations created a significant conundrum for the National Assembly.

Nor did parliamentarians speak with a single voice on the floor of the National Assembly. Eighteen MPs spoke about the quota in ways that further complicated the passage of the bill. Four MPs argued that the quota bill should be kept intact. The other fourteen orators, however, proposed a wide range of amendments and alternatives to the quota bill. Six MPs suggested lowering the quota for elected posts, whereas three proposed eliminating the quota for elected office. Four MPs suggested that instead of creating a legal gender quota, Niger should install a reserved seats system like that of Uganda. By the end of the speeches, it was almost midnight.

How did the male-dominated assembly come to disagree over the gender quota? One area of contention concerned the quota's implications for democracy. Some MPs argued that the creation of a quota would be good for democracy. An "essential element of democracy" is women's participation in running the country, stated the report from the Finance Committee, and the quota would help improve women's participation.[104] The Rural Development and Environment Committee's report said that the quota was "indispensible for improving and stabilizing democracy."[105] "A real democracy cannot last if it marginalizes the full participation of the largest group in society," said the report from the Committee on General Affairs and Institutions. On the floor of the National Assembly, three MPs and three political party leaders also invoked democracy to support the quota. "Democracy," said MP Amadou "Bonkano" Oumarou (MNSD-Niamey), "requires that all members of society participate. Since women are already participating, I don't see how we can stop the evolution of our country. All of us, including women, chose democracy. . . . It is absolutely necessary to vote for the bill."[106]

Detractors argued that quotas would undermine democracy. The quota is "a word that is in flagrant contradiction with the mission of democracy," stated the report from the Committee on Social and Cultural Affairs. More specifically, some MPs asserted that quotas for elected office subverted the democratic nature of competitive elections. Though Niger's electoral system is such that the electorate votes for a party list and not individual candidates, candidates still run campaigns to cultivate a following and impress party elites. When composing the party lists and deciding who will occupy a seat, party leaders take into account the financial resources and popularity of those vying for a seat. The Foreign Affairs Committee's report illustrates this concern with quotas for elected office:

> In a representative democracy, access to elected office proceeds from the free expression of individual will to come before the voters, to campaign, to fight and get the votes of the people. Furthermore, all the national laws require that to reach elected office, one must have been elected.[107]

On the floor, five MPs similarly invoked democracy to oppose the gender quota for elected office. MP Abdou Bako (CDS-Zinder) said, "In a democracy, we elect. We don't nominate. So the 25 percent quota is not democratic. Only for nominations can we give a percentage." Mamane Salissou (CDS-Maradi) said that it was not fair if a man invested millions of CFA francs in a campaign, only to see a woman get elected. Another MP agreed and told the assembly, "We cannot take away votes from a man to give them to a woman, just so she can be an MP."

Arriving at a Consensus on the Quota

Although a cacophony of voices emerged over the gender quota, the assembly did end up adopting the government bill. Throwing out the bill would have violated Niger's consensus doctrine, a belief that political elites should accommodate each other for the sake of political stability.

Political elites had sought to institutionalize the consensus doctrine when they wrote the 1999 Constitution, which was designed in part to encourage cooperation between the president and the National Assembly. The president, elected by popular vote, is required to work closely with a prime minister, who is chosen by the majority party or coalition of the assembly.[108] The president has the power to appoint and dismiss ministers to the executive cabinet, but the prime minister proposes the names of cabinet appointees.[109] The president calls cabinet meetings, but the president and prime minister jointly establish the agenda. Whereas the executive cabinet sets the national policy agenda, the National Assembly votes on the national budget, can reject the government's national policy, and can amend bills.[110] The president can call a period of exceptional power, but the National Assembly can bring an end to it with a majority vote.[111] Power, however, tips in the favor of the president, who can dissolve the National Assembly.[112] In practice, the National Assembly has observed the consensus doctrine: up until 1999, Niger's parliament had never voted against a government bill.[113]

The influence of the consensus doctrine can be seen on the floor of the National Assembly. Indeed, the first orator, MP Moumouni Adamou Djermakoye, called for consensus on the gender quota bill.

Djermakoye: I notice that the committees' opinions diverge. But in my humble opinion, I think it's possible to find some consensus around this problem. Politically, it would be disastrous to reject the bill even if we do not have to accept it. The proposed quota, we can find a middle-ground solution to satisfy our sisters. Because to reject this bill, the consequences in my opinion risk harming our parliament's reputation in addition to that of our country. So that is the proposition that I wish to make. I think we can reach a solution through consensus . . .

An unidentified MP: Always bringing up consensus!

The unidentified MP's retort is a lighthearted jab toward Djermakoye. Djermakoye, upon passing away in 2009, was commemorated for being "a man of consensus."[114] He was the president of the National Assembly between 1993 and 1994 and knew all too well what could happen in the event of political deadlock. Like many prominent politicians of his generation, he served in the military and as a minister in Kountché's government. Upon Niger's transition to democratic rule, Djermakoye split from the MNSD and founded the Alliance Nigérienne pour la Démocratie et le Progrès (ANDP). A smaller party (Djermakoye unsuccessfully ran for president in 1993, 1996, 1999, and 2004), the ANDP nevertheless was an important ally for other parties, having a foothold in the Dosso region. That the word "consensus" was made into a joke also indicates the widespread use of the word in national politics.

Djermakoye was not the only MP to call for consensus. MP Soumana Sanda (MNSD-Niamey), a rising star in the party, also invoked the importance of listening to the women's claim for a gender quota law:

Our Nigérien mothers, our sisters, our wives, they have asked, have made only one demand, a 25 percent quota and through these speeches I am realizing that you want to bluntly refuse them, I'd say that's not fair.

"To bluntly refuse" their mothers', sisters', and wives' "only one demand," as Sanda put it, would contradict the doctrine of consensus.

Parliamentarians, in addition to wanting to meet women's demands, did not want to be out of step with the international consensus on women's representation. As Djermakoye said, rejecting the gender quota bill would "risk harming our parliament's reputation in addition to that of our country." Other MPs raised similar concerns. As MP Boureima Gado (MNSD-Tillaberï) stated, "We in Niger we have to avoid being put at the bottom of the class. . . . Today the situation is such that everywhere we go, we do not feel comfortable with having just one female MP. Let's try to correct that." Parliamentarians did not want to violate what they saw to be the international consensus.

Earlier, I showed that women's activists emphasized that women made up more than 50 percent of Niger's population and therefore should have a greater political presence in Niger's democracy. Parliamentarians repeated this argument. When I asked one MP—a Muslim and a former middle-school teacher—whether he voted for the quota bill, he replied, "Yes. Fifty-two percent of the Nigérien population is women. In managing the country, we have to include them. They are the majority."[115] Along the same lines, the head of the CDS parliamentary group said at the end of the plenary debate:

> Mr. President [of the National Assembly], women represent more than 50 percent of Niger's population, but we find that this majority is still today, for several reasons, including socio-economic challenges, a social minority. Faced with this situation, the government proposes to help our wives, our sisters, our daughters, to be able to exercise a little more of their rights, which stem from their demographic weight and the fact that Niger is a constitutional state. Mr. President, if we assume that democracy can be a dictatorship of the majority, democracy must also take into account the interests of minorities.

If democracy meant rule by the majority, then it made sense to many MPs to include more women in politics through a gender quota.

Nigérien women's activists also influenced the debate over gender quotas by arguing that women deserved to be in politics. Picking up the language of women's activists, MPs argued that women deserved to be included under the umbrella of consensus. Aïssata Karidjo Mounkaïla (MNSD-Niamey), speaking on behalf of Nigérien women, emphasized that women deserved to be included in positions of power. Her speech is quoted at length here:

> The contribution that women have made to culture and in ancient civilization is unquestionable. . . . As I observed in "Women of Niger" in September '86, and I quote, women do not go to politics, it is politics that comes to them. The first women campaigned in the shadow of their husbands and brothers, end quote.

That is to say in politics, Nigérien women have always fought alongside men, and continue to do so with determination. Mr. President, honorable male colleagues-MPs, today it is no secret and easy to verify that Nigérien women are the fiercest campaigners and least prone to political nomadism. But if we analyze the integration of women in decision-making processes, in light of existing practices in Niger, much remains to be done. That is why I think the government in submitting the bill establishing a quota system in elective function in government and administration of the state asks us to look inside ourselves and our conviction to be fair. Mr. President, honorable MPs, concerned about the problems that beset our brave women who work determinedly for the welfare of the Nigérien people as we are required to do as MPs, we ask this august Assembly to overwhelmingly vote for this bill. . . . Mr. President, honorable MPs, once again we ask in the name of God, in the name of the Prophet, to vote for this bill for us. Thank you Mr. President.

Mounkaïla, in line with women's activists, argued that women were "the fiercest campaigners" and therefore earned a seat at the political table.

Men MPs, too, argued that Nigérien women deserved to be in politics. Following a discussion about whether only so-called privileged or elite women would benefit from the gender quota, MP Bonkano Maifada (MNSD-Banibangou) said this:

I still remember those that perhaps some call privileged women. When on January 11, we were arrested, it was right in the middle of the cold season. It was extremely cold. The women came with their children and protested in front of Camp Baneau. Even the police begged us to convince the women to go back home with their children so that they wouldn't get sick. Yet, there were plenty of men in Niamey and none of them dared come to Camp Baneau. So I think it is only fair that we find the best way to increase women's representation.

The MP referred to the time of Baré's tumultuous presidency, in 1997, when more than one hundred opposition leaders in the Front pour la Restauration et la Défense de la Démocratie (FRDD), including President of the National Assembly Mahamane Ousmane (CDS-Zinder), were arrested, among them at least nine women.[116] Women and men protested against the arrests, and some of the protesters were tear-gassed or beaten.[117] Women of the opposition further staged a protest at the camp where some of the opposition leaders were being held.[118]

In spite of the widespread agreement that women had earned a place in politics, a "coalition for change," to use a term developed by political scientist

Joel Barkan, challenged the consensus doctrine.[119] A coalition for change is a group of MPs who want to reform the legislature from a rubber-stamping institution to an autonomous one. This coalition consisted of three MPs from the Maradi region, a major economic zone. In the 2000s, wealthy merchant traders from the region who had provided funding to political parties vied for political office. The coalition for change opposed the executive branch's interference in electoral politics. Sani Souley Dangara (MNSD-Maradi) argued that an electoral quota would risk creating an "unmanageable situation." The local population chooses the MPs, not the central government, and to interfere with that process would "run the risk of doing evil," said Salissou Abdou.

Senior-ranking politicians in the National Assembly did not want to ignore the coalition for change. To meet both the opposing MPs and the women's activists' demands, the parliament had to "find a middle-ground solution," as Djermakoye put it. Others in the National Assembly agreed. The chairman of the CDS parliamentary group said the following:

> Democracy is also the search for compromise. Here, it seems that compromise is what the government is seeking by proposing a quota for elected, government and administrative posts. In our opinion, this compromise can be a reality if it has the support of political parties. That is why, notwithstanding the amendments that almost the entire session has accepted, including the 10 percent quota for elected office, my group will vote yes for the bill in question.

Achieving consensus was more important than following the party line. The strongest opposition to the quota bill came from the president's coalition of the MNSD and CDS. MPs from Minister Foumakoye's own party, the CDS, opposed the quota bill.[120] The strongest supporters of the bill came from the opposition party, the PNDS. Two MPs from the PNDS who spoke on the floor backed the government's original proposal. Indeed, no one from the opposition spoke against the gender quota during the general discussion.

By now, it should be clear what one woman meant when she said that lobbying for the quota in the National Assembly was "quite a challenge." Eighty-two male Muslim MPs disagreed about gender-based affirmative action.

The Absence of Countermobilization

One might wonder if there was conservative religious resistance to the adoption of the gender quota in Niger. After all, conservative activists mobilized against the proposed family law reform in 1994, the ratification of CEDAW in 1999, and the ratification of the African Union's treaty on women's rights in 2006. Opposition to those reforms was predicated on the idea that the reforms were "foreign" impositions brought in by "elite intellectual women." Conservative religious activists could have advanced a similar argument against the gender quota, which was lobbied for by the same women who advocated for family law reform and the ratification of international women's rights treaties.

There was, however, little resistance to the adoption of the gender quota law from conservative religious activists. In fact, officials at the Ministry of Social Development said that there was no resistance from conservative religious activists.[121] After the quota's adoption, some conservative religious women did question whether women ought to participate in politics.[122] Other conservative religious women, however, argued that women needed to be involved in politics. Consider one conservative activist I interviewed, a woman who helped organize protests against the Maputo Protocol. When I asked for her opinion about women serving as ministers, she responded, "Who will defend the women's cause if there are no women?"[123] To my knowledge, conservative activists did not organize any protests or issue any declarations against the gender quota. Collective action against the quota was limited.

Why the lack of conservative opposition to the gender quota and the "elite intellectual women" who supported it? To answer this question, I interviewed MPs who had a reputation of being Islamist. Some of them voted against the ratification of the Maputo Protocol but, generally speaking, support the use of gender quotas. One MP from RDP who voted against the Maputo Protocol said that he would support increasing the gender quota for elected office to 20 or 30 percent. He reasoned that not encouraging women's participation in politics was akin to hindering women from entering the workforce: "Why prevent women from working? In Algeria, there are nine thousand women in the police. Why should we keep things the same?"[124] As a parliamentarian from PNDS who voted against the Maputo Protocol told me:

> Niger is a democracy. Everyone has a right to their rights, women and children. I am not against women's rights. . . . Women should have their quota of 10 percent. Thanks to the law, we see that and in all the ministries, too.[125]

A third parliamentarian, from CDS, who voted against the Maputo Protocol said that the quota was a good idea "because women are mothers and are our children."[126] Adopting the language of women's activists, ostensibly Islamist MPs saw the gender quota issue as a matter of "democracy" and according women their "rights."

To further make sense of the absence of countermobilization, I examined the parliamentary transcripts for how MPs talked about culture and found that they invoked it in multifaceted ways. Some argued that Nigérien culture made it difficult for women to run for office; thus, a gender quota would be impossible to enforce. Because of "cultural obstacles," the quota could never be implemented at 30 percent and would thus have to be reduced to 10 percent. Other MPs argued that Niger's patriarchal culture gave the National Assembly even more reason to adopt a gender quota.

Looking at the national political context, it is important to recall that women had been visible in public life and that women's activists framed women's participation in politics as "natural" dating back to precolonial Niger. A 2001 study conducted by Hadiza Djibo found that approximately 68 percent of 127 surveyed women in Niamey said that it was a good thing for women to work outside the home, and slightly more than 63 percent agreed that it was important for women to participate in politics.[127] Furthermore, the presence of Muslim women in public life had been on the rise.[128] Private radio and television stations that emerged in the democratic transition featured Muslim women, such as the conservative Malama Houda (on the privately owned Radio Ténéré), feminist Malama Zeinab Hadara (on the privately owned Radio Anfani), and Malama Zaharaou (on the state-supported ORTN), articulating their own interpretations of Islam. The idea of including women in decision-making posts was thinkable, particularly by 2000, when the quota reached the National Assembly.

In sum, women's activists in and outside the state helped construct women's underrepresentation as a public problem and proposed gender quotas as a thinkable solution. In advocating for more women in politics, women's activists encountered relatively little opposition from conservative religious activists. Parliamentarians accepted the women's activists' arguments that having more women in politics would be democratic and that women had earned a place at the political table. Yet some parliamentarians argued that establishing a quota for elected offices was undemocratic. A compromise was reached in the name of consensus building, and the proposed 25 percent quota for elected office was lowered to 10 percent.

Additional and Alternative Explanations

In explaining how Niger came to adopt a gender quota law, I have focused on the role of women's mobilization, the absence of countermobilization, and the veto power of the National Assembly. This section considers four kinds of additional and alternative explanations for the adoption of gender quota laws.

International Influence

Scholars agree that the international dimension is critical for understanding how countries adopt gender quotas.[129] This chapter does not contest the importance of international influence. Much information sharing about gender quotas happens at international conferences. Indeed, CONGAFEN's president learned about gender quotas while attending the meeting of the Commission on the Status of Women in New York City in the late 1990s.[130] International meetings can have an impact on people who are not in attendance. In March 1994, the Inter-Parliamentary Union (IPU) adopted a Plan of Action to Correct Present Imbalances in the Participation of Men and Women in Political Life. The Action Plan lists nearly every possible measure that advocates, political parties, and state officials can employ to address gender imbalances in politics. Minister Foumakoye was inspired by the IPU's Action Plan to seek a gender quota.[131] Her ministry developed the language of the quota bill using the Action Plan as a guide.

Niger's leading politicians were also influenced by what was happening at the international level. Djermakoye did not want to reject the gender quota partly because he worried that doing so would damage Niger's international reputation. One MP worried about his country being denied international funding. In the absence of both international meetings through which women's activists could learn about quotas and an international climate that praised countries with high percentages of women in politics, it is less likely that Niger would have adopted a gender quota law.

Domestic actors can also learn about new rules and practices from countries in the region. Egypt's 1979 adoption of reserved seats for women for parliament and local, district, and provincial councils was partly based on Sudan's system of reserved seats for women.[132] Rwanda's adoption of a gender quota can be partly attributed to Uganda's use of reserved seats; before taking power in 1994, leaders of Rwanda's ruling party, the RPF, lived in exile in Uganda.[133] Neighborly learning can help explain regional and subregional trends, such as the prevalence of reserved seats in East Africa. In Niger, politicians were aware of Uganda's reserved seat system, and some MPs proposed that Niger take on a similar system. Although the MPs ultimately decided to keep the proposal to create a legal quota, Uganda's example helped make the adoption of such a law thinkable.

Explanations that focus on the international context, however, can only get us so far. For one, international factors do not fully explain why Niger adopted a gender quota in 2000 and not earlier, when there was already concerted international support for gender quotas. As I have shown in this chapter, women's activism influenced the timing of reform. Women did not publicly call for a gender quota until 1999; only after 1999 did the issue of gender quotas become a national concern.

Moreover, the international context does not fully explain the content of Niger's gender quota. Recall that there are many types of gender quotas, from voluntary party quotas to reserved seats. How did Niger adopt a mandatory gender quota law, as opposed to letting political parties voluntarily set their own quotas, especially when other African countries had only voluntary party quotas? Why does Niger's quota law require a 10 percent minimum for seats won rather than for candidate lists, which is the more common form of legal gender quotas? To answer these questions, one must examine the actions of a range of domestic actors. Women's activists in the Ministry of Social Development and the prime minister decided to ask for a legal gender quota and proposed a 25 percent minimum for both elected and nominated posts. Although parliamentarians worried that the rejection of the quota bill would be bad for the country's international reputation, they nevertheless lowered the quota for elected office to 10 percent to compromise with the coalition for change. Global trends only become meaningful when they are picked up and debated by domestic actors.

Party Ideology, Electoral Institutions, and Political Transitions

The chapter reinforces existing arguments about the role of domestic politics in the adoption of gender quotas. The scholarship on quotas suggests that countries with a dominant socialist or left-leaning party are less likely to adopt legal gender quotas. This is counterintuitive in that socialist parties are often believed to promote gender equality. It is important to note, however, that socialist or left-leaning parties tend to adopt voluntary party quotas.[134] Socialist parties in Africa, such as FRELIMO in Mozambique, have a voluntary party quota. (FRELIMO also belongs to the Socialist International network, which encourages its members to advance gender equality.) If a socialist party is dominant and already has a gender quota in place for the party, there may not be much perceived need or interest in superseding the party's quota with a legal quota. Niger, lacking a strong socialist party at the time, adopted a gender quota law.

Studies further suggest that countries with a PR electoral system are more likely to adopt gender quota laws than are countries that use a majoritarian electoral system.[135] In PR systems, a party can win multiple seats in an electoral district, which makes elections less of a zero-sum game. Thus, in PR systems, parties are more likely to be open to putting newcomers on the ticket and accepting of gender quota laws. In majoritarian electoral systems, like that in the United States, only one candidate can win a seat in an electoral district. This makes electoral politics a zero-sum game, one in which parties are less open to allowing newcomers such as women to run for office through the adoption of gender quota laws. Niger's adoption of a gender quota law lends support to this electoral argument, as 105 out of 113 seats in the National Assembly are chosen through proportional representation.

The best available evidence suggests that countries that recently experienced a major political transition are more likely to adopt legal gender quotas or reserved seats for women.[136] This is because the political opportunity structure, to borrow a concept from the study of social movements, opens up in times of major change. Women's movements take advantage of this opportunity to push for women-friendly policy, including gender quotas, while leaders look to improve the country's reputation and be seen as a stable country or liberal democracy. Following the end of civil war, in particular, countries typically rewrite constitutions and electoral codes. Legal gender quotas and reserved seats have been adopted in post-conflict countries like Afghanistan, Iraq, Burundi, Mauritania, Rwanda, and South Sudan, and in countries with recently revised constitutions, like Kenya. By contrast, countries that have not witnessed a significant political transition, such as Botswana, have not adopted legal gender quotas or reserved seats for women.[137] Niger adopted a gender quota law shortly after its transition from military rule under Wanké to democratic rule under Tandja.

Public Opinion

Public opinion, for some scholars, is important for understanding Muslim politics. Yet attempts to generalize what Muslims think about women's rights wash over the diversity of opinions expressed the day the gender quota was discussed in the National Assembly.

M. Steven Fish argues, "Muslims express more traditional views toward gender-based inequality than non-Muslims do."[138] He finds that a Muslim man living in a country that is 95 percent Muslim and 5 percent Christian has a predicted 72 to 77 percent chance of agreeing with the statement, "On the whole, men make better political leaders than women do."[139] A Muslim woman has a 56 to 63 percent chance of agreeing with that statement. Whereas in a country that is 95 percent Christian and 5 percent Muslim, a Muslim man has a predicted 45 to 47 percent chance of agreeing with the statement, and a Muslim woman 29 to 31 percent chance of agreeing that men make better political leaders than do women.[140] This might lead one to expect that public opinion made the adoption of the gender quota more difficult.

Did public opinion on women's access to political power obstruct the adoption of the gender quota law in Niger? Data from a Gallup poll in 2007 suggest that Nigériens prefer male to female leaders. In response to the statement, "Men make better political leaders than women do," 85 percent agreed or strongly agreed. Yet in an Afrobarometer poll conducted in Niger in 2013, 48 percent of respondents said that they agree or strongly agree with the statement, "Men make better political leaders than women, and should be elected rather than women."[141] And 51 percent of respondents agreed or strongly agreed with the statement, "Women should have the same chance of being elected to political office as men."

Examining the 2007 and 2013 polls, one arrives at two observations about public opinion in a predominantly Muslim country such as Niger. The first is that public opinion can significantly change among Muslim publics, and such changes in attitudes toward gender equality in politics require explanation. The second is that Muslim respondents can be discerning in their opinions about gender equality.[142] A survey respondent could prefer that a man take a leadership position over women, yet she may also support the adoption of a gender quota to even the playing field among the sexes.

Supply-Side Explanations

It is possible that as more women enter into the formal workforce, greater numbers of women would be "qualified" to run for office, which might help make the adoption of gender quotas thinkable.[143] If this were the case, then one would expect the timing of the adoption of the gender quota to coincide with a rise of women in pipeline professions. In Niger, a significant proportion of MPs in the 1990s were teachers, civil servants, businesspeople, and traders

Table 1. Distribution of seats in Niger's National Assembly according to profession, 1993 and 1995

PROFESSION	1993	1995
Teachers	23 (28%)	20 (24%)
Civil servants (including retired)	16 (19%)	25 (30%)
Businesspeople, traders	15 (18%)	24 (29%)
Engineers, technicians	13 (16%)	
Agricultural sector	4 (5%)	
Military, police officers	3 (4%)	
Farmers, cattle rearers		7 (8%)
Private sector employees		7 (8%)
Other	9 (11%)	

Note: Inter-Parliamentary Union, "Niger: Election Archives."

(see Table 1). Among the winners of the 1993 parliamentary elections, approximately 28 percent were teachers, 19 percent were civil servants, and 18 percent were businesspersons.[144] Again, in the 1995 parliamentary election results, teachers constituted approximately 24 percent of elected MPs. Perhaps more women were entering into the fields of education and business in the 1980s and 1990s, thus making a gender quota system seem feasible to Nigériens?

Changes in women's employment in Niger's formal labor force do seem to correspond with the adoption of the gender quota. Women's employment as primary and secondary school teachers remained relatively flat from the 1970s through the 2000s (see Figure 9). In the 1970s, women made up approximately 29 and 22 percent of primary school and secondary school teachers, respectively. In the 1980s, the average presence of women among primary school teachers was almost 33 percent, but the average presence of women among secondary school teachers declined to less than 18 percent. These figures remained relatively stable in the 1990s and 2000s, when women were between 32 and 37 percent of primary school teachers and 17 and 18 percent of secondary school teachers.

Women's presence in the formal labor force steadily grew over the 1990s. In 1990, women constituted more than 22 percent of the formal labor force. By 1999, that number had grown to 30 percent. It is possible that the steady or increasing proportion of women in pipeline professions helped make the gender quota thinkable, but as shown earlier in this chapter, women's activists emphasized women's grassroots contribution to political parties in calling for a gender quota, not the rise of women in the labor force per se.

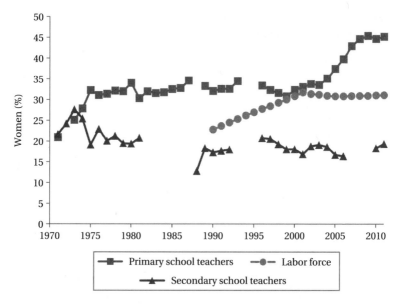

Figure 9. Women's presence in the pipeline professions, 1970–2011

Note: World Bank, "World Development Indicators." Gaps indicate missing data. The values for the percentage of primary school teachers, the labor force, and secondary school teachers who are women are from indicator codes SE.PRM.TCHR.FE.ZS, SL.TLF.TOTL.FE.ZS, and SE.SEC.TCHR.FE.ZS, respectively.

Enforcing the Gender Quota

In this section, we will see that the gender quota law has been implemented for positions in the National Assembly and executive cabinet thanks in part to women's mobilization. Furthermore, women's activists in and outside the state have expanded their purview to address other elected offices and positions in public administration, including governor, prefect, and even high school principal.

To clarify how the gender quota would be enforced, President Tandja passed a decree on the application of the quota law on February 28, 2001. Thereafter, women's activists in and outside the state worked to spread word of the quota law. In March 2002, CONGAFEN and a network of female ministers and parliamentarians—the Réseau des Femmes Africaines Ministres et Parlementaires (REFAM/P)—organized a conference to discuss how to increase awareness of the quota, along with how best to implement the quota law.[145] The following year, the Institut PANOS Afrique de l'Ouest—a West African organization—commissioned national newspapers to write about the quota.[146] Radio Saraounia FM aired a discussion titled "The Women's Quota

Law in Niger: Myth or Reality" in January 2004.[147] To hold these consciousness-raising activities, CONGAFEN and other groups solicited funding from such international organizations as the American-based National Democratic Institute (NDI), the Netherlands Development Organization (SNV), and UNFPA.

Concerned that the political parties would not give a sufficient number of seats to women to meet the 10 percent minimum requirement, women's activists appealed to the Constitutional Court. In 2004, women's activists from CONGAFEN and AFN and women from political parties released a press statement through the state radio and television stations asking the court to ensure that the quota law was being respected.[148] The Constitutional Court reportedly invalidated party lists that did not respect the gender quota law, though I have not found evidence of this in the existing archives of the Constitutional Court.[149]

Political parties for the most part have preemptively respected the quota to avoid receiving a formal sanction from the Constitutional Court. A woman who ran in the 2004 elections told Institut Panos:

> My candidacy was motivated by the quota law. So as not to see its list rejected by the Constitutional Court, our party asked all of its members with some education and capable of mobilizing people to offer their names. With the support of the party and some women's organizations, I wasn't afraid to jump into the water.[150]

I heard one political party official say that the Constitutional Court can block a party's list; for example, if a list has twelve candidates, there must be three women.[151] This shows that parties are concerned about the Constitutional Court, which has a record of invalidating party lists for a variety of reasons, such as not filing the necessary paperwork or putting one candidate on multiple lists.

In 2004, in the first legislative elections following the adoption of the gender quota, political parties put both men and women on their candidate lists, not a significant departure from previous multiparty elections. What differed was that each party that won ten or more seats in the National Assembly gave at least one seat to a woman. Of the two parties that formed the governing coalition, the MNSD won forty-seven seats and gave 17.0 percent to women (8). The CDS gave 13.6 percent of its seats to women (3 out of 22). In the opposition camp, the PNDS gave 8.0 percent of its seats to women (2 out of 25). The ANDP gave 20.0 percent to women (1 out of 5).[152] The RDP, RSD, and PSDN won fewer than ten seats and did not give any of them to women. Overall,

12.4 percent of the 113 MPs were women (14). This marked the first time women's presence in parliament surpassed 10 percent.

In the 2009 and 2011 legislative elections, women won 9.7 percent and 13.3 percent of the seats, respectively. Opposition parties boycotted the 2009 elections, so I will not examine those results in depth. In the 2011 race, the PNDS gave 18.9 percent of its seats to women, Mouvement Démocratique Nigérien (MODEN) gave 8.0 percent of its seats to women, the MNSD gave 7.7 percent of its seats to women, the RDP gave 28.6 percent of its seats to women, the ANDP gave 12.5 percent of its seats to women, and Union pour la Démocratie et la République (UDR) gave 16.7 percent of its seats to women. The CDS and Union des Nigériens Indépendants (UNI) won three and one seats, respectively, and did not give any seats to women.[153]

Gains in parliament aside, Nigériens have many criticisms about the electoral process. Some are worried that political party leaders are interpreting the 10 percent quota as a ceiling for women in elective office. People disapprove of the "elite" composition of the women in the National Assembly. No female domestic servants, market women, or female subsistence farmers had served in parliament.[154] The same can be said, however, for male MPs, who come from an "elite" pool of former state employees, chiefs, or wealthy merchant-traders.[155] Many lament that running for office has become an expensive endeavor, with only the wealthy being able to gain the attention of party elites. Another concern is with whether women are able to hold positions of influence within the parties. "Some notable gains have been made," said Niger's first female minister, Aïssata Moumouni, in a 2011 interview with *Aïcha*, "but on the quota law, within political parties, especially in the top positions, are women sufficiently represented? That is the real question!"[156] Little systematic research on the intersection of money, gender, and advancement in parties in Niger (and other African democracies) has been done to back these claims, but they point to future lines of inquiry.

When it came to the quota's provision on cabinet appointments, women's activists focused their efforts on monitoring and public shaming. Activists released public declarations via the state's radio and television stations when the government did not follow the gender quota law. In November 2002, CONGAFEN released a declaration on the gendered composition of the new government, pointing out that women made up 14 percent of the cabinet, whereas the quota called for either sex to make up 25 percent or more of the government.[157] In 2004, before the announcement of the new executive cabinet, CONGAFEN released a statement calling on the president, the prime minister, and the heads of political parties to implement the gender quota and appoint a sufficient number of women to the new cabinet.[158] Women in CONGAFEN issued similar statements in 2007 and 2011.

Women's activists also shamed the government in international venues. In 2007, women's activists from AFJN, ANDDH, CONGAFEN, ONG Dimol, SOS Femmes et Enfants Victimes de Violence Familiale (SOS FEVVF), and other organizations submitted a report to the United Nations Committee on the Elimination of Discrimination against Women. In the report, women's organizations wrote, "The quota law is not respected," and they called for the quota's application.[159] Thus, women's activists used state and private media, UN reporting mechanisms, and, in a democratic political context, the Constitutional Court to enforce the gender quota.

When I visited Niger in 2011, women's activists shifted their focus from cabinet posts, where the quota was respected, to appointments and promotions in public administration. Activists noted that out of fifty advisers to the president, only three were women; that an insufficient number of female teachers were being promoted to high school principals; and that out of twenty chairpersons of parastatal companies, only three were women.[160] Of particular concern was the lack of female prefects in the country. (An issue for prefects, according to a number of interviewees, is that prefects lead or take part in the prayer that precedes a religious holiday, typically a male role.) A sociologist conducted a study on the application of the quota in Niger, which found that its enforcement was weakest in the Ministry of Defense and in the Ministry of the Interior. Women's activists presented the study to Mahamadou Issoufou on the day of his presidential inauguration in 2011.

By the end of the 2000s, high-ranking government officials were keeping track of women's representation in public life as if it were the normal thing to do. As a former minister of agriculture and animal husbandry noted,

> When the cabinet met to review appointments, we'd count the number of women and men being nominated for promotion. [With his finger, he motions going down an imaginary list.] If women weren't on the list of names, we'd send it back to the minister. The female ministers were vigilant about this. The women were the most vigilant, but the men would count, too.[161]

Other ministers further volunteered that Minister of Social Development Barry Bibata, in particular, reminded the cabinet to look for women in appointments and promotions. "Nowadays, if a committee is being put together and has no women, someone will say there must be a woman," said one former minister to me.[162] Though not always the case, one can see increasingly the inclusion of women in politics. Consider Niger's Commission Electorale

Nationale Indépendante (CENI), which oversees the running of the country's elections. Before the adoption of the gender quota law, the CENI was not required to have a woman on the commission. Following the adoption of the gender quota, the CENI was required to include a representative from an umbrella women's association and a representative of the Office on the Advancement of Women.[163] Consider also the Conseil Supérieur de la Communication (CSC), which regulates the media. Article 161 of the 2011 Constitution stipulates that out of fifteen members of the CSC, there must be at least three women (one representing private media, one representing public media, and one elected by women's umbrella associations).[164] These changes are undoubtedly linked to the adoption of the gender quota law.

Conclusion

As I have shown in this chapter, Niger's adoption of a gender quota law was inextricably linked to women's mobilization in and outside the state. Women's activists constructed the lack of women in formal politics as a public problem and quotas as a thinkable solution. The nonmobilization of conservative religious activists also helped make the adoption of a quota possible. Nigérien women, however, did not mobilize in a political vacuum. Taking women's activists by surprise, a relatively autonomous National Assembly modified the quota bill, lowering the minimum requirement for elected office.

When I teach about women and politics in Lincoln, Nebraska, my students are struck by how poorly women's numerical representation in the United States compares to that of the rest of the world, but very few of them immediately call for the adoption of an affirmative action law. Women's activists in the United States expend significant amounts of energy recruiting women to run for office, training women how to run, and helping women raise campaign funds. Rarely, however, do they mobilize for the adoption of a legal gender quota. Whether one is in Nebraska or in Washington, D.C., the adoption of a gender-based affirmative action law seems unthinkable. Those who see the United States as exceptional might attribute the lack of a gender quota to the country's imperviousness to global trends and unique political culture.

Democracies like the United States and Niger do have something in common: people wrestle with what makes for an appropriate democracy. Nigériens, both men and women, continue to debate about the gender quota and democracy. Can the quota be enforced in all elected offices, including elections for prefects? Why aren't more women agreeing to run for office? Do women in office represent women's interests? Do any of the parliamentarians represent their constituents?

In the summer of 2011, the National Assembly's radio station, which broadcasts the plenary sessions, temporarily closed. Riding in a shared taxi one day, I listened to the driver and passengers complain about the station's shutdown. After the other passengers alighted, I asked the driver if anyone even listens to the station. "Sometimes I do," he said, monitoring the traffic and pedestrians in front of him, "but in any case, we're a democracy. The National Assembly is for the people." For all the frustrations that Nigériens have with the National Assembly, they want it to work. With this hope, women's activists in the 1990s and 2000s sought to promote a more representative democracy in Niger.

4 BRINGING RIGHTS HOME

How Niger Ratified CEDAW and Rejected the Maputo Protocol

ON A SATURDAY EVENING on June 3, 2006, the last day of the spring session, the scene at the National Assembly was one of confusion. MPs were voting on a bill to ratify the African Union's (AU) Protocol to the African Charter on Human and Peoples' Rights on the Rights of Women in Africa (hereafter Maputo Protocol, named after the city where it was adopted). Representatives of the Ministry of Women's Advancement, civil society, and international donors sat in the wings to observe. The first tally went in favor of the bill, but the number of votes counted exceeded the number of seats in the assembly. A recount was ordered, and the result stunned the audience. The bill was voted down: a reported forty-two MPs decided against the bill, thirty-one decided in its favor, and four abstained.[1] In doing so, Niger became the first country to reject the AU treaty on women's rights. The observers were taken aback, having thought that President Tandja's support for the bill would guarantee the treaty's ratification.

International women's rights treaties are important because countries that ratify such agreements generally see improvements in women's access to education, employment, and elected office.[2] Once ratified, these treaties become part of a moral and legal arsenal that activists, bureaucrats, and judges can draw on.[3] The National Assembly's rejection of the women's rights treaty is surprising because only seven years earlier, in 1999, Niger ratified another women's rights treaty: the United Nations Convention on the Elimination of All Forms of Discrimination Against Women (CEDAW). How did Niger ratify CEDAW and not the Maputo Protocol?

A dominant explanation for why countries ratify women's rights treaties focuses on international reputation. According to this explanation, countries that want to boost their standing and legitimacy on the world stage are more likely to ratify human rights treaties.[4] Two scholars, Christine Wotipka and Francisco Ramirez, lend strong evidence to this world polity approach.[5] Countries are more likely to ratify CEDAW shortly before and after United Nations women's conferences, as international conferences are where countries define, inspire, and seek to display "good state" behavior. Wotipka and Ramirez also find that as the number of countries that ratify CEDAW increases, the more others join the bandwagon and ratify the convention. By this logic, Niger should have ratified both CEDAW and the Maputo Protocol.

To understand how Niger ratified one women's rights treaty and not another, one must consider mobilization and the national political context. Women's activists in and outside the state helped put the issue of CEDAW and the Maputo Protocol on the national agenda. During the CEDAW debates, women's advocates helped make ratification thinkable by arguing that it would help the country meet international and regional standards. Women's activists, however, were internally divided on the issue of the Maputo Protocol, limiting their ability to mount a concerted campaign. Conservative religious activists sought to make the ratification of both treaties unthinkable by constructing stark dichotomies between international women's rights law and Islamic law, Nigérien women and "foreign" women, and ordinary Nigériens and "intellectuals." The conservative movement against CEDAW, however, was internally split, unlike the cohesive conservative movement against the Maputo Protocol.

The national political contexts during the CEDAW and Maputo Protocol debates differed in one important aspect: there was no parliamentary veto player during the CEDAW controversy. As stipulated in Niger's constitution, treaties with international organizations that either modify internal laws or involve a financial commitment require that the National Assembly pass a bill authorizing ratification.[6] During the Maputo Protocol debates, the National Assembly exercised its veto powers and voted down the bill of ratification. By contrast, in 1999, a coup d'état had dissolved the National Assembly. With no parliament in place, Niger's military leaders were able to ratify CEDAW by military decree. Edward Mansfield and his colleagues have found that when the preferences of two or more veto players diverge, the ratification of bilateral investment treaties and preferential trade agreements is less likely.[7] I suggest that the same is true in the ratification of international women's rights treaties. The ratification of women's rights treaties is a two-level game in which leaders balance their concerns about international reputation with the power and demands of domestic actors.[8]

Next I will examine the politics behind CEDAW's ratification in Niger, then explain how the Maputo Protocol was rejected. The last major section considers alternative and additional explanations for how Niger ratified CEDAW and not the Maputo Protocol.

The Convention on the Elimination of All Forms of Discrimination Against Women

Niger ratified CEDAW in 1999 with reservations on Articles 2, 5, 15, 16, and 29, which leads to two specific questions that motivate this section. First, why did it take Niger twenty years to ratify CEDAW? Adopted by the United Nations in 1979, CEDAW is one of the fastest international human rights treaties to have come into force. Forty-six out of fifty-three countries in Africa had ratified the convention by the time Niger did, including Muslim-majority countries such as Egypt in 1981, Guinea in 1982, Mali in 1985, Senegal in 1985, and Algeria in 1996.[9] Second, why did Niger ratify CEDAW with reservations? A reservation is a statement a country issues to modify the effect of specific provisions of the treaty for that country. Scholars find that predominantly Muslim countries tend to issue more reservations on human rights treaties than do non-Muslim countries.[10] Indeed, Muslim-majority countries such as Algeria and Egypt ratified CEDAW with reservations, but others, such as Guinea, Mali, and Senegal, did not.[11] Thus, the issuing of reservations on women's rights treaties does not simply boil down to whether a country is predominantly Muslim and requires explanation.

Women's Mobilization

Women's mobilization is critical for understanding Niger's ratification of CEDAW. Niger ratified the convention *only after* women in and outside the state formed a pro-CEDAW coalition.

Women's activists did not mobilize for the ratification of CEDAW in the 1980s, which helps explain why Niger did not ratify it before 1999. In the 1980s, the AFN considered campaigning for the ratification of CEDAW but opted against it. The decision not to act was based on AFN's understanding of the political context. Created by Seyni Kountché's military regime, the AFN was reluctant to step out of line. As a high-ranking member of the AFN told me, women's leaders wanted to mobilize women but also wanted to create "an association that was not political." The AFN was aware that "Kountché had always said that [CEDAW] was not the most urgent thing."[12] Instead of pursuing CEDAW's ratification, the AFN focused its efforts on lobbying for the creation of a ministry for women.[13] Indeed, the AFN did help advance the issue of a women's ministry. Kountché's government created an Office on the Status of Women in 1987, which then became part of the Ministry of Social Development in 1989.

Just as the AFN did not pressure the state to ratify CEDAW in the 1980s, international donors and organizations did not push Kountché to ratify the convention. A Nigérien woman who worked for the United Nations Economic Commission for Africa (ECA) said that before Niger's democratic transition, "nobody talked about [CEDAW]" in Niger.[14] That is not to say that international organizations such as the ECA made no effort to promote the ratification of CEDAW in other venues. The ECA helped spread the word about the treaty in Africa as early as 1978, during the preparatory meetings on the finalization of CEDAW in Nouakchott, Mauritania. CEDAW was also a prominent topic of discussion at the United Nations Second World Conference on Women in Copenhagen in 1980 and at the United Nations Third World Conference on Women in Nairobi in 1985. Yet in terms of directly lobbying rulers in Niger to ratify the convention, the ECA "didn't apply any pressure."[15] Thus, the 1980s can be described as a period of nonmobilization for CEDAW's ratification in Niger, and this nonmobilization helps explain why Niger did not ratify the treaty during this decade.

The democratic transition in the early 1990s marks an important turning point for women's organizing for CEDAW. At a May 1994 conference on Niger's new and independent women's associations and NGOs, Nigérien women called for CEDAW's ratification. In November of the same year, women in civil society and officials from the Ministry of Social Development met to prepare for a women's regional conference and identified Niger's nonratification of the convention as a key issue.[16] In 1995, those who had participated in the May 1994 conference created CONGAFEN, which selected CEDAW as the theme for its second general assembly. To promote CEDAW, CONGAFEN—along with other civil society groups such as Fédération Kassaï—helped organize training sessions on it for judges, civil servants, and leaders of Islamic associations in the late 1990s.[17] Women's activists took advantage of the first democratic transition to expand the national agenda and to include the issue of the convention.

Inside the state, women and men mobilized for the ratification of CEDAW. In March 1994, female MP Aïchatou Nana Foumakoye (CDS-Zinder) wrote to the minister of social development asking what was blocking the ratification of CEDAW.[18] To gain the religious community's approval for the convention, the Ministry of Social Development invited religious leaders to attend private meetings and public seminars about the treaty. The ministry's efforts to ratify CEDAW continued after the 1996 coup d'état brought in Ibrahim Baré Maïnassara. In March 1998, the Ministry of Social Development organized a mass education campaign to raise the population's awareness about CEDAW. The ministry also commissioned studies on the convention, particularly on whether it was compatible with Islamic law.[19]

During this period, international donors supported the activists' campaign for the ratification of CEDAW. UNIFEM had helped sponsor the May 1994 conference on women's associations and NGOs, in which attendees identified CEDAW as a key issue. In 1997, a study conducted for Coopération Suisse encouraged women's associations and donors to organize a workshop to identify potential solutions to resistance to CEDAW.[20] The following year, a report on Islam in Niger written for the Embassy of Canada encouraged the Canadian representation to "talk with the Nigérien government and encourage it towards ratifying CEDAW."[21] In 1999, USAID sponsored a seminar on women's rights and democracy. During the seminar, participants discussed the issue of CEDAW's ratification.[22] International donors, then, helped provide a space in which Nigérien women could meet and strategize about CEDAW.

In spite of the efforts of women in civil society, women in the Ministry of Social Development, and international donors to bring about the ratification of CEDAW, political leaders in the 1990s were unresponsive. President Mahamane Ousmane and Prime Minister Mahamadou Issoufou's struggling government did not answer the women's demands. President Baré's government was also not amenable to ratifying the convention. Between 1996 and 1999, the minister of social development repeatedly asked President Baré to ratify CEDAW. Yet "everytime the Minister proposed it, she was told to 'wait, wait,'" one women's leader told me. "I remember one time we were doing a tour of the country, and [Baré] said he didn't even know what the document was about."[23] Ratification would not happen instantaneously.

Then, on April 9, 1999, President Baré was shot and killed by members of his presidential guard. The head of Baré's security, Daouda Malam Wanké, became the country's interim president. Wanké set up a caretaker government called the Conseil de Reconciliation Nationale (CRN) and promised to organize free and fair presidential and legislative elections by the end of the year.[24] Niger's National Assembly and Supreme Court were dissolved, and an interim consultative body was established to help guide the country back to civilian rule.

Women's activists took advantage of the 1999 coup. Shortly after coming to power, Wanké invited leaders of Niger's national women's associations to the presidential palace, presumably to cultivate their support for the transitional government.[25] Thus, the president, secretary-general, and treasurer of CONGAFEN; the president of Fédération Kassaï; and leaders of other women's associations came together at the presidential palace. During the gathering, CONGAFEN's president gave Wanké a dossier on CEDAW, which included the text of the treaty and a report commissioned by the Ministry of Social Development that found that CEDAW did not contradict Islamic law. CONGAFEN's president wanted to ensure that "[Wanké] couldn't say that he had never heard of this document. He had the dossier on CEDAW. I told him that the women's associations, everyone, were hoping he could do something."[26] After the meeting, some of the women who had attended were excited about the prospects of the convention's ratification. Other attendees, however, admonished CONGAFEN's president for being too bold. "It was a risk that I was willing to take," said the then president. "Even after my death, I will be proud of this history and what CONGAFEN did. It was in the name of CONGAFEN, in the name of the conviction that I had for CONGAFEN, that I dared do this."[27]

Shortly after the installation of the caretaker government, two female ministers also moved to advance the issue of CEDAW's ratification.[28] In May 1999, Minister of Social Development Aïchatou Nana Foumakoye (the same female MP in 1994 mentioned earlier) reactivated the Réseau des Femmes Africaines Ministres et Parlementaires (REFAM/P), which had been dormant the previous four years.[29] A key member of REFAM/P was the only other woman in the twenty-member transitional cabinet, Minister of Foreign Affairs Aïchatou Mindaoudou.[30] The ministry of foreign affairs was charged with studying and recommending the ratification of international agreements to the president and his cabinet. Incidentally, the minister of foreign affairs was an ardent advocate of women's rights and had served as minister of social development from 1995 to 1996. Acting together with Foumakoye, Mindaoudou wrote to Wanké about the ratification of CEDAW. Wanké invited Minister Mindaoudou to present a proposal to ratify the treaty to the cabinet. At that meeting, the cabinet approved its ratification. Speaking about the two female ministers, the then president of CONGAFEN said, "They really made an effort." Mindaoudou, in particular, "worked a lot on [CEDAW] and knew a lot about it."[31]

To help make the ratification of CEDAW thinkable, women's activists advanced a causal story that ratifying the convention would help the country fall in line with the rest of the world. For example, a Ministry of Social

Development official told *Le Démocrat* in 1998, "Niger cannot remain on the sidelines of the international community and of progress. In this country that is more than 90 percent Muslim, everyone is a believer, but we are no more religious than others who have already ratified the text."[32] Nigériens who supported the convention's ratification referred in particular to other West African countries and Muslim-majority countries that had ratified it. A male judge who worked with RIDD-Fitila, a women's association, was quoted in May 1999 in *Le Sahel:* "Unfortunately, to this day, our country has not yet ratified this convention and thus it is not applicable in Niger. By contrast, it is applicable in some African countries like Côte d'Ivoire and European countries like France and Canada. Several African states, including Senegal, have adopted and ratified this convention."[33] This discourse helped make the ratification seem thinkable to Niger's military leaders. "Wanké said that there was no question [about ratifying CEDAW] because everyone else was doing it," said the then minister of social development.[34]

In the face of anti-CEDAW mobilization, pro-CEDAW advocates in the Ministry of Social Development tried to keep ratification thinkable by offering reservations as a solution for the deadlock between the state and conservative religious activists. The director of the Office on the Advancement of Women, who was at the same time president of CONGAFEN, told *Le Démocrate* in 1998, "The treaty allows for the ratification with reservations as long as they do not undermine the goal of the treaty."[35] Ministry officials again referred to the example of other Muslim-majority countries. Another official in the Ministry of Social Development told *Le Démocrate*, "A number of Arab-Muslim and African countries had ratified the convention with amendments," and the article went on to cite Iran, Egypt, Morocco, Nigeria, Mali, and Senegal.[36] This compromise option would appeal to Wanké in 1999.

Six years of pro-CEDAW advocacy by women in and outside the state helped put the issue of the convention on the national agenda and make its ratification thinkable. Ratification, however, did not happen automatically. Advocacy for CEDAW spanned one democratically elected government, one transitional government, and one questionably elected government. The mobilization of an anti-CEDAW coalition was part of the reason for the delay.

Countermobilization

If the democratic transition in the early 1990s created new opportunities for women to call for the ratification of CEDAW, it also created opportunities for conservative religious mobilization against the convention. Comparatively free of the constraints that military rulers imposed on formal religious associational life in the 1980s, Muslims (as well as Christians) formed dozens of religious organizations in the 1990s. Niger went from having one centralized state-controlled Islamic association in 1989 (AIN) to having at least twenty-three officially recognized independent Islamic associations by 1999.[37] Like the new women's associations, the new Islamic associations could identify their own list of problems to adddress.

Opposition in civil society to the ratification of CEDAW emerged soon after women's activists moved on the treaty. In 1995, the minister of social development met for three days with the presidents of various Islamic associations to discuss the contents of CEDAW, article by article.[38] At this encounter, leaders of some of the Islamic associations questioned whether the contents of CEDAW violated their interpretation of Islamic law.[39] For the rest of the 1990s, the debate between the Ministry of Social Development and conservative Islamic groups continued. When the Ministry of Social Development started its public education campaign on CEDAW in 1998, conservative religious activists organized protests against it.[40] In the same year, a coalition of ten Islamic associations met with President Baré to oppose the ratification of the convention.[41] As a journalist for Le Démocrate wrote in 1998, "[CEDAW] is today a topic of real arm wrestling between the ministry of social affairs and certain Islamic organizations."[42]

The anti-CEDAW coalition included not just men but also women. On May 9, 1999, the women's wings of six conservative Islamic associations—AEMUN, ADINI Islam, AJMN, ANASI, ARCI, and UFMN—held a special general assembly at the mosque of the Grand Marché in Niamey, during which they read four declarations denouncing CEDAW as well as family planning programs.[43] Conservative women's leaders at the meeting urged Muslims to "enjoin what is good and forbid the reprehensible," with CEDAW falling into the latter category.

To help make the ratification of CEDAW unthinkable, opponents constructed a stark dichotomy between the convention and Islamic jurisprudence. To this point, conservative religious activists presented Islamic law as a set of rigid dictates, overlooking classical Islamic legal theory's interest in human agency, pluralism, and debate.[44] As a spokesperson for conservative Islamic associations said in 1998, "We do not respect anything that does not respect Islamic law. This convention does not respect Islamic law, so we reject it."[45] According to conservative activists, the ratification of CEDAW threatened to violate Islamic precepts, creating a genderless society with no special place carved out for either men or women. A member of AEMUN was quoted in Le

Démocrate: "In the convention, there are several parts that contradict Islamic principles, such as the parts on equality between men and women. Islam sees the issue in terms of justice, in terms of complementarity."[46] Islamists reified and idealized Islamic jurisprudence.

Conservative activists presented the public not with a nuanced reading of international women's rights law or Islamic jurisprudence but with a simple one that would resonate with Nigériens. Opponents to CEDAW asserted that Islam provides stable and indisputable guidelines on equality between the sexes *(égalité)* and inheritance *(héritage)*, "two words to which the associations remain very allergic," wrote one journalist.[47] The word *equality* appears more than twenty times in the convention. *Inheritance*, however, does not appear at all in the treaty. Still, conservative activists talked about CEDAW as if it would have immediate and serious implications for how Nigériens handle matters of inheritance, connecting it to the previously vilified family code. Indeed, some members of the anti-CEDAW lobby argued that ratifying the treaty meant that the government could then impose the previously contested and abandoned family code.

In addition to advancing a simplified understanding of Islamic jurisprudence in their criticism of the convention, anti-CEDAW activists attacked the convention from a nationalistic point of view. CEDAW, according to the opponents to the convention, was a foreign law being forced on a sovereign population. As one male opponent told me, "CEDAW did not come from Africa. They imposed it on us."[48] For the conservative activists, the ratification of CEDAW required the consent of all Nigériens, including that of the new Islamic associations. A female opponent to CEDAW said to me, "We have multiple religions. They too don't want a law imposed on them that violates their religion."[49]

From this nationalistic perspective, CEDAW's opponents argued that there was nothing wrong with Niger's reputation to begin with, that there was no problem to be fixed. As Amina Rabiou, a female opponent to CEDAW, asked *Le Sahel* in May 1999, "Are Nigérien women really the object of discrimination?"[50] Rabiou further tells the newspaper, "The convention and other family planning policies were brought in by our feminist sisters who continue to fire on all cylinders to tarnish the image of Islam." The debate in civil society over CEDAW was as much, if not more, about defending Niger's reputation as it was about religion.

Not all Islamic associations opposed CEDAW. In 1998, *Le Démocrate* wrote, "Islamic associations no longer all speak with the same voice."[51] The director of the Groupement des Associations Islamiques pour les Activités en matière de Planification Familiale et de Promotion de la Femme (GAIPF)—a coalition of pro-family planning Islamic associations—told *Le Sahel* in a August 24, 1999 interview that it was acceptable to ratify the convention with reservations, and that the spirit of CEDAW did not necessarily undermine Islamic law. In response to the argument that ratifying the treaty meant that the government could then adopt a family code, the director of GAIPF made a clear distinction between the two, contending that CEDAW and the family code were not one and the same.[52] Some of the leaders of the *Tijaniyya* Muslim sect told me that they had "no problem" with CEDAW.[53] Outside Niamey, in the town of Diffa, Muslim leaders debated over the ratification of CEDAW.[54] It was becoming increasingly difficult for opponents to claim that they represented all of Niger's public opinion. After the convention was ratified, leaders of Niger's national Islamic associations continued to be split over the issue.

Bargaining with Women's Activists and Conservative Religious Activists

Amid mobilization of both women's activists and conservative religious activists over the treaty, Niger's transitional government ratified CEDAW on August 13, 1999.[55] A key difference between the transitional government and previous ones was that it did not need the approval of a National Assembly to ratify the convention (see Figure 10).[56] With the dissolution of the National Assembly, the transitional government had one fewer veto player to deal with. Women's activists recognized this when the opportunity to meet with Wanké arose in April 1999. As one member of the AFN said, "When there was a coup d'état, CONGAFEN reacted. Right away. It was not necessary to go all the way to the National Assembly. They were clever!"[57]

This is not to say that Wanké's presidency was smooth or predictable. A journalist in neighboring Burkina Faso described the period of transition as "chaotic," plagued by the fact that civil servants received no salary during the nine months Wanké was in power.[58] Analysts of Niger were wary of Wanké's intentions, wondering if he would fulfill his promise of transferring power to a democratically elected government. Observers were well aware that Wanké's predecessor, Baré, had also come to power in a military coup and then remained there through rigged presidential elections.

Nevertheless, compared to previous presidents, Wanké was in a position of relatively strong bargaining power. As one interviewee told me: "Wanké didn't need voters."[59] The transitional government successfully organized a constitutional referendum and presidential and legislative elections. On July 18, 1999,

1979	United Nations adopts CEDAW
1981	CEDAW enters into force
1991	National Conference
1993	Mahamane Ousmane elected president
1996	Ousmane removed in a coup d'état Ibrahim Baré Maïnassara becomes transitional president Baré elected president
1999	Baré killed in a coup d'état Malam Daouda Wanké becomes transitional president Niger ratifies CEDAW with reservations

Figure 10. Political context during the CEDAW debates, 1979–99

nearly 90 percent of voters approved the new constitution in what was deemed to be a fair and free process, though turnout was low, at 31 percent.[60] Article 141 of the new constitution granted amnesty to Wanké and other instigators of the January 27, 1996, and April 9, 1999 coups.[61] Later, it would become clear that Wanké had interest not in staying in power but in becoming a businessman.

In explaining the decision to ratify CEDAW, the transitional government adopted the causal story of the pro-CEDAW coalition. Earlier, I showed that women's activists framed CEDAW's ratification as something that would help bring Niger in line with peer countries and thus boost Niger's international reputation. Eleven days after ratifying CEDAW, the government's secretary-general published the following justification in *Le Sahel*:

> This decision [to ratify CEDAW] was influenced by the notable evolution of the international situation and by the fact that Niger was until recently the only African country to have not joined the convention. Furthermore, the majority of Muslim countries that follow Shari'a have adhered to the convention (Iran, Indonesia, Algeria, Egypt, Bangladesh, the Islamic Republic of Comoros, the Islamic Republic of Mauritania, Pakistan, Yemen, India, Turkey, etc.).[62]

The representative makes two mistakes here: Iran had not ratified CEDAW, and Mauritania would ratify CEDAW later, in 2001. Following the pro-CEDAW activists' lead, the government, albeit incorrectly, compared Niger to other African countries and to other Muslim countries.[63]

Given the government's concern with Niger's international reputation and its relatively strong bargaining position, it is striking that the military leaders placed any reservations on the convention at all. Wanké had come to power through undemocratic means, had secured amnesty for himself and his colleagues, did not need the approval of the National Assembly, and had little interest in staying in politics. Yet the government took pains to make sure that the Nigérien public knew that the government ratified CEDAW with reservations. For instance, the state-backed paper, *Le Sahel*, devoted nearly all of the front page and two additional full pages of its August 24 issue to the ratification of CEDAW with amendments. *Le Sahel* included the text of the military decree, which lists the reservations for all to see—an unusual move for the paper.[64] In the paper, the secretary-general of the government clarified that CEDAW had nothing to do with the family code and that "adhering [to CEDAW] will change absolutely nothing at all of current practices in our country."[65] CEDAW, according to the secretary-general, would certainly not affect inheritance practices, even though, as mentioned earlier, the convention did not contain any articles directly addressing inheritance. Further, the newspaper strategically placed on the same page a "message of condolences" from Wanké to King Fahd of Saudi Arabia on the death of the king's oldest son. The military government adopted a public, conciliatory stance toward conservative Islamic associations.

Historian Kimba Idrissa helps us make sense of the transitional government's compromise with both women's activists and conservative religious activists. Idrissa argues that contrary to what one might expect, there is no inherent difference between how military rulers and civilian rulers in Niger behave. This is because both military and civilian rulers need to rely on a coterie of elites to stay in power. Military rulers, as Idrissa writes, "sealed the same alliances with select, influential members of pressure groups, were held hostage by them, and exclusively used them for their own interests."[66] On the issue of CEDAW, these pressure groups included women's activists as well as conservative Islamic activists, and they influenced both military and civilian rulers.

Following the government's ratification of CEDAW, conservative religious activists demanded that the government rescind its ratification. Anti-CEDAW organizations met with Wanké on August 23, 1999, to express their dissatisfaction with the decree. In September, conservative Islamic associations met with the CRN's spokesperson, Djibrilla Hima Hamidou, at CRN headquarters to further complain about the ratification.[67] Conservative Islamic associations also asked their members to observe three days of fasting to bring God's curse on Wanké for ratifying CEDAW.[68] A curse was also invoked against Moussa Souleymane, a preacher who supported the presidential palace on the issue of the convention.[69] On September 25, 1999, at the mosque of the Grand

Marché in Niamey, preachers denounced CEDAW as a satanic text and distributed pamphlets in French and Arabic calling on Muslims to mobilize against "those who continue to plot against Islam."[70] In October, approximately two hundred to four hundred *"intégristes"* in Maradi "besieged" the state radio station, where a marabout had just discussed the contents and benefits of the convention.[71] The rioters burned tires, vandalized the radio station, and broke the windows of the prefect's car.

In the face of anti-CEDAW organizing in September and October 1999, the transitional government created an ad hoc interministerial committee to manage what one former minister called "the crisis."[72] The committee launched a public relations campaign, airing programs about CEDAW on television and radio to help inform the public of its benefits, making sure to invite moderate Muslim leaders.[73] Wanké told conservative religious activists that he was open to placing additional reservations on the convention provided that the activists specify which articles merited amendments.[74] Further, the caretaker government asked Cheick Oumarou Ismael, president of the AIN, to reign in the anti-CEDAW fervor. On September 22, 1999, Cheick Ismael went on national television and said that the military assured him that they would never adopt a text that went against Islam. "Those who have reservations about the text are asked to send them to me," said AIN's president. "I will be sure to send them to the CRN."[75] The hardliners, the most conservative members of the Islamic associations, however, would not be mollified. After Cheick Ismael's television appearance, a leader of the AEMUN grumbled that its members rejected the reservations because "man as a simple human being has no right to make laws. All legislation is in the hands of God. Take it or leave it, there are no half-measures."[76]

Once ratified, however, there was no going back on the issue of CEDAW. In September, the transitional government released a public statement: "Neither the CRN nor the government intend to revisit this issue on Niger's ratification of the Convention."[77] Members of the conservative Islamic associations saw that they had been outmaneuvered. As one female anti-CEDAW activist noted, "Secular women . . . persevered by changing their strategy" and proposing that the government issue reservations on the convention.[78] The hardliners' relatively extreme measures against the state did not change Wanké's mind. When the rioters attacked the radio station in Maradi, the state brought in the police and army to put an end to the violence.

In sum, the mobilization of women in and outside the state in the mid-1990s helps explain Niger's ratification of CEDAW. And while conservative

Islamic associations mobilized against the convention, there was no National Assembly for the government to contend with in the ratification of the international agreement. Yet, falling in line with Niger's practice of partial power sharing with religious actors and ideal of building consensus, Wanké's military transitional government compromised with the anti-CEDAW coalition and ratified CEDAW with reservations.

The Protocol on the Rights of Women in Africa

Women's activists in Niger and across the African continent mobilized for the ratification of CEDAW, but they also believed that the convention did not go far enough in addressing African women's needs. Starting in the mid-1990s, women's activists across the continent advocated for the creation of an Africa-specific women's rights treaty.[79] In July 2003, their efforts were answered when the African Union's heads of state adopted the Maputo Protocol. The protocol reaches beyond CEDAW, requiring that states ensure women's right to choose any method of contraception; adopt legislation prohibiting female genital cutting; and, in cases of rape, incest, or the endangerment of the mother's mental or physical health, protect the rights of women to medical abortion. It further calls on states to protect the rights of women in prison, women living with disabilities, and elderly women, none of which were explicitly addressed in CEDAW.[80] The protocol entered into force on November 25, 2005, thirty days after the fifteenth ratification. As of the end of 2012, Niger has yet to ratify the Maputo Protocol.

Women's Mobilization

As was the case for CEDAW, women's activists helped put the issue of the Maputo Protocol on the national agenda. Women's activists in Niger knew about the Maputo Protocol and mobilized for its ratification even before the African Union officially adopted the treaty. In particular, ONG Dimol, a member of CONGAFEN that focuses on women's reproductive health, led the early struggle for the ratification of the protocol. In 2000, representatives of ONG Dimol and ANDDH met with activists from Burkina Faso, Guinea, Ivory Coast, Mali, and Senegal in Lomé, Togo, to strategize about the Maputo Protocol. Their goal was to find ways to convince the African Union's heads of state to adopt the protocol and to brainstorm how to persuade their country's leaders to ratify the treaty.[81] Shortly thereafter, ONG Dimol and ANDDH, along with the AFN, CONGAFEN, Fédération Kassaï, representatives of ministries, and female representatives of the major political parties, formed the Coalition sur le Plaidoyer sur le Protocole (Coalition for the Lobbying of the Protocol).[82]

International donors supported activists who called for the ratification of the Maputo Protocol. The Canadian International Development Agency (CIDA) and nonprofit Canadian Centre for International Studies and Cooperation helped finance the 2000 meeting in Lomé on the Maputo Protocol.[83] In the years leading up to the June 2006 vote, international organizations—in particular, UNFPA and SNV—financed seminars for women's advocacy groups, Islamic associations, and Catholic associations to arrive at a common understanding on the protocol.[84]

Advocacy for the Maputo Protocol's ratification, however, was relatively limited compared to that for CEDAW's ratification. A formal coalition was established, but it appeared to exist in name only. Meanwhile, women's activists pursued broader or different women's issues. For instance, in February 2006, AFJN organized a workshop on gender and lobbying, but it did not call specifically for the Maputo Protocol's ratification.[85] In hindsight, women's activists, including the president of ONG Dimol, reasoned that not enough consciousness raising or lobbying had been done for the protocol.[86]

Mobilization for the protocol was limited before the June 2006 vote, as two types of divisions plagued women's activists. One split arose between pro-protocol activists in civil society and the minister of women's advancement. (Between December 30, 2004, and March 1, 2010, the Ministry of Social Development was split into a Ministry of Social Development and a stand-alone Ministry of Women's Advancement and Child Protection.) According to one leader of the pro-protocol coalition, the minister of women's advancement refused to join the Coalition for the Lobbying of the Protocol.[87] The Ministry of Foreign Affairs and the Ministry of Land and Territory, in contrast, had joined the coalition.[88] Some of the pro-protocol activists felt that the minister of women's advancement did not want to work with women in civil society because she wanted to be able to take all the credit for the ratification of the Maputo Protocol.[89] These strained relations may have also hampered coalition building among female ministers at the time. Minister of Foreign Affairs Mindaoudou, for instance, did not personally sign the government's October 2005 *exposé des motifs,* which was to accompany the bill of ratification. Instead, it was one Hassane Souley who signed the document.[90] The minister of foreign affairs also reportedly did not attend the plenary debate on the Maputo Protocol in the National Assembly. Instead, it was the minister of women's advancement who addressed the assembly and gave her support to the treaty.

Women's activists also split among those who wanted to pursue the removal of the reservations on CEDAW and those who wanted to pursue the ratification of the Maputo Protocol. Some women's activists wanted to put the removal of CEDAW's reservations first. Indeed, at a conference organized by SNV in 2005, it was agreed that CONGAFEN would take the lead on campaigning for the removal of the reservations on CEDAW.[91] Others thought that it was more important to ratify the Maputo Protocol. Still others thought that they could combine the two issues into one campaign. In that spirit, in March 2006, the coalitions on the Protocol and on CEDAW ostensibly merged together. Some activists felt that members of the pro-protocol coalition themselves were not entirely convinced that it was worth the effort, money, and time to ratify the AU treaty.[92] As a representative of an international donor agency that supported the protocol's ratification told me, "There was no common front from the beginning. Within this context we worked and tried to get them together on the Protocol and on CEDAW."[93]

Some of the energy and donor money that might have gone into campaigning for the Maputo Protocol's ratification went toward the campaign to remove CEDAW's reservations. In November 2005, the Ministry of Women's Advancement and Child Protection issued a report that sought to justify why the state should lift its amendments on CEDAW.[94] (UNFPA helped fund the writing of this report.) In the same month, the government organized a "day of awareness-raising" for MPs on the benefits of removing the reservations on the convention.[95] (UNDP and Coopération Belge financed the day of awareness raising.) Yet at the same time, ONG Dimol and others were trying to organize a campaign for the ratification of the Maputo Protocol.

In spite of the difficulties that the coalition for the protocol encountered, President Tandja signed the Maputo Protocol on July 6, 2004. The cabinet then reviewed the bill of ratification, which made it onto the National Assembly's 2006 calendar. The pro-protocol coalition did not know that difficulties surrounding the ratification of the treaty were just beginning.

The National Assembly

Unlike Wanké, President Tandja was required to obtain the approval of the National Assembly for the ratification of the Maputo Protocol, for the National Assembly had been reinstated after the October and November 1999 presidential and legislative elections (see Figure 11). In 2004, Tandja was reelected

2003	African Union adopts the Protocol
2004	President Mamadou Tandja signs the Protocol
2005	The Protocol enters into force Bill of ratification is sent to the National Assembly
2006	National Assembly rejects the bill of ratification
2007	Subsequent attempts to send a bill of ratification fail

Figure 11. Political context during the Maputo Protocol debates, 2003–11

president, with 65.5 percent of the second-round votes. Tandja's party, the MNSD, and its allies held a significant majority in the National Assembly (77.9 percent). MNSD won 47 of the 113 seats (41.6 percent) in the National Assembly. Four parties allied with the MNSD won 41 seats: the CDS won twenty-two seats, the RSD won seven seats, the RDP won six seats, the ANDP won five seats, and the PSDN won one seat. The PNDS and its allies won the remaining 25 seats.[96]

In spite of holding the majority in parliament, MPs exercised their veto powers and voted against the government bill for the Protocol's ratification because they felt that the legislative process had been tampered with. Indeed, at least two versions of the bill had been presented to the National Assembly. One earlier version issued reservations on Articles 6, 14(b), 14(c), and 21 in the protocol.[97] When parliamentary committees met in March 2006 to discuss the bill of ratification, they used the initial version, the one with reservations.[98] Article 6 concerns marriage. Of its ten subsections, two in particular interested the MPs. Article 6(b) states that countries that ratify the protocol "shall enact appropriate national legislative measures to guarantee that . . . the minimum age of marriage for women shall be eighteen years."[99] Article 6(e) states that "the husband and wife shall, by mutual agreement, choose their matrimonial regime and place of residence." Next, Article 14 focuses on women's health and reproductive rights. Article 14(b) states that women have "the right to decide whether to have children, the number of children and the spacing of children." Article 14(c) states that women have "the right to choose any method of contraception." Finally, Article 21 concerns women's right to inherit property. It states, "A widow shall have the right to an equitable share in the inheritance of the property of her husband" and "shall have the right to continue to live in the matrimonial house." Furthermore, "Women and men shall have the right to inherit, in equitable shares, their parents' properties."

An April 2006 version of the bill, however, did not propose to levy reservations on the protocol.[100] That is, no explicit reference to Articles 6, 14, or 21 was made. According to available sources, the April version of the bill was the one that MPs voted on in June 2006.[101] The MPs, then, were voting on a bill different from the one they had discussed weeks earlier in committee. This caused considerable confusion and consternation on the floor. MPs in Tandja's own MNSD party as well as MPs in opposition parties were dissatisfied with the perceived sleight of hand. To this day, it is unclear why the assembly voted on a different version of the bill. I heard people speculate that the government, not wanting reservations, intentionally switched bills in the hopes that the MPs would not notice the change. Others felt that the government purposively sabotaged the process because it did not want the Protocol's ratification in the first place. From my reading of the available evidence, the Ministry of Women's Advancement carried out its task clumsily, but it remains unclear precisely how the executive cabinet or the assembly's executive office allowed a different version of the bill to arrive on the floor.

To express their discontent with the switching of the bills, MPs voted against the proposal to ratify the protocol. This point of dissatisfaction came up repeatedly in my interviews with MPs and led me to question the story that the bill was rejected by "illiterate" and "rural" MPs. Consider one MP's (PNDS-Tahaoua) argument for why he voted against the bill:

> When you bring in a proposed law, you have to arrange it properly. You can't remove even one part of the bill. It's for that reason the bill was rejected. If there had been the reservations on the Protocol, we could have passed it.[102]

Note that this MP was considered an illiterate. Yet when my research assistant and I arrived at his office in Niamey, the MP was at his computer working on several spreadsheets. During the interview, we were frequently interrupted by assistants seeking his signature on various documents. It turned out that the MP, an oil importer and owner of several gas stations, had attended Qur'anic schools and received several years of formal schooling. He appeared to understand not only the contents of the Maputo Protocol but also the legislative process.

Another MP, a former public school teacher with two wives (CDS-Maradi), said to me that the removal of reservations troubled him. Note that this MP belonged to Tandja's coalition of parties:

> I voted against it. . . . I was a member of the committee that studied the bill. We examined it in great depth. . . . There were reservations that the government put

on certain articles. We wanted those reservations. . . . Curiously, they took out the reservations. That first vote failed. The majority of [the National Assembly] was in agreement but with reservations on five points.[103]

MP Kalla Ankourao (PNDS-Maradi) told the *Le Républicain* shortly after the vote that the government's "hemming and hawing over the text, including whether to put reservations on certain articles, led members to have doubts about the document."[104] Had the final version of the bill contained reservations on the protocol, the bill might have passed.

In arguing for reservations on the Maputo Protocol, MPs adopted the language of conservative religious activists who had opposed the family code and the ratification of CEDAW. These MPs socially constructed a black-and-white dichotomy between international law, on the one hand, and Islamic law, on the other. "We here, we are ninety-five percent Muslim," said one MP (PNDS-Tahaoua) to me. "It is necessary that the law conform to religion."[105] The following excerpt from an interview with a businessman and MP (RSD-Zinder) is illustrative:

AJK: What was your vote on the Additional Protocol?

MP: Against. I don't agree with the contents.

AJK: Which contents?

MP: Those that had to do with our tradition, our religion. On inheritance rights. Our religion clearly defined how to split up inheritance.[106]

Note, however, that in the original bill submitted to the National Assembly, the government offered to place an amendment on Article 21 on inheritance.

Like the conservative religious activists who had opposed the ratification of CEDAW, some MPs invoked anti-Western rhetoric to oppose the Maputo Protocol. These MPs portrayed the protocol as a foreign imposition. One businessman and MP (CDS-Tahoua) told me that Nigériens deserve the freedom of choice, and that "no one should be obligated to do this or that."[107] His stance on the protocol appears firm:

I'd rather die than vote for the adoption of the Protocol. . . . The women who want the Protocol, they are female intellectuals. . . . If you want to support the Protocol, that's for intellectuals, city-folk, or those who come from the West.

Following the discourse of conservative religious activists, MPs such as the one quoted here created a false dichotomy between "female intellectuals" and the rest of the population, between "city-folk" and the rural population, and between "the West" and Niger.

In general, female MPs in the National Assembly supported the ratification of the Maputo Protocol, though it is important not to oversimplify the differences between female and male MPs. A female MP (PNDS-Tahoua)—an active union member and member of the RDFN with two co-wives—voted for the protocol, but she also argued that parts of it merited reservations: "I voted for it. All that was in those laws go with my wishes. There were, though, two or three religious things that I didn't agree with. We could have had reservations, but those articles were taken out."[108] Still, for this female MP, Article 6(c), which promoted a woman's right to have a say in where to live, made sense to her. "The men [in the National Assembly] were creating all these unnecessary problems," said the female MP to me. "When married, I had my own place. I don't rest in the same house as the other wives."

Some female MPs went further and argued against placing any reservations on the Maputo Protocol. The Committee on Social and Cultural Affairs, whose president and vice president were both female MPs, stated in its report on the protocol that "the reservations expressed in the explanatory memorandum that allude to Articles 6, 14(b, c) and 21 of the Protocol have no raison d'être."[109] The report points out that "Niger just adopted a law on reproductive health that states that couples have the right to make their own decisions concerning fertility, such as the number and spacing of births." Thus, for the committee, no reservations were needed on Article 14. The committee further argued that Article 21 on inheritance does not contradict Islamic law because the article calls for the fair, and not necessarily equal, partition of property: "Fair does not mean 'equal.'" The committee also questioned the reservation on Article 16, contending that "it is natural that . . . the State accept that the widow can remain in the marital home."

After the vote, the government's spokesperson expressed disappointment with the assembly's rejection of the protocol bill.[110] The government pledged to resubmit a bill of ratification for the Maputo Protocol later that year. However, getting the National Assembly to reconsider the issue of the Maputo Protocol would prove to be difficult.

Countermobilization

Following the National Assembly's rejection of the bill of ratification, conservative activists, worried that Tandja and the government would try to submit another bill of ratification to the National Assembly, mounted a concerted campaign against the Maputo Protocol. This countermobilization helped stall subsequent bills of ratification.

Activists against the Maputo Protocol formed a coalition more cohesive than the anti-CEDAW coalition. In October 2006, two umbrella organizations—CASIN and the Groupement des Associations Islamiques en matière de Planning Familial et Développement Social (GAIP/DS; formerly GAIPF, which sided with women's activists on the issue of CEDAW)—issued a declaration against the protocol following a government meeting on the treaty.[111] In the declaration, conservative religious associations denounced the use of reservations as "a new form of trickery to lull the Muslim population." In December of that year, Cheick Oumarou Ismael—the president of AIN who sided with Wanké during the CEDAW debates—gave an interview to the conservative Islamic newspaper *As-Salam,* in which he opposed the ratification of the protocol.[112] Opponents also had the well-known politician Sanoussi Tambari Jackou on their side.[113]

Conservative women formed a common and sustained front on the issue of the Maputo Protocol. Three months after the rejection of the protocol bill, in September, several hundred women assembled in front of the National Assembly at the meeting in Niamey to denounce the protocol.[114] Three women's associations organized the demonstration: the women's section of ANASI, the Association des Femmes Musulmanes pour les Œuvres de Bienfaisance et de Développement (AFMBD), and UFMN. Outside Niamey, dozens of women in regional towns including Zinder protested against the protocol, recruiting demonstrators through the radio and women's Qur'anic schools.[115] In December, conservative women in the towns of Dosso and Zinder released declarations against the protocol.[116] Upon hearing that the National Assembly might consider another bill of ratification, conservative Muslim women in Niamey issued another declaration in March 2007 that asked MPs to reject the bill.[117] On National Women's Day (May 13), several hundred women that belonged to conservative associations gathered at the Centre Culturel Oumarou Ganda.[118] Conservative women leaders called on women to pray that God thwart the ratification of the "lesbian Protocol."[119]

In opposing the Maputo Protocol, opponents adapted the anti-CEDAW causal narrative and constructed a stark dichotomy between international women's rights law and Islamic law. The following excerpt from a 2006 *As-Salam* interview with AIN president Cheick Oumarou Ismaël is illustrative:

There are two opposing camps: those who want the decision of Allah and those who are dissatisfied with the law of God. And I say, when God and his Prophet decide upon something, Muslims have no further choice to make. Those who, by contrast, believe that God's laws are outdated, they should know that they have declared war on God.[120]

Anti-protocol activists made it seem as if Nigériens had only two options: to be a "good Muslim" and oppose the treaty in its entirety or to be a "bad Muslim" and support it.

Anti-protocol activists further portrayed international women's rights law as inferior to Islamic law. "Islam has given more rights to women than any other religion," argued CASIN and GAIP/DS.[121] Conservative women agreed. As a spokesperson for conservative Muslim women told Le Républicain in September 2006, "For us Muslims, nothing is more favorable to the real emancipation of women as is the Qur'an and the Sunnah of the Prophet."[122] Anti-protocol women repeatedly told me that under Islam, all of women's needs are taken care of. Once widowed or divorced, women under Islamic law are cared for by their uncles, cousins, and brothers. As a thirty-year-old woman and contractual teacher who protested against the Maputo Protocol in Zinder said, "Even if the husband is poor, and the wife is rich, the responsibility [of taking care of the family] is on him."[123] Like their anti-CEDAW counterparts, anti-protocol activists challenged Niger's low ranking in the world, defensively arguing that by situating Niger at the bottom, one was also ranking Islam at the bottom of all world religions.

International women's rights laws, particularly for conservative women, imposed ideals that did not fit with Nigérien realities. Fixing the age of marriage at eighteen would punish girls who have a child out of wedlock before then. "Why should one wait until 18 when they are messing around up until the point they have a baby outside marriage?" said the thirty-year-old protester. "Why prevent them from getting married?"[124] Similarly, in explaining why she was opposed to setting a minimum age of marriage at eighteen, one conservative woman, who worked for a ministry, recounted to a fellow researcher and me a story she had heard from friends in the town of Diffa. In this story, a father was concerned about his daughter's unruly behavior and decided that it would be better to have her marry to head off a scandal. Local authorities learned that the father was planning for his daughter to marry before she was eighteen and arrested the father. By the end of the year, the daughter became pregnant.[125] For the conservative activist who told me this story, it would be better to allow girls to marry, because the reality was that teenage girls could get, and were getting, pregnant. Allowing girls to have children out of wedlock, warned a 2007 document sent by the Comité des Associations Islamiques Nigériennes Opposées au Protocole to the minister of women's advancement, "dangerously threatens our society."[126]

Unlike their anti-CEDAW counterparts, anti-protocol activists adapted to the democratic political context. Conservative women at the September 2006 meeting in front of the National Assembly defended the legislative body: "We applaud the vigilance of the people's representatives who rejected the ratification of this text and we encourage them to persevere in this direction."[127] CASIN and GAIP/DS argued that sending another bill of ratification to the National Assembly implied that "the MPs didn't know what they were doing in protecting the Nigérien people."[128] In addition to defending the National Assembly, conservative activists directly appealed to parliamentarians to reject the treaty. When conservative religious women in Dosso and Zinder issued declarations against the Maputo Protocol in December 2006, they wrote, "We ask our honorable representatives in the National Assembly to reject again the Protocol, which could plunge Niger and its people into an abyss of discord and tumult."[129] In the same year, Zada Ali, a conservative Muslim leader, wrote an open letter to the National Assembly asking them to "relieve Muslims from their suffering and in large numbers reject the Maputo Protocol."[130]

Anti-protocol activists also adapted to the political context by framing the Maputo Protocol as antithetical to so-called public opinion, which ought to matter in a democracy. The conservative women's declaration of May 13, 2007, invoked the principle of democratic majority rule:

> "If democracy," according to Abraham Lincoln, "is the government of the people, by the people, and for the people," then we want to know for the history books who benefits from having this Protocol as law in Niger? Which politician? Which political party? Or which civil society organization?[131]

The protocol was "rejected by the majority of Nigériens," said anti-protocol activists in an earlier declaration.[132] *As-Salam* framed the Maputo Protocol later in October 2007 as "not respecting popular will."[133] While anti-protocol activists depicted MPs as respecting the desires of the majority, conservatives depicted the "feminists" who support the Maputo Protocol as "working against the Muslim people of Niger."[134] Although the protocol makes no reference to gay rights, Zada Ali asks MPs to remember that "on the one hand you have Allah, the Qur'an, and the Prophet Mohammed and the Muslims that elected you, and on the other hand feminist Nigériens, the international lesbian movement, and their international donors."[135] In other words, conservative religious activists painted women's activists as the minority, a fringe movement. These rhetorical strategies helped make the ratification of the Maputo Protocol unthinkable.

Bargaining with Women's Activists, Conservative Religious Activists, and the National Assembly

Whereas Wanké and the transitional government had to contend with women's activists and conservative religious activists, Tandja was confronted with women's activists, conservative religious activists, *and* representatives in the National Assembly. Tandja sought to bargain with all three groups.

Following the June 2006 vote, pro-protocol activists mobilized for the treaty's ratification, hoping that a second bill would pass if MPs and conservative associations better understood the contents of the protocol. In December 2006, the AFJN organized a roundtable consisting of the president of the AFJN, Muslim leader Cheick Yahaya Abdou, a representative of the Association des Chefs Traditionnels du Niger (ACTN), and a journalist on the Maputo Protocol, which was aired on Télé Sahel.[136] (Representatives of the National Assembly and the Ministry of Women's Advancement and Child Protection, however, "were unable to attend" AFJN's roundtable.)[137] The AFJN also developed radio spots and a short film in French, Hausa, and Zarma on the consequences of early marriage to favorably influence public opinion on the protocol. In contrast to the pre-2006 period, women's activists and the Ministry of Women's Advancement and Child Protection worked together; the president of ONG Dimol was quoted in 2007, "The Women's affairs ministry pulled out all the stops for a participative approach in order to bring together the positions of NGOs and Islamic associations [on the Maputo Protocol]."[138] Tandja also reportedly provided funds to female ministers and parliamentarians to organize consciousness-raising activities on the protocol.

Tandja and cabinet ministers tried to negotiate with conservative religious activists. In December 2006, on the occasion of Maoulid, a major Muslim holiday, Tandja met with Muslim leaders in Agadez to seek common ground on the Maputo Protocol.[139] The minister of women's advancement and the minister of the interior helped organize that meeting. The Ministry of Women's Advancement and Child Protection also invited CASIN and GAIP/DS to write a report on the Maputo Protocol from their point of view. Adapting to the conservative religious view that Islamic jurisprudence consisted of fixed dictates, the ministry asked CASIN and GAIP/DS to assess whether Articles 6, 14, and 21 of the treaty could be reconciled with Islamic precepts.[140]

President Tandja also tried to work with the National Assembly. In October 2006, the government submitted another bill of ratification to the legislature.[141] In April 2007, the Ministry of Foreign Affairs wrote a new *exposé des motifs* for the ratification of the Maputo Protocol. Seeking to mollify the MPs, the statement of purpose explicitly mentioned that the government consulted religious scholars, CASIN, and GAIP/DS on the protocol.[142] According to *La Griffe*, the National Assembly was scheduled to vote on the resubmitted bill on June 2, 2007. The government, however, decided to withdraw the bill in late May out of fear that it might be voted down again.[143]

Tandja's bargaining position vis-à-vis the National Assembly and civil society further weakened as new political scandals, civil society protests unrelated to the Maputo Protocol, and armed rebellion arose. In 2006, two former ministers were arrested along with others on the charge of stealing four billion CFA francs from an education project.[144] That same year, labor unions and civil society groups organized national strikes to oppose increases in the cost of living. Relations between Tandja and Prime Minister Hama Amadou increasingly soured as Tandja made it clearer that he was planning to run for a third term. In 2007, 62 of 113 parliamentarians voted to remove Amadou from office, effectively dissolving the government. In February of that year, a militia group, the Mouvement des Nigériens pour la Justice, attacked an army base in northern Niger, and similar raids continued into 2008.[145] Amid the turmoil, the ratification of the Maputo Protocol was set aside.

In sum, several factors impeded the ratification of the Maputo Protocol. Women's advocacy for the protocol was limited due to divisions among women's activists. The National Assembly utilized its veto power and voted down the bill of ratification, specifically the version of the bill that contained no reservations. Anti-protocol activists, by invoking democracy, drawing on a pared-down version of Islamic law, and targeting their messages to the National Assembly, used the national political context to their advantage.

Additional and Alternative Explanations

Women's mobilization, conservative religious mobilization, and the national political context help us understand how Niger ratified CEDAW and not the Maputo Protocol. Other factors, however, may be at play. Here I will focus on how international influence, regime type, political ideology, and the content of the treaties may have affected Niger's commitment to international women's rights law.

International Influence

Perhaps varying levels of international donor pressure could explain how Niger ratified CEDAW and not the Maputo Protocol. As an aid-dependent country, Niger's leaders may have wanted to show international donors that they were committed to protecting women's rights, which donors explicitly supported. This chapter has shown that international donors backed the ratification of CEDAW *and* the Maputo Protocol. International organizations (e.g., UNIFEM), embassies representing wealthy countries (e.g., the United States), and aid organizations of wealthy countries (e.g., USAID) provided money and moral support in the 1990s and 2000s to help activists lobby for the ratification of both women's rights treaties. International donors ramped up their lobbying for the Maputo Protocol's ratification after the 2006 vote. After the vote, representatives of European and U.S. delegations pledged to ask government officials and MPs to readdress the issue of the Maputo Protocol, and yet no ratification occurred.[146]

Transnational advocacy networks also mobilized for the ratification of the Maputo Protocol, but to no avail. Following the 2006 vote, a representative of the pan-African women's network Solidarity for African Women's Rights (SOAWR) declared its regret over the decision and shamed the MPs for having set a "dangerous precedent."[147] In February 2007, the Fédération Internationale des Ligues de Droits de l'Homme (FIDH) sent a mission to Niger.[148] The delegation met with First Lady Laraba Tandja, the minister of women's advancement, and the minister of social development. "FIDH urges Nigérien MPs to follow the recommendations of Niger's vibrant civil society, including its women's organizations, and adopt the Protocol without reservations," stated the human rights organization in its report.[149] FIDH promised that it would make the same recommendation before the UN Committee on the Elimination of Discrimination against Women in New York. Four years later, in 2011, a delegate from the regional organization Réseau Interafricain pour les Femmes, Media, Genre et Développement (FAMEDEV) visited with Nigérien authorities, including the minister of justice, to persuade them to ratify the Maputo Protocol.[150] No number of international human rights or women's rights groups, however, would induce the government to resubmit a bill of ratification or the National Assembly to put the Maputo Protocol's ratification on its calendar.

I do not want to minimize the importance of the international context on women's rights policymaking. It was during the preparatory meetings for the UN World Conference on Women in Beijing that women's activists in Niger first publicly called for the ratification of CEDAW. Women's activists argued for the ratification by pointing out that many other countries in the region had already ratified the convention. Pro-protocol activists met with activists from other West African countries to discuss strategies for the ratification of the protocol. Women's activists received international funding to help raise the public's consciousness about both the UN convention and the AU treaty. Women's activists used what was happening at the global level to inform their advocacy at the national level.

Yet it is also important not to overstate the role of international influence. Five years after my first trip to Niger, I returned to Niamey to present my findings to women's leaders and hear their feedback. At one point during the presentation, a new and relatively young member of CONGAFEN's executive board asked if I thought international donors imposed their preferences on Niger's leaders. A former president of CONGAFEN responded:

> Donors can't impose what they want. It's not even good that donors try to impose laws. Because it's Nigérien women who know their problems. [Nigérien women] ask maybe for logistical help, financial help to try and go forward. UNICEF gave us money to lobby on the reservations on CEDAW. And that was all. It's us that had proposed the idea. And them, they give support.

Given that it would have been easy to blame international donors for not doing enough or for imposing their will on women's activists, I was surprised to hear the former president say that it was CONGAFEN who proposed the unsuccessful campaign to remove the reservations on CEDAW. In cases in which there is no foreign occupation, it may be more accurate to describe the impact of international influence on women's rights policy adoption as indirect rather than direct.

One is also in danger of oversimplifying the effect of international forces on women's rights policies. International pressure and discourse had an unintended consequence of providing fodder to conservative religious activists, who framed international women's rights treaties as "foreign impositions." To return to the FIDH delegation that visited Niger in 2007, the mission included French comedian Marie-Christine Barrault. In the context of her visit to Niamey, Barrault was infamously quoted as saying that "a dog in

France has more rights than a woman in Niger."[151] This quotation only angered conservative activists. Anti-CEDAW and anti-protocol activists argued that the world polity unduly ranked Niger—and, by extension, Islam—low compared to other countries and religions. Thus, international pressure had multiple effects, both positive and negative, on the ratification of women's rights treaties in Niger.

Democracies vs. Autocracies

Scholars suggest that regime type—that is, whether a country is authoritarian, transitioning to a democracy, or democratic—helps account for states' decisions to ratify international human rights agreements.[152] Democratizing regimes may be more likely to ratify human rights treaties, particularly those with a better chance of being enforced, to signal their commitment to democracy.[153] Stable democracies may be less likely to ratify human rights treaties because democratic institutions can hold rulers accountable to the terms of the international agreement, thereby making ratification costly. By contrast, with no institutions to hold them accountable, authoritarian countries may be more likely to ratify international treaties because doing so offers a low-cost way of boosting their reputation.[154]

A transitioning regime ratified CEDAW and a democratic regime rejected the Maputo Protocol, which provides support for the argument that countries undergoing democratic transitions are more likely to commit to global norms of women's rights. CEDAW, moreover, has stronger enforcement mechanisms than does the Maputo Protocol. When a country ratifies CEDAW, it is required to submit periodic reports to a UN committee in New York, specifically tasked with evaluating the country's progress toward enforcing the treaty. The Maputo Protocol asks state parties to describe how they are enforcing the treaty in periodic reports, but no special committee was created for the task, and no details were made in the treaty in terms of how often state parties should submit their reports.[155]

Yet in this and other chapters of the book, I suggest that the adoption of women's rights policies does not simply boil down to whether countries are democratic, authoritarian, or transitioning. Women's activists played an important role in bringing the ratification of CEDAW to the attention of then president Wanké and in offering reservations as a solution to the deadlock with conservative religious activists. Across authoritarian, transitioning, and democratic Niger, leaders sought to accommodate conservative religious activists. And in democratizing and democratic contexts, opportunities open up for both pro- and anti-women's rights mobilization. The story of international women's rights law in Niger is further complicated by such factors as activists' relative unity or fragmentation, and their success in framing policy proposals as thinkable.

Ideology of the Leader or Party in Power

It may be that Niger ratified CEDAW and not the Maputo Protocol because President Wanké was ideologically more committed to promoting women's rights than was President Tandja. The evidence, however, suggests that Wanké and Tandja held similar ideologies. Neither president espoused Marxist or socialist sentiments that might lead him to promote gender equality. Both rose to political power through their service in the military, where they were socialized to protect the status quo of secular rule.[156] When I expressed skepticism about Tandja's commitment to promoting women's rights, people not affiliated with Tandja's party responded in his defense, pointing to the opening of a women's bank during his time in office. "The government is really behind [the Maputo Protocol]," said one representative of a foreign delegation.[157] Tandja "cares about women," said a woman's activist not affiliated with the MNSD.[158]

If Niger had had a left-leaning party in power, then perhaps it would have ratified both CEDAW and the Maputo Protocol. Until 2011, Niger has not had a leftist or socialist president or party in control of the government. Since winning the presidency, the country's longest-standing socialist party, the PNDS, has yet to demonstrate that it is ideologically committed to promoting women's rights. As previously mentioned, MPs from the PNDS voted against the bill for the ratification of the Maputo Protocol. Thus, the ideology of the leader or power in party alone does not appear to explain the outcomes examined in this chapter.

Differences in Content

CEDAW, which contains thirty articles, and the Maputo Protocol, which contains thirty-two articles, differ in content, which might help account for the outcomes analyzed in this chapter. As mentioned earlier, some scholars suggest that democratizing countries may be more likely to ratify treaties if the treaties have relatively strong enforcement mechanisms. CEDAW has clearer rules about enforcement than does the Maputo Protocol. The Maputo Protocol is ostensibly a more radical document. The protocol explicitly sets a minimum age of marriage for women, whereas CEDAW does not. Earlier, I showed that conservative religious women opposed Article 6 of the protocol, which sets a minimum age of marriage for women at eighteen years. The protocol also explicitly calls for states to protect women's rights to inheritance and abortion as well as widow's rights, unlike CEDAW. Conservative activists as well as MPs disapproved of the Protocol's call for equal inheritance rights among men and women. Thus, leaders may find the convention more appealing to ratify than the protocol.

Comparing the contents of the treaties is helpful but limiting because there are predominantly Muslim countries that have ratified both CEDAW and the Maputo Protocol. I have found it more illuminating to examine how activists and others interpret the policy and policymaking process. Recall that MPs were prepared to vote for the ratification of the protocol before the June 2006 vote, but it was the mysterious removal of reservations that pushed them to vote against it. MPs did not vote against the Maputo Protocol solely because of its content. It is possible that had the Maputo Protocol avoided the issues of marriage and inheritance, that no reservations would have been seen as necessary in the first place. Yet recall that conservative religious activists argued that CEDAW violated Islamic law by calling for equal inheritance rights. Anti-CEDAW activists, in doing so, misread the convention, which does not explicitly make any reference to a deceased person's distribution of property.

Conclusion

At the United Nations headquarters in New York City, twenty-three experts on the Committee on the Elimination of All Forms of Discrimination against Women met on May 29, 2007, to evaluate progress in eliminating discrimination against women in Niger and seven other countries. The state of Niger submitted a sixty-nine-page report to the committee.[159] The state also sent seventeen representatives to UN headquarters to respond to the committee's questions and hear the committee's remarks. The Nigérien representatives included Minister of Women's Advancement and Child Protection Zeinabou Moulaye Ousmane, a female MP, Niger's ambassador to the United Nations, the president's adviser on issues relating to gender, a representative of the prime minister, and representatives of the Ministry of Health and Ministry of Education.

The UN experts, chosen for their "high moral standing and competence," praised Niger in their concluding comments for submitting its report and for sending such a high-powered delegation. The committee commended "the constructive dialogue" that took place between the delegation and the committee. It deplored, however, the reservations that Niger issued on CEDAW. The committee recommended that Niger lift its reservations on CEDAW "within a concrete time frame."[160] The experts also criticized Niger for having not ratified the Maputo Protocol. It urged Niger "to accelerate the process of ratification of the Protocol."[161]

This chapter demonstrated that the ratification of international women's rights treaties does not happen automatically, even in the face of international pressure. Just two weeks before the UN meeting in New York, hundreds of women in Niamey protested against the Maputo Protocol, citing Abraham Lincoln's definition of democracy as government of the people, by the people, and for the people. Conservative religious activists framed international women's rights treaties as anathema to Islamic law. National institutions like the National Assembly have veto power. Collective action by women's activists can be effective in putting new issues on the national political agenda but can also be weakened by internal division. Although the experts who met in New York in 2007 may have had good intentions in chiding the Nigérien representatives for Niger's reservations on CEDAW and the lack of ratification of the Maputo Protocol, the UN committee lacked a basic understanding of politics.

CONCLUSION

Rethinking Women's Activism

LOOKING BACK ON MY FIRST TRIP TO NIGER IN 2006, I see that the field of actors involved in women's rights policymaking was much more diverse than I had anticipated. Nigérien women's activists mobilized for women's rights reforms through many kinds of organizations, from the statist Association des Femmes du Niger to the autonomous umbrella women's group CONGAFEN. Beyond civil society, women mobilized for women's rights from within the Ministry of Social Development and the Ministry of Foreign Affairs and sought to represent women's interests in the National Assembly. Moreover, it was difficult to differentiate between women's activists in civil society and women in the state. Advocates for women's rights moved fluidly across different occupations. Over the course of her lifetime, a woman could be a feminist activist, a parliamentarian, and a minister.

The relationships among women's activists were complex and ever shifting. At times, women's activists were united, as in the 1991 protest at the National Conference. At other times, as during the 1996 military coup, internal divisions sharpened. The division between women's rights activists and conservative religious women was not all that clear-cut or stable. Some of the women I interviewed in Zinder belonged to both secular and religious women's associations. One woman was a member of the statist AFN and the conservative UFMN, in addition to being a *militante* of the CDS political party. A feminist activist could be friendly officemates with a conservative religious female activist. Women's activists were sometimes united and sometimes divided, depending on the issue at hand and what was happening in national-level politics.

Religious actors also mobilized through a wide range of organizations, from the Association Islamique du Niger to autonomous umbrella groups, such as CASIN and GAIP/DS. Like the women's movement, the division between religious civil society and the state was often blurred. The AIN's quasi-statist regulation of family disputes is emblematic of the blurry line between state and religion in Niger. Religious activists served on state bodies, like the Conseil Islamique du Niger, while leading their own independent religious associations. Female conservative activists, who worked as ministry officials or at the national post office, organized anti-feminist rallies that challenged the very government they were working for. Like women's activists, religious activists were sometimes united around a common issue, such as the Maputo Protocol. At other times, religious activists internally split over women's issues, such as the ratification of CEDAW.

Actors inside the state who were in a position to influence women's rights policymaking were also diverse. From the president and prime minister to the ministries to the National Assembly, state actors themselves debated over women's policy proposals. The distinct constellation of actors, the decisions they made, and the political context in which they operated resulted in a wide range of women's rights policy outcomes, from outright rejection to negotiated adoption.

Summary of Main Findings

In examining the micropolitics of the adoption and rejection of women's rights policies, this book advanced three main findings. The first is that the adoption of women's rights policies is more likely when women's activists mobilize for them. Women's activists are particularly effective when activists in civil society and in the state come together and persistently seek reform. Women in CONGAFEN, the Ministry of Social Development, and the National Assembly lobbied for the gender quota law in the late 1990s. This multipronged effort helped push the gender quota through the executive cabinet and eventually the National Assembly. Similarly, women in CONGAFEN, the Ministry of Social Development, the Ministry of Foreign Affairs, and the National Assembly advocated for the ratification of CEDAW. When it was time for the National Assembly to vote on the ratification of the Maputo Protocol, however, women's activists in civil society were internally divided, and they were also at odds with the Ministry of Women's Advancement. Consequently, women's mobilization for the protocol before the National Assembly's vote was limited.

Women's activists influence policy adoption by helping put—and keep—new issues on the national political agenda. Under authoritarian rule, both the UFN and the AFN brought the issue of family law reform to the attention of Niger's presidents. Later, in democratic Niger, the RDFN, UPFN, AFJN, and Ministry of Social Development raised family law reform again as an issue of national import. Looking beyond the issue of family law, women's activists were the first to name the issue of women's underrepresentation as a public problem. Women's activists were also among the first to call for gender-based affirmative action, the ratification of CEDAW, and the ratification of the Maputo Protocol.

Furthermore, women's activists help make reform thinkable by invoking politically valid concepts and using meaningful symbols and narratives. Although the symbols may sometimes be ambiguous and the narratives not always accurate, they appeal to commonsense understandings among policy-makers and ordinary Nigériens. Women in and outside the Ministry of Social Development helped make a gender quota law thinkable by contending that women were "deserving" candidates of affirmative action and that a gender quota was "democratic." In advocating for the ratification of CEDAW, women's activists used other countries' ratification of the convention as a symbolic reference point. At times, however, women's activists failed to identify salient arguments and meaningful symbols for their cause. This was the case during the family law and Maputo Protocol debates.

Second, this book has found that women's rights policy adoption can be blocked when opposing activists mobilize. Activists are more effective in blocking reform when they mobilize repeatedly in and outside the state. During the 1999 military transition, the state-affiliated AIN decided to ally with Wanké and support the ratification of CEDAW. When the AIN sided with conservative Islamic associations, however, the state was more reluctant to adopt women's rights reforms. This was the case in the early 1990s during the family code debates, in the 2000s during the Maputo Protocol controversy, and again in 2011 during the debate over the *Statut Personnel*. The AIN's support may not have been necessary for conservative activists to succeed, but it did lend extra legitimacy to what could have been portrayed as an extremist movement.

When opposed to reform, conservative activists influence policymaking by presenting policies as unthinkable. In their efforts to oppose proposed reform, activists invoke politically valid concepts and use locally meaningful symbols and counternarratives. The power of public rituals in making reforms unthinkable is particularly clear in the chapter on family law reform. In the early 1990s, conservative activists branded the proposed family law reform as satanic, and extremist activists publicly issued a curse against prominent women's activists, making the reform politically untouchable. Following this success, conservative activists vilified other proposed reforms, namely, the ratification of CEDAW and the Maputo Protocol, by linking them to the family code, which had become a charged symbol in and of itself. Even fifteen years later, the *Statut Personnel* was abandoned in 2011, demonized through ritual and tainted by its association with the family code.

Like that of women's activists, the political language of conservative activists need not be correct in all details for it to effectively make women's rights reform unthinkable. Symbols, narratives, and rituals merely need to resonate with the target audience. Conservative activists presented Islamic law as an unchangeable set of dictates rather than a flexible field of debate and inquiry. Similarly, conservative activists argued against the ratification of CEDAW and the Maputo Protocol by creating a stark binary between international law and Islamic law. Other binaries that served conservative activists well pitted ordinary Nigérien Muslims against "foreign," "feminist," and "intellectual" women.

Third, this book emphasized that the domestic political context affects women's rights policymaking in ways that have yet to be fully appreciated in the study of Muslim-majority countries. In democratic contexts, state actors other than the executive may inform the adoption of women's rights reform. When it was relatively autonomous from the president, Niger's National Assembly exercised its veto powers and modified the content of the gender quota bill. In the case of the Maputo Protocol, MPs—while expressing a wide range of opinions about the treaty—rejected its proposed ratification in large part because the government had bungled the review of the bill in the assembly. Thus, in predominantly Muslim democracies, the relations between the executive and the legislature merit more attention, at least more than analysts currently give it.

The relationship between the state and religious society constitutes another important part of the political context in whether religious authorities have a say over women's rights legislation. In time periods and countries in which the state is strictly or assertively secular, religious authorities have limited weight in policymaking. By contrast, in contexts in which the state is loosely or passively secular, religious leaders or institutions may enjoy formal or informal veto power. As described earlier in this book, Niger inherited a passive secular state administration from the French. State rulers in and following independence uneasily allied with and relied on religious and traditional leaders. In democratizing Niger, religious and traditional rulers continued to exercise partial influence on the state. The AIN complied with Wanké's government and backed the ratification of CEDAW, whereas the same organization sided with conservative activists and opposed the ratification of the Maputo Protocol. To understand the conditions under which states adopt women's rights policy, one needs to examine state and religious society relations.

Broader Implications

This book is about women and politics in a Muslim-majority African country, but it carries implications not limited to Niger. These broader implications speak to what we know about women in Muslim-majority countries, the political consequences of women's movements, and the diffusion of international women's rights norms.

Women's Agency in Muslim Societies

What is the significance of this book for understanding the agency of women living in Muslim-majority countries more generally? A central implication is that *women in predominantly Muslim societies can and do influence policymaking*. The majority of the women's activists discussed in this book are Muslim, as are the conservative women's activists. Of the women ministers, ministry officials, and parliamentarians mentioned in this book, the greater part were Muslim. That is not to say that all the women were Muslim; Muslim women's activists agitated alongside Christian women as well.

Previous research has shown that women in Muslim societies, contrary to conventional wisdom, do have agency. Nearly twenty years ago, Lila Abu-Lughod argued in her ethnography of a Bedouin Egyptian community, "Veiling is both voluntary and situational."[1] Women decide for themselves when to cover their faces, "motivated by a desire to embody the good—that which wins respect, confers respectability, and allows for self-respect." Since the publication of Abu-Lughod's landmark study, scholars have shown that Muslim women use their agency to interpret Islam through many (including feminist) lenses, to support secular and Islamic political parties, to run for national- and local-level elected office, and to mobilize for peace and economic and social justice.[2] Indeed, as Abu-Lughod argued in the wake of the U.S. invasion of Afghanistan and Iraq, Muslim women do not need saving.[3]

Although scholars have given us a deeper appreciation of Muslim women's agency in various aspects of life, few have made the impact of women in policymaking in democratic contexts their central problematic. Thus, this book contributes to the scholarship on women and Islam by demonstrating how women in predominantly Muslim democracies may influence policy adoption. Exercising their agency, Muslim women may help put new issues on the national agenda. Muslim women's activists may help make reform thinkable by publicly invoking politically legitimate concepts, deploying meaningful symbols, and advancing resonant causal stories. As ministers and ministry officials, Muslim women inside the state may help draw up legislation and lobby presidents and prime ministers to move bills from the executive cabinet into the legislature. In parliament, Muslim women MPs may speak up in favor of reform and vote for its passage.

Additionally, it is worth pointing out that Muslim women are not a monolithic group. Some adhered to the *Tijaniyya* Sufi congregation, some followed *Wahhabist* teachings, and others still were open to different interpretations of Islam, not having a strict affiliation with any one sect. As discussed in this book, conservative Muslim women mobilized against women's rights policy proposals, helping to block reform. It is important to note here that these conservative female activists were not the dupes of conservative men. Muslim women were part of the founding of the new conservative Islamic associations. Conservative women were active students and teachers of Islam themselves, some creating conservative associations not tied to male-dominated ones.

When Women's Movements Influence Policy

More than two decades of scholarship have examined the political consequences of women's mobilization, but in this book, I look at the policy impact of women's mobilization with a slightly wider angle. I examine what happens when actors in addition to women's activists and the state seek to influence reform. Having included conservative activists in the analysis, I conclude that *women's activists are more likely to influence policy adoption in the absence of conservative mobilization. This is especially the case in political contexts in which the separation between church and state is ambiguous.*

This three-actor approach contributes to the scholarship on women and politics that has, to date, either focused on the impact of religious and traditional actors or on the impact of women's movements on women's rights policymaking. That is, some studies on variation in women's rights policy outcomes temporarily put aside women's mobilization and focus on the importance of church-state relations (e.g., Mounira Charrad's study of family law in North Africa, Mala Htun's research on divorce law in Latin America, and Kimberly Morgan's study of work-family policy in the United States and Europe). Other studies on women's rights policy set aside church-state relations and focus on women's movements (e.g., Kathleen Fallon's study of women's movements in Ghana and S. Laurel Weldon's work on women's movements in high-income countries) or women in elected office (e.g., Michele Swers's study of women and men in the U.S. Congress).

Some studies have examined the interplay of women's mobilization, religious mobilization, and politics. Merike Blofield's study of abortion and divorce policy in Argentina, Chile, and Spain argues that the impact of feminist activists on policymaking depends on the number of economic resources and amount of political access they have relative to the Catholic Church.[4] In Niger, the closest equivalent to the Catholic Church is the Association Islamique du Niger. The AIN had resources and access to the state. When it was opposed to a women's rights policy proposal, the AIN helped block the policy's adoption, which supports Blofield's argument. This book contributes to Blofield's findings by identifying cases where the engine of conservative mobilization was not a centralized religious authority but a loose network of younger, autonomous religious associations. Based on the available evidence, I am skeptical that the new conservative associations, though rumored to have had connections with wealthy traders and Middle Eastern countries, were significantly wealthier than women's associations. The power of hardliner conservative activists, rather, lay in their ability to deploy salient symbols and causal narratives and enact meaningful public rituals that silence debate. Thus, I suggest that scholars of women's movement impact pay attention not just to the country's major religious authority but also to smaller, hardline conservative associations.

Another major implication for understanding when women's movements influence policymaking concerns democracy. Scholars have long sought to identify why women's movements struggle to achieve policy change following a transition to democracy.[5] Following a wave of transitions from authoritarian to democratic rule in the 1980s and 1990s, scholars wondered whether and how women would benefit from democratization. There was good reason to believe that women's lives would improve with the arrival of democratic freedoms and institutions. Political transitions from authoritarian to democratic rule provide opportunities for rewriting constitutions and introducing major bodies of legislation. During moments of transition, women's activists can seek out the inclusion of women-friendly texts. In countries where women mobilized for change, one would expect women to be well placed to press for greater freedoms. And in a democratic context, elected representatives would be more responsive to women's interests than would unelected or noncompetitively elected officials.

Having experienced authoritarian, transitioning, and democratic rule in a relatively short period, Niger provides a natural experiment in which to evaluate the impact of democracy on women's movements. This book helps identify why there are unexpected and contradictory repercussions of democratization on the ability of women's movements to influence reform. The first reason is that democratization enables the mobilization of competing groups. In Niger, conservative activists mobilized during and shortly after democratic transition. Moreover, religious activists made use of newly privatized media outlets, such as the newspaper *As-Salam,* to defame the proposed ratification of the Maputo Protocol. Though non-statist newspapers such as *Le Démocrate* and *Le Républicain* initially looked on conservative religious activists with derision, they, too, became an outlet through which religious activists could disseminate their arguments.

Second, the ability of women's movements to inform policymaking in democratizing and democratic regimes is complicated because democracy can be made to mean different things. Democracy was invoked in Niger to justify positions for and against women's rights reforms. To back their demands for a gender quota, women's activists argued that in a democracy, the country's largest and most politically active group deserved to hold positions of political power. Yet in opposing the gender quota for elective office, parliamentarians also invoked democracy, much more so than they did Islam and culture, arguing that voters should determine who gets into office. Conservative activists invoked the principle of democratic majority rule in opposing women's rights reforms.

Women's activists and conservative religious activists, however, were also constrained by conditions that enabled their ascent. Activists have to contend with potentially new veto players, such as the National Assembly. As discussed in this book, the National Assembly struck down the bill to ratify the Maputo Protocol in 2006. Although the assembly's rejection was not anticipated by women's or religious activists, the vote was widely considered to be a sign of democracy. To apply this observation beyond Niger, one need only go south to Benin, where the Constitutional Court exercised its veto powers and altered the content of family law reform (the court called for the abolishment of polygyny on the basis that in a gender-equal society, women should be allowed to take multiple husbands).[6] The Constitutional Court also signaled that it would reject any gender quota bill that did not call for parity among women and men on the grounds that the constitution calls for equality between the sexes.[7] Although at a distance it may look as though democratization does not promote women's rights, it still could—just in ways that are more complicated than expected.

The Spread of International Women's Rights Norms

Examining Niger, which seems to defy global trends and the preferences of international donors, provides new insight into how international women's rights norms spread. The country's experience with women's rights policy suggests that governmental concerns about reputation and funding are mediated by national-level political actors and dynamics.

This book follows Sally Engle Merry's insight that *international women's rights norms spread through a process of vernacularization.* Merry examines the intermediary role of women's rights activists in Hawaii, Delhi, Beijing, Fiji, and Hong Kong in translating global discourse on violence against women into locally meaningful terms. Merry argues,

> In order for human rights ideas to be effective, however, they need to be translated into local terms and situated within local contexts of power and meaning. They need, in other words, to be remade in the vernacular. How does this happen? . . . Examining this process is crucial to understanding the way human rights act in the contemporary world.[8]

Merry identifies three ways through which local actors vernacularize international women's rights norms: (1) activists frame international norms so that they resonate with the local population, (2) activists design interventions that work within the existing constraints, and (3) activists identify an appropriate target population.

Building on Merry's work, this book shows that local actors may arrive at different understandings of international women's rights norms, resulting in *multiple vernacularizations.* As demonstrated in previous chapters, once women's activists take up and bring international ideas home, other actors, including other women's activists, may challenge them, reinterpreting the meaning of international norms. After women's activists mobilized for the ratification of CEDAW and the Maputo Protocol, opponents argued that women's rights treaties were foreign impositions and that the women's activists who supported them were Westernized intellectuals. Like the women's activists that Merry and this book studied, conservative activists designed interventions that fit with the existing context, using curses, sermons, and prayer in addition to state-controlled and new privately owned media outlets.

Finally, conservative activists identified the right population to target, meeting with presidents and prime ministers. As we can see, the vernacularization of women's rights norms is multivocal.

Given how often I hear colleagues and friends in Niger and the United States talk about the power of international donors, I feel obliged to discuss the broader relevance of this book to the study of foreign aid. What role do international donors play in spreading women's rights norms? To borrow Joel Barkan's insight about the international diffusion of democracy, I contend that external efforts to spread women's rights norms "are at best programs that operate at the margin of the process—as facilitators of transition that are driven mainly by the internal dynamics of the societies in which they occur and/or by the internal dynamics of the regimes that govern these societies."[9] External attempts to promote women's rights are limited, not because of religion or culture, as many have posited, but because of politics.

That said, the international context matters, but to understand how, *one needs to disaggregate international influence.* International influence on the spread of norms may be direct in the presence of a foreign occupation or military. Sarah Bush, for instance, finds that countries with a liberalizing UN peacekeeping mission are more likely to adopt legal gender quotas. A study by Mona Lena Krook and her colleagues, however, finds that the adoption of gender quotas in Afghanistan and Iraq happened through different processes: the quota's adoption was a top-down affair in Afghanistan, whereas women mobilized from below for the quota in Iraq.[10] Most countries in the 1990s and 2000s, however, were not occupied by an international peacekeeping force or foreign country.

Peer pressure is a different form of international influence. This book has shown that Nigérien leaders care about their reputation abroad. This was particularly evident in the adoption of the gender quota law and ratification of CEDAW. The attention of Niger's leaders to their country's international image is not limited to worrying about what France or the United States thinks; it includes a concern with how African and predominantly Muslim countries behave. Yet if peer pressure were consistently at work, Niger should have ratified the Maputo Protocol and adopted a family code. Peer pressure influences domestic policymaking, but this type of explanation is partial at best.

International funding constitutes another form of international influence. Beginning in the early 1990s, World Bank officials encouraged African countries to modernize (in their words) their legal systems. The World Bank believed that legal unification and rationalization would help empower women economically in Africa, which would then lift African countries out of poverty. The agencies of the United Nations supported this theory and gave money for family law reform in Niger. Yet in spite of concerted international support for the reform of family law, Niger has consistently refused to change the status quo. This suggests that the influence of foreign aid, like peer pressure, is indirect. International organizations such as UNIFEM and the World Bank helped fund the Ministry of Social Development, which, to a certain degree, decided on its own policy priorities. Donors helped provide a space in which women activists could meet and strategize about the policies they cared about.

International contact is the last form of international influence that deserves its own spotlight. Traveling abroad, attending conferences, and even reading women's rights manifestos at home provide a source of inspiration to local activists. Women's activists were inspired to create CONGAFEN after learning about women's coalition building at a workshop in Canada in the early 1990s. CONGAFEN got the inspiration to propose a gender quota law after learning about the use of gender quotas in Latin America at a UN Commission on the Status of Women meeting in New York. The minister of social development was inspired by the Inter-Parliamentary Union's 1994 Action Plan to push for a quota and to frame it as gender neutral. Exposure to innovations abroad help inspire activism at home.

Questions for the Future

Having examined the politics of women's rights policymaking in Niger, this book raises new questions that scholars of women's movements, Islam and politics, and African politics have yet to adequately address.

Are Curses Democratic?

There remains a critical need for activists, policymakers, and scholars to discuss whether particular kinds of anti-women's rights tactics are undemocratic. More specifically, does an individual or group violate democratic principles when it issues a malediction against a fellow individual? I am particularly thinking of the 1994 deployment of a curse on three women's activists amid the family code debates. The curse effectively, albeit temporarily, silenced women's activists on the issue of family law reform. In the words of one of the targeted women, the curse was traumatic; it caused considerable fear and distress. Yet never did I hear activists or policymakers suggest that curses ought to be subject to critical public discussion or regulation; democratically elected leaders seem to tolerate the use of curses in public life.

If democracy, following Alfred Stepan's minimum definition, ensures that all individuals and groups enjoy the right to advance their interests, then a curse that effectively forestalls the mobilization for one's interests ought to be considered undemocratic.[11] Yet there is a conundrum here. Stepan argues that in a democracy, religious authorities respect democratic principles, but in addition the state respects the freedoms of religious individuals and groups. When these "twin tolerations" are in effect, in Stepan's phrase, democracy prevails. By regulating the deployment of curses, a state may be impinging on the freedoms of religious individuals and groups. Policymakers and scholars, then, need to weigh the benefits and costs of regulating the use of curses for all individuals and groups.

Political scientist Denise Walsh offers one avenue out of this quandary. Walsh argues that when conditions of public debate are closed, the quality of democracy diminishes.[12] By contrast, the quality of democracy is high when there is "just debate," when "everyone who wishes to exchange ideas about issues of common concern has the opportunity to do so."[13] Following Walsh, rather than ask whether curses are undemocratic, it might be more fruitful to examine the effect of curses on debate conditions. Do curses exclude those who are targeted from accessing the public sphere and voicing their concerns? If so, then the regulation of curses may be justified with the goal of improving the quality of democracy.

Speaking directly to the political implications of curses, Adam Ashforth unequivocally argues that the unabated use of witchcraft in South Africa undermines the quality of democracy.[14] For Ashforth, the "spiritual insecurity" that witchcraft creates is an injustice. By ignoring the problem of witchcraft, leaders may be perceived to be complicit with witches, undermining the legitimacy of democracy. "African democrats who know these evil forces of witchcraft as real and present dangers," Ashforth writes, "cannot deny that government has a role to play in these matters, a role akin to that of providing safety, security, and justice in relation to ordinary crimes and violence."[15] Yet the question of what a democratically elected government ought to do to promote "just debate" and "spiritual security" for all individuals and groups remains.

When Do Countermovements Emerge?

While conservative mobilization is prominently featured in this book, concerted mobilization against women's rights does not occur everywhere and at all times. This book has shown that there are several nuances to consider when it comes to countermobilization. For one, conservative activists mobilize against certain women's rights policy proposals but not against others. Conservatives did not mobilize against the adoption or the implementation of the gender quota law in Niger. Indeed, at times, women's and conservative activists work together to develop policy proposals. Women of CONGAFEN and ANASI came together in the early 2000s to combat the practice of repudiation. Second, conservative activism emerges in specific periods and not in others. Mobilization against pro-women policy proposals was limited in authoritarian Niger. Third, across countries, conservative activists react differently to similar policy proposals. There remains a need to closely compare countermovement emergence and nonemergence across issue, time, and countries.

The scholarship on countermovements in the United States provides some starting points by suggesting that countermobilization often only emerges after a liberal movement has made partial gains.[16] The logic here is that when liberal movements make little progress, they do not appear threatening to conservative actors. By achieving initial victories, liberal movements appear to conservatives as on the verge of effecting radical change. Kenneth Andrews's research on countermovements during the civil rights era shows that resistance to desegregation, in the formation of predominantly white private schools, emerges as a result of three factors: when there is a credible threat of successful desegregation, when civil rights activists have the capacity to mobilize, and when whites have the capacity to mobilize.[17] Yet few studies of this kind have been conducted outside the United States.

Karen Kampwirth's work on antifeminism in Central America similarly finds that conservative activists mobilize when feminists make initial gains. She further suggests that one look at not only domestic but also global politics to account for the emergence of conservative movements.[18] Kampwirth finds that backlash movements—specifically, the rise of antifeminist organizations in Nicaragua—emerge partly as a response to organized domestic and international feminist movements and partly because of growing links with conservative organizations in other countries. Conservative activists in Nicaragua, like conservatives in Niger, adopted a nationalist stance, opposing family planning programs as a form of imperialism. Some conservative leaders, moreover, had ties to conservative international Catholic organizations, such as Opus Dei. Conservative, U.S.-based organizations, such as Focus on the Family, the Heritage Foundation, and Vida Humana International provided money and other forms of support to conservative, pro-life organizations in

Nicaragua. International conservative organizations, then, helped enhance domestic conservatives' capacity to mobilize.

Taking a step back, we see commonalities in the emergence of counter-movements in the United States, Nicaragua, and Niger. Conservative activists in Niger emerged at the cusp of women's movement victories. Opponents mobilized right when the draft family code was about to be disseminated across the country in 1994, just when the Ministry of Social Development started talking openly about the ratification of CEDAW, and immediately following the national meeting on the *Statut Personnel* in 2011. Still, this focus on movement-countermovement dynamics does not explain the absence of countermobilization on women's issues in other times, when women's activists made initial gains. Nor does it explain why international connections between conservatives emerge in the first place. Further research into the emergence, and nonemergence, of anti-women's rights activists needs to be done.

When Are Women's Rights Policies Implemented?

This book emphasized the politics of policy adoption, leaving open the question of women's rights policy implementation. Once adopted, under what conditions are women's rights reforms implemented?

First and foremost, if women's activists affect the uptake of new reforms, then women's activists in and outside the state may also affect the implementation of reform. Earlier in this book, I showed that women in civil society, across the ministries, in the Constitutional Court, and in political parties helped enforce Niger's gender quota law. Women's activists closely monitored the appointment of women to the executive cabinet and shamed leaders when they did not respect the cabinet quota. Thus, a hypothesis that emerges from this book is that implementation is more likely when women in civil society and in the state mobilize for it.[19]

A second insight from this book that may help answer the implementation question is that states are not unitary actors. In terms of policy adoption, the president, prime minister, executive cabinet, and National Assembly all played a key role. It is likely that policy implementation, then, hinges on the commitment and cooperation of multiple entities within the state. Which state entities affect policy implementation will depend on the policy issue, as research by the Laboratoire d'Études et de Recherche sur les Dynamiques Sociales et le Développement Local (LASDEL) has ably demonstrated.[20] Susan Hirsch examined how family laws are interpreted and applied in Islamic courts in Kenya, but to my knowledge, few have studied women and family law in official and semiofficial courts in Niger. Thus much work remains to be done on whether and how women's rights policies are implemented at both the national and local levels.

Bargaining for Women's Rights

Under what conditions do states adopt women's rights policy? Contrary to conventional wisdom, this book suggests that a so-called Islamic heritage does not predict what Muslim-majority states do about women's issues. Religion may play an important role in people's day-to-day lives, but it does not determine policy. As shown in this book, French colonial authorities formed uneasy alliances with religious and traditional elites and invented customary-cum-Islamic law, creating a dictotomy between French-based civil law and so-called customary law. Niger's leaders maintained this passive secularist state. Conservative religious actors also socially constructed Islamic jurisprudence as if it were fixed and undisputable. Presenting Islamic jurisprudence as if it were easily knowable, whether through pamphlets sold in pharmacies, street sermons, or radio shows, is how, in large part, conservative activists influenced women's rights debates in Niger.

Seeking to eschew simple stereotypes about Islam, Africa, and women, this book offers an analytic framework for understanding women and politics that places particular emphasis on the agency of women's activists and conservative activists. It further situates activists on a political stage, where multiple veto players within the state debate over women's rights. Once mobilized, societal actors and state actors negotiate with each other in an iterative and unpredictable process. By bringing mobilization and politics to the fore in a place that external observers often deem agentless and devoid of political contestation, *Bargaining for Women's Rights* shines light on human agency and struggle in a Muslim-majority African democracy.

APPENDIX

Research Methods

COMBINED, THE INTERVIEWS, primary sources, secondary sources, and personal observations provide an invaluable depth of information about debates over women's rights in Niger, allowing us to better evaluate which factors encourage and which factors inhibit the passage of women's rights policy.

Women's Activists

To find the women's activists who mobilized for the four proposed reforms examined in this book, I used several strategies. Previous scholarship points to three major women's associations in Niger in the 1990s.[1] They are the Association des Femmes du Niger (AFN), CONGAFEN, and Fédération Kassaï, and they come up many times in this book. In addition, I used the country's newspaper of record, *Le Sahel,* to make a list of potential women's activists to interview, reading stories from years in which there was public debate over women's rights: 1993 and 1994 (the family code controversy), 1999 (the CEDAW controversy), and 2006 (the Maputo Protocol controversy). I also looked for activists in *Le Sahel* surrounding women's rights milestones: 1974 and 1975 (United Nations International Year of the Woman), 1991 (women's protest during Niger's first democratic transition), and 1994 and 1995 (United Nations World Conference on Women in Beijing). A list of formally recognized women's associations published by the Ministry of the Interior (36 associations in 2006) was also helpful at the start of my fieldwork, though I eventually found that many women's associations on the list did not directly lobby for policy change. Last, I asked interviewees for suggestions for additional people to contact.

The personal documents of women's activists as well as annual reports, brochures, financial records, and advocacy materials produced by women's associates helped me fill in gaps, cross-check information, and identify new lines of inquiry. In particular, I relied on *Aïcha,* a women's magazine that publishes stories on fashion, food, health, and politics, with advertising revenue and support from the United Nations Population Fund (UNFPA). I also used *Matan Niger,* the magazine of the AFN during the authoritarian era, which came out several times a year beginning in 1975. My access to *Matan Niger* was incomplete, and there were a couple of breaks during which production came to a halt. Starting in 2001, CONGAFEN published *Matan Daga* until 2008. Last, I presented summaries of my case studies to women's leaders in Niamey in 2011 and received their feedback on the book.

Conservative Activists

Countermobilization figures centrally in this project. Speaking with religious leaders, members of religious associations, editors of religious newspapers, and religious radio personalities helped me understand when, why, and how religious actors mobilized around women's rights policy. To identify which religious actors sought to draft, monitor, promote, and contest women's rights policies, I used the same strategies I used to identify women's activists. In addition to interviewing religious activists, I read religious pamphlets and speeches produced by religious leaders and listened to radio shows and debates to better understand the various stances of religious elites on women's rights issues.

I was also interested to hear how different religious actors talked about women's rights, to discover where Muslim leaders shared opinions about the state and women's rights, and where they diverged. The overwhelming majority of Muslims in Niger are Sunni. Among Sunni Muslims are adherents to different Sufi orders, particularly the *Qadiriyya* (whose origins can be traced to Mauritania) and the *Tijaniyya* (whose origins can be traced to Morocco). Sunni Muslims also include adherents to the *Wahhabi* or *Salafi* movements. Because of the diversity of Muslims in Niger, I tried to ensure that the interviewees came from a range of orders. Thus, I spoke with members of the formerly statist Association Islamique du Niger (AIN), the *Salafi* Jama'atu Izalatul bid'a wa Iqamatul Sunna (Izala, Organization for the Removal of Unlawful Innovations and the Reestablishment of the Sunna), and the *Tijaniyya* order.

State Actors and Institutions

To better understand policymaking, I sought out a wide range of state actors, including low- and high-ranking officials in the Ministry of Social Development, the Ministry of Justice, and the Ministry of Foreign Affairs. I also interviewed judges who served on local courts, the Supreme Court, and the Constitutional Court.

In the national legislature, I interviewed MPs from eight political parties. These parties include the MNSD, which had the highest proportion of seats in the National Assembly in the 1990s and 2000s. The MNSD was the party of the military-led government in the late 1980s. The Convention Démocratique et Sociale (CDS Rahama, or CDS) is another major political party whose representatives I interviewed. The first democratically elected president in the 1990s, Mahamane Ousmane, was a member of CDS. The Parti Nigérien pour la Démocratie et le Socialisme-Tarayya (PNDS Tarayya, or PNDS) is Niger's main left-leaning party; in 2011, long-time member Mahamadou Issoufou was elected president. PNDS's historical base is Tahoua, though its roots can also be traced to a class of engineers and *intellectuels*. Smaller parties with whom I spoke include the Alliance Nigérienne pour la Démocratie et le Progrès (ANDP Zaman Lahiya, or ANDP), Parti Progressiste Nigérien (PPN-RDA), Rassemblement pour la Démocratie et le Progrès (RDP Jama'a), Rassemblement Social-Démocratique (RSD Gaskiya), and Parti Nigérien pour l'Autogestion (PNA). I also interviewed five female members of parliament (representing the MNSD, CDS, PNDS, and ANDP) and a few of the legislature's staff.

In talking with state actors and politicians, I asked when they had first heard of the issue or proposed reform, about the activists and organizations they encountered, and about the factors that influenced their vote or decision.

To analyze women's rights debates in parliament, I obtained cassette recordings of the plenary session for the gender quota debate. Recordings of the Maputo Protocol debates were not available. In English-speaking African countries, one would consult the Hansard, an edited transcription of parliamentary proceedings. Indeed, in principle, open-air parliamentary debates ought to be transcribed. When I was conducting research at the National Assembly in 2008, however, relatively few of the debates had been converted to text. I hired a team of research assistants to transcribe the debates. The debates took place in Hausa in addition to French. Given my limited understanding of Hausa, the team also translated the portions of the debates that were in Hausa into French. These transcripts of parliamentary debates, rarely used in the study of Muslim or African politics, provide an animated glimpse into how states make women's rights policy. To trace state and religious society relations over time, I rely on secondary sources and newspaper articles as well as *Africa Research Bulletin* and *Africa Confidential*.

International Actors and Institutions

While in Niger, I spoke with international representatives from the U.S. representation to Niger, CARE, Coopération Suisse, DANIDA, NDI, Oxfam, Netherlands Development Organization (SNV), UNDP, UNFPA, and UN Women. For a bottom-up perspective on the influence of the international context and international donors on policymaking, I asked Nigérien actors to describe when they first were inspired to pursue (or oppose) reform, to tell me about their international travels, and to identify which international organizations and donors provided assistance at what points in time. When actors mentioned a specific international conference or document that was important in their advocacy, I tracked down those documents. I also collected materials that came out of the major international conferences on women to see whether and how Nigérien actors use international discourse about women's rights.

Whether, how, and how much international organizations supported women's rights policy was gauged by collecting international donors' assessments, budgets, lending agreements, and project reports from Niger's major donors. For most donors, this information was available online or in the resource libraries of the SNV and the United Nations Children's Fund (UNICEF) in Niamey.

As reported by the Organization for Economic Cooperation and Development (OECD), Niger's largest multilateral donors between 1995 and 2011 were the European Union's institutions ($1.42 billion), the World Bank's International Development Association (IDA) ($1.25 billion), and the African Development Fund of the African Development Bank (ADF) ($335 million).[2] Among multilateral donors, the following gave the most amount of money to women's equality organizations and institutions between 1995 and 2011: UNICEF ($150 million), UNDP ($75 million), and UNFPA ($28 million). Niger's largest bilateral donors between 1995 and 2011 were France ($1.16 billion), the United States ($483 million), Belgium ($295 million), Japan ($283 million), Germany ($273 million), Switzerland ($158 million), and Canada ($138 million). The largest bilateral donors, however, were not the most active in funding women's civil society. Most of the aid earmarked for women's civil society came from Belgium ($13.2 million), Spain ($6.7 million), Norway ($5.2 million), Italy ($1.7 million), Switzerland ($1.0 million), and Denmark ($0.8 million). The United States gave significantly less funding ($0.17 million) to women's organizations than did their European counterparts. These figures suggest which donors were most active in supporting change.

Watching the evening news with friends, talking before and after meals in peoples' homes, and attending baptisms and weddings provided a different glimpse into the politics of women's rights. These day-to-day events helped me better understand the ways in which the institutions of gender, patriarchy, and family are constructed on a quotidian basis. It surprised me how often family issues—issues of polygyny, mothers-in-law, aunts, and divorce—came up. I also attended religious celebrations, namely the festivities surrounding the end of Ramadan and the celebration of Tabaski. During these holidays, one can see the close connections between the ostensibly secular state and religious authority.

The overwhelming majority of people I encountered were generous with their time and highly respectful, including conservative religious activists. Of the 136 people whom I approached to interview, only 3 declined to speak with me: a female midlevel official in the Ministry of Social Development, a male midlevel official in the Ministry of Justice, and a female conservative religious activist.

Some interviewees gave me permission to use their names in the book, whereas others wanted to be referred to by their associational affiliation only. Thus, I refrain from naming any of these individuals, referring to their associational affiliation instead. If an individual is identified by name in a newspaper or some other source, then I use that person's name.

List of Associations Interviewed

Women's Rights Associations

Association des Femmes Juristes du Niger

Association des Femmes du Niger

Alliance Nigérienne des Educatrices pour le Developpement

Coordination des Organisations Non Gouvernementales et Associations Féminines Nigériennes

Comité Nigérien sur les Pratiques Traditionnelles

Fédération Kassaï

Maillon Africain pour la Paix et le Développement

ONG Centre Reines Daura

ONG Dimol

Rassemblement Démocratique des Femmes du Niger

Réseau Interafricain pour les Femmes, Media, Genre et Développement

RIDD-Fitila

Union des Femmes du Niger

Islamic and Islamic Women's Associations

Association des Femmes Musulmanes pour les Œuvres de Bienfaisance et de
Développement

Association Islamique du Niger

Association Nigérienne pour l'Appel et la Solidarité Islamique / ANASI-Femmes

Association pour le Rassemblement et la Foi Islamique

Collectif des Associations Islamiques du Niger

Groupement des Associations Islamiques en matière de Planning Familial et
Développement Social

Jamiyat Nassirat-Dine

Union des Femmes Musulmanes du Niger

Other Associations

Association des Chefs Traditionnels du Niger

Association Nigérienne pour la Défense des Droits de l'Homme

NOTES

Introduction

1. At the request of the leaders of CONGAFEN, I refer to individuals in the organization by their position rather than by their personal name. After some heated debate on the issue, the leaders agreed that their work was done in the name of the organization and Nigérien women, not for themselves. Meeting at CONGAFEN's headquarters in Niamey on June 30, 2011.

2. This narrative is based on an interview with the then president of CONGAFEN, May 22, 2008, and an interview with the then minister of social development, December 28, 2012. Some of the events were verified at a public presentation of the study's findings at the American Cultural Center in Niamey on July 3, 2008; at a meeting at CONGAFEN's headquarters in Niamey on June 30, 2011; and in an interview with a former officer of CONGAFEN, who was also a journalist for the state's radio, January 3, 2013. All took place in Niamey.

3. "Military Controls Niger," *BBC News*, April 10, 1999, http://news.bbc.co.uk/2/hi /africa/316037.stm; "New Military Leader for Niger," *BBC News*, April 12, 1999, http:// news.bbc.co.uk/2/hi/africa/316956.stm.

4. Throughout the book, states refer to sovereign entities defined by territorial boundaries. Regimes refer to systems of rule, either democratic or authoritarian. Governments are groups of people. In this book, governments are headed by a prime minister during periods of democracy and by a president during periods of authoritarian rule.

5. *Nigérien* refers to the Republic of Niger, whereas *Nigerian* refers to Nigeria.

6. UN Treaty Collection (TC), "Convention on the Elimination of All Forms of Discrimination against Women."

7. Inglehart and Norris, *Rising Tide.*

8. MacLeod, *Accommodating Protest*; Alidou, *Engaging Modernity*; Shehabuddin, *Reshaping the Holy*; Rinaldo, *Mobilizing Piety.*

9. Charrad, *States and Women's Rights.*

10. An important exception is Brand, *Women, the State, and Political Liberalization.*

11. The population figure refers to 2006. World Bank, "World Development Indicators." Sources vary on the percentage of the population that is Muslim. The 2006 Demographic

Health Survey finds that 98 percent of survey respondents identified as Muslim. Ministère de l'Economie et des Finances, Enquête démographique et de santé et à indicateurs multiples 2006, 33. Another source, however, states that 80 percent of Niger's population is Muslim. Central Intelligence Agency, "World Factbook: Niger."

12. Tripp, *Women and Politics in Uganda.*

13. Abdullah, "Wifeism and Activism."

14. For example, see Tarrow, *Power in Movement.*

15. Lycklama à Nijeholt, Vargas, and Wieringa, eds., *Women's Movements and Public Policy,* 3–4.

16. Mazur, *Theorizing Feminist Policy,* 190–95.

17. Disney, *Women's Activism and Feminist Agency,* 124–31, 202–3.

18. Hassim, *Women's Organizations and Democracy,* 163; Meintjes, "The Politics of Engagement," 140–59; Waylen, *Engendering Transitions,* 77.

19. Banaszak, *The Women's Movement.*

20. Franceschet, "'State Feminism' and Women's Movements," 9–40. On the mutually beneficial relationship between women's movements and feminist policy agencies, see also Weldon, "Beyond Bodies."

21. Geisler, "Parliament Is Another Terrain of Struggle."

22. Schatzberg, *Political Legitimacy in Middle Africa.*

23. See McCammon, *The U.S. Women's Jury Movements and Strategic Adaptation*; Beckwith, "Women's Movements at Century's End."

24. For an overview of women's movements in Africa, see Tripp, Casimiro, Kwesiga, and Mungwa, *African Women's Movements.*

25. Recent examples include Shehabuddin, *Reshaping the Holy*; Rinaldo, *Mobilizing Piety*; Salime, *Between Feminism and Islam.*

26. Idrissa and Decalo, *Historical Dictionary of Niger,* 74–75.

27. Idrissa, "The Invention of Order," 230–34. For a comparative analysis of debates over secularism in the Sahel, see Villalón, "From Argument to Negotiation."

28. Wing, "Women Activists in Mali," 174.

29. Adamu, "A Double-Edged Sword."

30. Mills and Ssewakiryanga, "'That Beijing Thing.'"

31. Gal and Kligman, *The Politics of Gender after Socialism,* 98.

32. Bashevkin, *Women on the Defensive*; Mansbridge, *Why We Lost the ERA.*

33. This argument is skillfully constructed in Salime, *Between Feminism and Islam.*

34. Daloz, "'Big Men' in Sub-Saharan Africa"; Hyden, *African Politics in Comparative Perspective*; Van Cranenburgh, "'Big Men' Rule"; McCauley, "Africa's New Big Man Rule?"

35. Tsebelis, *Veto Players.*

36. Mezey, "The Functions of Legislatures in the Third World"; Barkan, "African Legislatures and the 'Third Wave,'" 10–12. Pointing to countries like Kenya and South Africa, Barkan finds that some African legislatures have asserted their autonomy from the executive in ways that would have been unheard of in the 1980s and early 1990s.

37. Thomas and Sissokho, "Liaison Legislature," 99. See also Beck, "Democratization and the Hidden Public"; Creevey, "Senegal"; Lindberg, "What Accountability Pressures."

38. Van de Walle, "Presidentialism and Clientelism," 309–11.

39. The distinction between passive and assertive secularism is made in Kuru, *Secularism and State Policies toward Religion.*

40. See Article 4 in the fourth, fifth, and sixth Constitutions of Niger and Article 3 of the seventh Constitution.

41. Miles, "Shari'a as De-Africanization."

42. See, for example, Masquelier, *Prayer Has Spoiled Everything*; Masquelier, *Women and Islamic Revival.*

43. Idrissa, *The Invention of Order,* 343–44.

44. Kuru, *Secularism and State Policies toward Religion*; Minkenberg, "The Policy Impact of Church-State Relations"; Morgan, *Working Mothers and the Welfare State.*

45. Charrad, *States and Women's Rights.* Similarly, Kimberly Morgan argues that France offered comprehensive child care in the absence of a strong women's movement because disputes between the state and religious society in the late 1800s resulted in an autonomous state. Morgan, *Working Mothers and the Welfare State.* See also Mala Htun, who argues that where there was conflict between the state and the Catholic Church (e.g., in authoritarian Brazil and democratic Argentina), politicians legalized divorce. When rulers were cordial with the Catholic Church, rulers were slower to legalize divorce (e.g., in democratic Chile, leaders were loyal to the church because the church supported them during the previous dictatorship). Htun, *Sex and the State.*

46. Levi, *Of Rule and Revenue,* 11.

47. Abu-Lughod, *Do Muslim Women Need Saving?*

48. Fish, "Islam and Authoritarianism," 24.

49. Inglehart and Norris, *Rising Tide,* 71.

50. Paxton, "Women in National Legislatures"; Rule, "Electoral Systems."

51. Kenworthy and Malami, "Gender Inequality in Political Representation"; Reynolds, "Women in the Legislatures and Executives of the World"; Paxton, Hughes, and Green, "The International Women's Movement."

52. Heckman, "Sample Selection Bias"; Berk, "An Introduction to Sample Selection Bias."

53. Stepan and Robertson, "An 'Arab' More Than 'Muslim' Electoral Gap"; Stepan and Robertson, "Arab, Not Muslim, Exceptionalism."

54. Donno and Russett, "Islam, Authoritarianism, and Female Empowerment"; Rizzo, Abdel-Latif, and Meyer, "The Relationship between Gender Equality and Democracy."

55. Poe, Wendel-Blunt, and Ho, "Global Patterns," 825.

56. Ross, "Oil, Islam, and Women."

57. Norris, "Petroleum Patriarchy?," 555-56.

58. Inglehart and Norris, *Rising Tide,* 62.

59. For an overview of family law, see Esposito, *Women in Muslim Family Law.* See also Mir-Hosseini, *Islam and Gender.*

60. Solivetti, "Family, Marriage and Divorce in a Hausa Community," 261–62.

61. Cooper, *Marriage in Maradi,* 33.

62. Hirsch, *Pronouncing and Persevering*; Roberts, "Representation, Structure and Agency"; Shereikis, "Customized Courts."

63. MacLeod, *Accommodating Protest.* See also Tohidi, "Gender and Islamic Fundamentalism."

64. Spierings, Smits, and Verloo, "On the Compatibility of Islam and Gender Equality."
65. An-Na'im, *African Constitutionalism*. On women's participation in a Sufi sect, see Bop, "Roles and the Position of Women"; Hanretta, "Gender and Agency in the History of a West African Sufi Community"; Mbow, "Les femmes, l'Islam et les associations religieuses." For an introduction to the history of Islam in Africa, see Robinson, *Muslim Societies in African History*.
66. Mir-Hosseini, *Islam and Gender*; Van Santen, " 'My 'Veil' Does Not Go with My Jeans.' " See also Kondo, *Crafting Selves*.
67. Van Allen, " 'Sitting on a Man,' " 180. Note, however, that Yoruba women adapted to these changes. See McIntosh, *Yoruba Women*. See also Fallon, *Democracy and the Rise of Women's Movements*, 28–30.
68. Hanson, "Queen Mothers and Good Government in Buganda."
69. Fallon, *Democracy and the Rise of Women's Movements*; Tidjani Alou, "Les politiques de formation en Afrique francophone."
70. Dahlerup and Freidenvall, "Quotas as a 'Fast Track' to Equal Political Representation for Women"; Jones, "Gender Quotas, Electoral Laws, and the Election of Women"; Tripp and Kang, "The Global Impact of Quotas."
71. Howard-Merriam, "Guaranteed Seats for Political Representation of Women." Tanzania had reserved seats for women in 1975. See Tripp, Konaté, and Lowe-Morna, "Sub-Saharan Africa," 113.
72. Ghana's Convention People's Party adopted a party quota in 1960. See Tripp, Konaté, and Lowe-Morna, "Sub-Saharan Africa," 113.
73. Simmons, *Mobilizing for Human Rights*, 102.
74. UN TC. "Convention on the Elimination of All Forms of Discrimination against Women."
75. S. Hale, *Gender Politics in Sudan*, 186.
76. Wotipka and Ramirez, "World Society and Human Rights."
77. Chan-Tiberghien, *Gender and Human Rights Politics in Japan*.
78. Goodliffe and Hawkins, "Explaining Commitment"; Hathaway, "Do Human Rights Treaties Make a Difference?"
79. Adams, " 'National Machineries' and Authoritarian Politics."
80. Bush, "International Politics."
81. E.g., Apodaca, "The Effects of Foreign Aid."
82. Keck and Sikkink, *Activists beyond Borders*; Hughes, Krook, and Paxton, "Transnational Women's Activism and the Global Diffusion of Gender Quotas."
83. For an exception, see Bob, *The Global Right Wing*. Bob's focus is on the rise of conservative TANs, however, and not on explaining variation in policy outcomes.
84. Risse-Kappen, Ropp, and Sikkink, for instance, acknowledge the presence of "blocking" factors in the domestication of international human rights norms, but they do not theorize where and why blocking factors influence domestic change. Risse-Kappen, Ropp, and Sikkink, *The Power of Human Rights*.
85. Cichowski, *The European Court and Civil Society*.
86. Duffy, "*Hadijatou Mani Koroua v Niger*."
87. Stetson, "Human Rights for Women"; Gray, Kittilson, and Sandholtz, "Women and Globalization."

88. Simmons, *Mobilizing for Human Rights*.

89. I am indebted to Crawford Young for pointing this out to me.

90. Katzenstein and Mueller, eds., *The Women's Movements of the United States and West-ern Europe*; Matland, "Institutional Variables Affecting Female Representation in National Legislatures"; Caul, "Political Parties and the Adoption of Candidate Gender Quotas."

91. See, for example, Burrell, *A Woman's Place Is in the House*; Swers, *The Difference Women Make*; Wolbrecht, *The Politics of Women's Rights*; but see Reingold, *Representing Women*.

92. Morgan, *Working Mothers and the Welfare State*.

93. Fallon, *Democracy and the Rise of Women's Movements*.

94. Walsh, *Women's Rights in Democratizing States*.

95. Htun and Weldon, "When Do Governments Promote Women's Rights?"

96. Htun, *Sex and the State*, 181; Htun and Power, "Gender, Parties, and Support."

97. Gelb and Palley, *Women and Public Policies*, 5–6; Blofield and Haas, "Defining a Democracy."

98. This approach is similar to that of several recent books, though this study compares adoption and non-adoption within one country, rather than across countries. See Charrad, *States and Women's Rights*; Htun, *Sex and the State*; Blofield, *The Politics of Moral Sin*. For a study that employs the within-country comparative case method in a Catholic, Latin American context, see Haas, *Feminist Policymaking in Chile*.

99. With a 10 representing a full democracy and a –10 representing a full autocracy, Polity IV gave Niger a score of –6 during Baré's presidency. Niger received a score of 8 under Ousmane's presidency and between 5 and 6 under Tandja's presidency (until 2009). See Polity IV, "Authority Trends, 1960–2010: Niger." For a similar ranking using a different definition of democracy, see Cheibub, Gandhi, and Vreeland, "Democracy and Dicta-torship Revisited." Freedom House also ranked Niger as "Partly Free" between 1993 and 2009, with the exception of the years of Baré's presidency, when Niger was rated "Not Free." See Freedom House, "Country Ratings and Status."

100. Yin, *Case Study Research*.

101. I arrived at the baseline estimate of forty-one by counting the number of reforms men-tioned in Niger's first report to the United Nations Committee on the Elimination of Discrimination against Women. The report was submitted to the UN in 2001. See UN CEDAW, "Initial et deuxième rapports du Niger."

102. I was in Niger May to July 2006, September 2007 to July 2008, June to July 2011, and December 2012 to January 2013.

103. This number does not add up to 133 because some interviewees belong to multiple groups (e.g., a parliamentarian who also served as a minister). Some interviewees do not easily fall under any of these groups (e.g., housewives).

104. Mohanty, "'Under Western Eyes' Revisited."

105. Wolbrecht, *The Politics of Women's Rights*, 19, italics in the original.

106. Alternatively, "feminist legislation seeks to eliminate all forms of economic, political, social, and cultural inequalities between women and men." See Haas, *Feminist Policy-making in Chile*, 7.

107. Ewig, "Hijacking Global Feminism."

1. A French Colonial Legacy

1. Collier and Collier, *Shaping the Political Arena*, 29. Idrissa's brilliant dissertation "The Invention of Order" provides an alternative historical interpretation, one that traces the origins of the Nigérien state to the influence of French Republicanism as well as Sudanic Sufism, both of which provided "normative matrices" of political order.

2. Bayart, *The State in Africa*, 55.

3. Cooper, "Gender and Religion in Hausaland," 21–37; K. Idrissa, "La dynamique de la gouvernance," 15–84; Masquelier, *Prayer Has Spoiled Everything*, 32, 35.

4. Alidou, *Engaging Modernity*; Fuglestad, *A History of Niger*, 33; F. Mounkaïla, *Le mythe et l'histoire*, 200–202; Olivier de Sardan, *Les sociétés songhay-zarma*; Streicker, "On Being Zarma," 43.

5. For an introduction to precolonial Niger, see Abadie, *Afrique centrale*; Fuglestad, *A History of Niger*; Salifou, *Histoire du Niger*; Urvoy, *Histoire des populations du Soudan central*.

6. On the Songhai Empire (ca. 900–1500), see Abadie, *Afrique central*, 103–5; Fuglestad, *A History of Niger*, 35–37; Mounkaïla, *Le mythe et l'histoire*; Rouch, *Les Songhay*; Salifou, *Histoire du Niger*, 33–46; Urvoy, *Histoire des populations du Soudan central*, 28–63.

7. Fuglestad, *A History of Niger*, 41; K. Idrissa, *Guerres et sociétés*; Olivier de Sardan, *Les sociétés songhay-zarma*.

8. For an example, see Adamou, *Agadez et sa région*.

9. Bonte, *Production et échanges*; Fuglestad, *A History of Niger*, 48–49; D. Hamani, *L'Adar précolonial*.

10. Cooper, "Gender and Religion in Hausaland"; G. Nicolas, *Dynamique sociale et apprehension*.

11. Zakari, *Contribution à l'histoire*.

12. Cooper, *Evangelical Christians in the Muslim Sahel*, 153–54.

13. Dunbar, "Damagaram (Zinder, Niger)," xii. In Hausa, *sarki* can mean chief of a village or town, ruler more generally, or king or emir of large entities. I use the words *sultan, ruler,* and *emir* interchangeably.

14. Ibid., 165.

15. Gado, *Miroir du passé*, 50.

16. Dunbar, "Damagaram (Zinder, Niger)," 160; Salifou, *Le Damagaram ou le sultanat de Zinder au XIX siècle*.

17. Dunbar, "Damagaram (Zinder, Niger)," 157–59; Salifou, *Le Damagaram ou le sultanat de Zinder au XIX siècle*, 138, 141.

18. Dunbar, "Damagaram (Zinder, Niger)," 157.

19. For explanations for why trans-Saharan trading networks shifted from Katsina to Kano in Nigeria, thereby moving trading posts in Niger toward Zinder, see Dunbar, "Damagaram (Zinder, Niger)"; Fuglestad, *A History of Niger*, 47; Salifou, *Le Damagaram ou le sultanat*.

20. Cooper, *Evangelical Christians in the Muslim Sahel*, 151.

21. Dunbar, "Damagaram (Zinder, Niger)," 161–62; Salifou, *Le Damagaram ou le sultanat*, 138–41. On the precolonial trade in salt, see Lovejoy, *Salt of the Desert Sun*.

22. Mounier, "La dynamique des interrelations politiques," 367–86; Dunbar, "Damagaram (Zinder, Niger)," 145; Salifou, *Le Damagaram ou le sultanat,* 118.

23. Dunbar, "Damagaram (Zinder, Niger)," 175–76, 149; see also Salifou, *Le Damagaram ou le sultanat,* 118.

24. K. Idrissa, "La dynamique de la gouvernance," 22. For a general history of the colonial period, consult Fuglestad, *A History of Niger.* Information about the establishment of a military and then civilian colony comes from Arzika, "Droit et société au Niger," 2, 274.

25. For example, in 1897, the French sent Captain Cazémajou to Damagaram with the goal of convincing Sarki Ahmadu to sign a treaty. Although Cazémajou was greeted warmly by traders in Zinder, Sarki Ahmadu suspected that the French would collude with the invader Rābīh and in 1898 executed Cazémajou. Fuglestad, *A History of Niger,* 54–55.

26. Fuglestad, *A History of Niger,* 70; K. Idrissa, *Guerres et sociétés;* Lovejoy and Hogendorn, "Revolutionary Mahdism," 217–44.

27. Fuglestad, *A History of Niger,* 65, 122.

28. On the change of capitals, see Abadie, *Afrique central,* 2; Fuglestad, *A History of Niger,* 80; Séré de Rivières, *Histoire du Niger,* 235–37.

29. The year is recorded as 1924 by Arzika in "Droit et société au Niger," 2.

30. Abba, "La chefferie traditionnelle en question," 53.

31. The remainder of this paragraph is based on Fuglestad, *A History of Niger,* 71–72, 126.

32. Information in this paragraph comes from Fuglestad, *A History of Niger,* 61, 73–4, 85, 126. Cooper notes that on average, the tenure of rulers in Maradi during the colonial period was longer than that of the late precolonial period. See Cooper, *Marriage in Maradi,* 112n4.

33. K. Idrissa, "La dynamique de la gouvernance," 281.

34. Cooper, *Evangelical Christians in the Muslim Sahel,* 151.

35. Cooper, "Gender and Religion in Hausaland," 32.

36. K. Idrissa, *Guerres et societies,* 104–06.

37. Olivier de Sardan, *Les sociétés songhay-zarma,* 20.

38. K. Idrissa, *Guerres et societies,* 78.

39. Fuglestad, *A History of Niger,* 41, italics in the original.

40. Ibid., 68; see also K. Idrissa, *Guerres et sociétés,* 105.

41. K. Idrissa, *Guerres et sociétés;* Fuglestad, *A History of Niger, 1850–1960,* 67, 74. The year is recorded as 1902 by Fuglestad.

42. Olivier de Sardan, *Les sociétés songhay-zarma,* 220.

43. For an introduction to the French colonial legal system in Niger and other French colonies in West Africa, see Salacuse, *An Introduction to Law in French-Speaking Africa.* For an overview of Niger's colonial legal system, see Arzika, "Droit et société au Niger."

44. Solus, *Traité de la condition des indigènes en droit privé,* 117.

45. Arzika, "Droit et société au Niger," 282n19(bis).

46. An overview of the 1903 decree's history can be found in the introduction to Jeppie, Moosa, and Roberts, *Muslim Family Law in Colonial and Postcolonial Africa.*

47. For a complete overview of Shari'a, see Hallaq, *Shari'a: Theory, Practice, Transformations.*

48. On the contemporary use of an oracle called the *gon,* see Kelley, "Exporting Western Law to the Developing World." An alternative legal system in used precolonial Maradi is described in Cooper, "Injudicious Intrusions: Chiefly Authority and Islamic Judicial

Practice in Maradi, Niger," 197–98. Cooper writes that nineteenth-century leaders in Maradi "worked to accommodate the practices of the Arna population that had proven so loyal to them in the face of the Sokoto jihad."

49. Cooper, "Injudicious Intrusions," 192.
50. Richard Roberts quoting Clozel. See Roberts, "Custom and Muslim Family Law," 101–2n47.
51. Cooper, "Gender and Religion in Hausaland," 12. That aristocratic men sought to use the codification of customary law for their own benefit is not unique to the colony of Niger. See Coquery-Vidrovitch, Les Africaines.
52. Cooper, Marriage in Maradi, 11–12.
53. Shereikis, "Customized Courts," 175.
54. Ibid., 208–9.
55. Lydon, "The Unraveling of a Neglected Source," 575.
56. Ibid.
57. D. Robinson, "Sénégal," 313. The caseload at the Tribunal Musulman de Saint-Louis varied from 48 to 203 between 1857 and the 1950s, averaging 100 to 125 cases per year.
58. Lydon, "The Unraveling of a Neglected Source," 575.
59. Cooper, Marriage in Maradi, 35.
60. Cooper, "Injudicious Intrusions," 191. For an important rereading of the significance of the 1903 decree, see Mann, "What Was the Indigénat?," 338. Mann argues that law provided an "alibi" for the colonial state against critics of colonialism. Law, then, provides a cover for the exercise of arbitrary state violence.
61. This discussion is based on Cooper, Marriage in Maradi, 22–34.
62. Osborn, " 'Circle of Iron,' " 38.
63. Olivier de Sardan, Les sociétés songhay-zarma, 220.
64. The Mandel Decree set minimum ages of marriage for each colony: in Mali, 15 for girls and 18 for boys; in Senegal, 16 for girls and 20 for boys; in Burkina Faso, 21 for both girls and boys. See Boye, Hill, Isaacs, and Gordis, "Marriage Law and Practice in the Sahel," 343–49.
65. Salacuse, quoted in Boye et al., "Marriage Law and Practice in the Sahel," 344.
66. In contrast to 70 in 1965 and 137 in 1985. Cooper, Marriage in Maradi, 73n15.
67. Arzika, "Droit et société au Niger," 288–89.
68. For an overview of the gendered implications of colonial rule in Africa, see Fallon, Democracy and the Rise of Women's Movements, chap. 2.
69. Dunbar, "Damagaram (Zinder, Niger)," 158.
70. Salifou, Le Damagaram ou le sultanat, 119.
71. Cooper, Marriage in Maradi, 65–68.
72. Nast, Concubines and Power.
73. Fuglestad, A History of Niger, 130.
74. Masquelier, Prayer Has Spoiled Everything, 162.
75. Cooper, Marriage in Maradi, 112, 119–20.
76. Alou, "Les politiques de formation en Afrique francophone," 56. The progression of schooling in 1922 went from the école de village, école régionale, école primaire supérieure, and then to one of the écoles du gouvernement général (école normale William

Ponty, école Faidherbe, école Pinet La parade, école des pupilles-mécaniciens, école Imprimeur de gouvernement général). This paragraph is based on Alou, 60–72.

77. Ibid., 63.
78. Cooper, *Marriage in Maradi,* 118.
79. Salifou, *Histoire du Niger,* 267.
80. Thom, "The Niger-Nigeria Boundary," 23, 35; Cooper, *Marriage in Maradi,* 24n3.
81. Grégoire, "Quelques aspects des échanges entre le Niger et le Nigeria," 154, 157; Thom, "The Niger-Nigeria Borderlands."
82. Abba, "La chefferie traditionnelle en question," 53–4; Fuglestad, *A History of Niger,* 161–2.
83. Abba, "La chefferie traditionnelle en question," 54; Idrissa and Decalo, *Historical Dictionary of Niger,* 186.
84. Fuglestad, "Djibo Bakary, the French, and the Referndum," 15.
85. Abba, "La chefferie traditionnelle en question," 54.
86. Hayter, "French Aid to Africa," 240.
87. Van Walraven, *Yearning for Relief.*
88. As quoted in Triaud, "L'Islam et l'État en République du Niger (Première partie)," 16n39.
89. Triaud, "L'Islam et l'État en République du Niger," 21 quoting Adamou Oumarou, "Interférences de la loi, la coutume et la 'Charia' islamique devant les juridictions nigériennes,' *Penant* 88, no. 764, April–June (1979): 129–33.

2. The Puzzle of Non-Adoption

1. Boubacar Nasser, "L'Association islamique rejette l'avant projet de code de la famille: Des manifestants brûlent le document 'satanique,' " *Le Démocrate,* March 1, 2011, 2; "Polémique autour du code de la famille," *Roue de l'Histoire,* March 3, 2011, 2.
2. Ousseini Issa, "Le gouvernement abandonne le statut personnel devant la fronde des islamistes," *Inter Press Service,* March 18, 2011, http://www.ips.org/fr/niger-le -gouvernement-abandonne-le-statut-personnel-devant-la-fronde-des-islamistes/.
3. Alidou, *Engaging Modernity,* 157, 164–68, 181, 190; Alio, "L'islam et la femme"; Masquelier, *Women and Islamic Revival,* 7, 30, 77, 108; F. Mounkaïla, "Femmes et politique au Niger"; Niandou-Souley and Alzouma, "Islamic Renewal in Niger"; Villalón, "The Moral and the Political in African Democratization."
4. Talfi, *Quel droit applicable à la famille au Niger?*
5. Charlick and Ousseini, *The Participation of Women in Nigérien Political Life.*
6. Alio, "L'Islam et la femme"; Cooper, *Marriage in Maradi*; Dunbar and Djibo, *Islam, Public Policy, and the Legal Status of Women in Niger*; Dunbar, "Islamic Values, the State, and 'the Development of Women' "; Villalón, "The Moral and the Political in African Democratization."
7. Cooper, *Marriage in Maradi,* 178, obtains this information from Clair, *Le Niger,* 134–40. See also Nicolas, *Don rituel et échange,* 108.
8. République du Niger, Loi No. 62–11 of March 16, 1962.
9. Cooper, "The Politics of Difference and Women's Associations in Niger," 864, italics in the original.
10. A. Mounkaïla, "Les obstacles à la participation," 43.

11. Mariama Alzouma, "Mme Sabo Fatouma Zara, présidente de la Congafen : Profiter de la prise en compte du genre pour se positionner," *Aïcha*, May–June 2009, 6.

12. Alidou, *Engaging Modernity*; Piault, *Contribution à l'étude*, 110–11.

13. Dunbar, "Islamic Values, the State, and 'the Development of Women,'" 78–79.

14. Interview, October 27, 2007, Niamey. For a comparison of the UFN and the AFN in Maradi, see Cooper, "The Politics of Difference and Women's Associations in Niger."

15. Interview with a retired nurse, May 6, 2008, Zinder.

16. Ibid.

17. Interview with a woman who was a member of the AFN in Dogondoutchi, October 27, 2007, Niamey.

18. Interview with a retired nurse, May 6, 2008, Zinder.

19. "Nous avons pris l'engagement de mener des actions de développement de notre pays," *Le Sahel*, May 30, 1977, 3.

20. "L'Association des femmes du Niger au débat national sur la santé," *Matan Niger*, July 1983, 28.

21. Illou, "Le rôle de l'information," 19.

22. Interview, June 12, 2008, Niamey.

23. Interview with a member of the AFN, June 12, 2008, Niamey. Abdourhaman, "Le code de la famille au Niger," 159, also says that in 1985, the AFN formally requested that the drafting of the code recommence. Unless otherwise noted, the discussion of the code's history from 1985 to 1992 is based on Villalón, "The Moral and the Political in African Democratization."

24. "Malgré les difficultés qu'elle rencontre, l'A.F.N. œuvre pour l'émancipation de la nigérienne," *Le Sahel*, December 12, 1976, 45.

25. Dunbar, "Islamic Values, the State, and 'the Development of Women,'" 80–81.

26. " 'Nous avons pris l'engagement de mener des actions de développement de notre pays," *Le Sahel*, May 30, 1977, 3.

27. Dunbar, "Islamic Values, the State, and 'the Development of Women,'" 80–81.

28. "Portrait de Mme veuve Omar Malé Hadijatou," *Matan Niger*, 1983, 33.

29. Interview with a member of the AFN since 1976, June 12, 2008, Niamey; interview with a member of the AFN since 1982, May 6, 2008, Zinder.

30. Sounaye, "God Made Me a Preacher," 67. For more information on the AIN, see Triaud, "L'Islam et l'État en République du Niger (Deuxième partie)"; Meunier, *Dynamique de l'enseignement islamique du Niger*; Zakari, *L'islam dans l'espace nigérien*, 68–74.

31. Hassane, "Contribution des associations islamiques."

32. See, for example, case studies in Olivier de Sardan and Tidjani Alou, eds., *Les pouvoirs locaux au Niger*, 268, 342–43.

33. Idrisssa and Decalo, *Historical Dictionary of Niger*, 75. The AIN may hear disputes pertaining to land as well.

34. Mariama Alzouma, "La répudiation : Une autre forme de violation des droits des femmes," *Aïcha* 17 (March–April 2010): 10–11.

35. Interview with Barry Bibata in "Au nom de la loi : Pour le meilleur et pour le pire !" *Haské*, September 9, 1991, 2.

36. Alzouma, "La répudiation."

37. The 2007 information was collected at Commune II and AIN's headquarters by the author in 2008.

38. Idrissa, "The Invention of Order," 184; Zakari, *L'islam dans l'espace nigérien*, 72; Nicolas, "Détours d'une conversion collective," 105.

39. Dunbar and Djibo, *Islam, Public Policy, and the Legal Status of Women in Niger*, 30; Anifa, "Femmes pionnières : L'itinéraire de Mme Souna Hadizatou Diallo," *Seeda* 40 (August 2007): 19.

40. Abdourhaman, "Le code de la famille au Niger," 159; Villalón, "The Moral and the Political in African Democratization," 51. Unless noted otherwise, information in this section comes from Villalón's study.

41. Dunbar and Djibo, *Islam, Public Policy, and the Legal Status of Women in Niger*, 31; Dunbar, "Islamic Values, the State, and 'the Development of Women,'" 82.

42. "L'Association des femmes du Niger au débat national sur la santé," *Matan Niger*, July 1983, 28.

43. Ibid.

44. Abdourhaman, "Le code de la famille au Niger," 159.

45. Interview with an official of the AIN, January 11, 2008, Niamey; interview with an opponent of the code in the 1990s, June 24, 2008, Niamey.

46. Villalón, "The Moral and the Political in African Democratization," 53.

47. République du Niger, Decree No. 89–50/PCSON/MAS/CF of September 1, 1989; Decree No. 88–390/PCMS/MSP/AS/CF of November 24, 1989.

48. Boye et al., "Marriage Law and Practice in the Sahel," citing Moumouni in *Sahel Dimanche*, December 15, 1989.

49. Illou, "Le rôle de l'information."

50. Tidjani Alou, "La dynamique de l'État post colonial au Niger," 111. See also P. Robinson, "Niger," 4.

51. Charrad, *States and Women's Rights*.

52. Charrad, *States and Women's Rights*, xix. Data on the Muslim population come from Pew Forum on Religion and Public Life, Mapping the Global Muslim Population.

53. Miles, "Traditional Rulers and Development Administration," 43.

54. Abba, "La chefferie traditionnelle en question," 55.

55. Ibid., 57.

56. Bivins, "Daura and Gender in the Creation of a Hausa National Epic," 2n4.

57. Fuglestad, *A History of Niger*, 18; Triaud, "L'Islam et l'État," 35–48.

58. Stoller, *Fusion of the Worlds*, 175.

59. Charlick, *Niger*; Miles, "Traditional Rulers and Development Administration," 35.

60. Abba, "La chefferie traditionnelle en question"; Miles, "Partitioned Royalty."

61. Toungara, "Inventing the African Family," 46.

62. Ibid., 52.

63. Niandou-Souley, "L'armée et le pouvoir."

64. On this period, see Illiassou and Tidjani Alou, "Processus électoral et démocratisation."

65. Adamou Imirane Maiga, "Leader du Rassemblement démocratique des femmes du Niger (RDFN) : Mme Bayard Mariama Gamatié," *Amina*, June 20, 1993, 20.

66. République du Niger, Ministère du Développement Social, de la Population et de la Promotion de la Femme, Direction de la promotion de la femme, La politique de promotion de la femme au Niger, 32.

67. "Reprise de la session ordinaire de l'Assemblée Nationale : La promotion de la femme en question," *Le Sahel*, April 6, 1994, 3; Foumakoye, "Dix-huit mois de vie parlementaire," Annex A.

68. Mallam Yaro, "Le code de la famille en question," *Haské*, October 7, 1991, 3.

69. "Nous sommes une génération de femmes sacrifiées," *Le Républicain*, May 6, 1993, 6.

70. "Assaita [sic] Bagnan : 'Le code de la famille, c'est notre cheval de bataille," *Amina*, March 1993.

71. Yaro, "Le code de la famille en question."

72. Interview, October 31, 2007, Niamey.

73. République du Niger, Ministère du Développement Social, de la Population et de la Promotion de la Femme, Direction de la promotion de la femme, Synthèses du projet de code de la famille, 1.

74. Yaro, "Le code de la famille en question."

75. Maiga, "Leader du Rassemblement démocratique des femmes du Niger (RDFN)."

76. Dunbar and Djibo, *Islam, Public Policy, and the Legal Status of Women in Niger*, 31–32, 36.

77. Villalón, "The Moral and the Political in African Democratization," 54.

78. "Mme Bayard Mariama Gamatié, secrétaire général du R.D.F.N. : Nous sommes une génération des femmes sacrifiées," *Le Républicain*, May 6, 1993, 6.

79. Zakari, *L'islam dans l'espace nigérien*, 136.

80. "Le comité de popularisation écrit au Premier ministre," *Le Républicain*, June 9, 1994, 3.

81. République du Niger, Ministère du Développement Social, de la Population et de la Promotion de la Femme, Direction de la promotion de la femme, Synthèses du projet de code de la famille.

82. Harouna Maimouna, AP/MDS/P/PF, "Projet de Code de la Famille : Préparation de la campagne de popularisation," *Le Sahel*, May 11, 1994, 3.

83. For an overview of the major Islamic associations in Niger in the 1990s, see Zakari, *L'islam dans l'espace nigérien*; Hassane, "Contribution des associations islamiques."

84. Zakari, *L'islam dans l'espace nigérien*, 108–9; Meunier, *Dynamique de l'enseignement au Niger*, 170.

85. Zakari, *L'islam dans l'espace nigérien*, quoting the declaration published in *Le Sahel*, May 31, 1993.

86. "Communiqué," *Le Sahel*, May 19, 1994, 2.

87. M. Moustapha, "Réunion du Collectif des six associations islamiques sur le code de la famille : Front commun contre le 'Code de la famille,' " *Le Sahel*, May 23, 1994, 3.

88. Interview with a member of ANASI, June 19, 2008, Niamey.

89. M. Moustapha, "Projet de code de la famille/Réunion des femmes musulmanes : Le droit à la différence," *Le Sahel*, June 6, 1994, 3.

90. "Communiqué de presse des sections féminines des Associations islamiques du Niger," *Le Sahel*, June 6, 1994, 3.

91. Interview, June 30, 2008, Niamey.

92. Article 7 of the Constitution of 1989 declares Niger to be *une république laïque*.

93. Collectif des associations islamiques du Niger, "Débat sur la laïcité : On écrit au '*Démocrate*,' " *Le Démocrate*, October 5, 1992, 6.

94. Zakari, *L'islam dans l'espace nigérien*, 130–1; on ANAUSI's split from ANASI, see 109.

95. For a more thorough analysis of this debate, see Idrissa, "The Invention of Order," 232–34; Villalón, "From Argument to Negotiation," 383–86. My comparison of voter turnout in the 1989 and 1992 constitutional referenda is based on Chaïbou, *Répertoire biographique*, 82, 96.

96. "Bello Tiousso Garba, président de l'UDP-Amintchi : 'Les marabouts . . . veulent utiliser l'islam pour s'emparer du pouvoir,'" *Le Républicain*, September 17, 1992, 4.

97. M. Abdou Galadima, "Débat sur la laïcité de l'État : Les réactions de l'Église," *Le Démocrate*, September 28, 1992.

98. "Allahou Akbar : Dieu est grand," *Le Démocrate*, September 21, 1992, 1.

99. Collectif des associations islamiques du Niger, "Débat sur la laïcité."

100. I am grateful to Barbara Cooper for pushing me to think about the connection between the secularism debate and the family code debate.

101. *L'Avenir* 2, May 7, 1994, quoted in F. Mounkaïla, "Femmes et politique du Niger," 384.

102. "Interview d'Umaru Sumaïla, Président de l'AIN," *Weybi* 1, Spécial code de la famille, 1994, 13; Al Hamet, *Anfani* 44 (June 1994): 6, quoted in Zakari, *L'islam dans l'espace nigérien*, 137.

103. "Quelques articles incrimines sur les 603 articles anti-islamiques du code de la famille du Niger qui compte au total 906 articles," *Le Sahel*, May 24, 1994, 4.

104. MMA, "Les islamistes ruent, le pouvoir s'efface," *Le Républicain*, June 9, 1994, 3.

105. Moustafa, "Liberal Rights versus Islamic Law?"

106. Quoted in Zakari, *L'islam dans l'espace nigérien*, 138.

107. Interview, June 30, 2008, Niamey.

108. Interview, June 24, 2008, Niamey.

109. "Quelques articles incrimines sur les 603 articles anti-islamiques," 4. For a nuanced analysis of the discourse surrounding shari'a and democracy in Niger's neighbor to the south, see Kendhammer, "The *Sharia* Controversy in Northern Nigeria."

110. "Droit de réponse : Précisions de Adini-Islam," *Le Républicain*, March 27, 1997, 7.

111. A. J. Jimm, "De la réalité d'un code," *Le Républicain*, July 1, 1993, 2–3.

112. Namaiwa Boubé, "Les intégristes à l'assaut du Niger," *Le Républicain*, January 21, 1993, 2–3.

113. "Bello Tiousso Garba, président de l'UDP-Amintchi."

114. Also mentioned in F. Mounkaïla, "Femmes et politique au Niger," 366. I do not know whether the marabout belonged to an anti-code association. An ANASI leader said that his association did not issue the curse. Interview, June 19, 2008, Niamey.

115. MMA, "Les islamistes ruent, le pouvoir s'efface."

116. "Le comité de popularisation écrit au Premier ministre." Fatimata Mounkaïla writes in reference to the curse, "The Nigérien political class who mobilized with fervor and enthusiasm for establishing democracy in the country stood out by its eloquent silence." F. Mounkaïla, "Femmes et politique au Niger," 384.

117. "West Africa: The Men of Power," *Africa Confidential*, December 2, 1987, 5–6.

118. Lund, "Precarious Democratization and Local Dynamics in Niger," 857.

119. Cassette recording of Malama Zeinabou's show, Radio Anfani, aired August 28, 1999; transcribed by Mahaman Ragi.

120. Cassette recording of "Certaines fautes chez les femmes" by Ousseini Hassane; transcribed by Roukyatou Idrissa.

121. Interview, May 23, 2008.

122. Pseudonym used. Interview with a women's activist, June 7, 2006, Niamey.

123. Interview with two female journalists, January 3, 2013, Niamey.

124. McCammon, *The U.S. Women's Jury Movements and Strategic Adaptation.*

125. "Déclaration du président de la république à propos du code de la famille," *Le Sahel,* May 30, 1994, 3.

126. Interview with a radio journalist, May 2, 2008, Zinder. F. Mounkaïla, "Femmes et politique au Niger," 384.

127. "Niger: Coup Rumours Scotched," *Africa Research Bulletin,* March 1–31, 1994, 11375A.

128. "Niger: Opposition Leaders Arrested," *Africa Research Bulletin,* April 1–30, 1994, 11401C.

129. Ibid., 11402A.

130. Gazibo, "Foreign Aid and Democratization."

131. F. Mounkaïla, "Femmes et politique au Niger," 384.

132. Interview, May 23, 2008.

133. Interview with the first president of CONGAFEN, July 2, 2011, Niamey; CONGAFEN, *Compte rendu de l'atelier sur le thème;* Amarou, "Female Organizations," 15. In 1996, the RDFN joined other women's associations to create Fédération Kassaï.

134. CONGAFEN, *Compte rendu de l'atelier sur le theme.*

135. Union pour la Promotion de la Femme Nigérienne (UPFN) (undated brochure, field notes February 11, 2008).

136. Interview with the president of the UPFN, February 11, 2008, Niamey. Unless otherwise noted, my discussion of the proposed Law on Marriage and Divorce is based on this interview, parts of which are substantiated in Joseph Seydou Allakaye, "Mariage et divorce au Niger : Sur le chemin d'une réglementation officielle," *Le Républicain,* February 2, 2006, 6.

137. UPFN, *Rapport des travaux de l'atelier,* 47.

138. UPFN, *Rapport final des travaux des sous commissions.*

139. Ibid.

140. Interview with the secretary-general of the ACTN, June 21, 2006, Niamey.

141. K.I., "Une loi sur le mariage et le divorce au Niger en cours de préparation," *La Griffe,* January 30, 2006.

142. Ibid. See also "Des efforts en faveur de l'instauration de l'équilibre familial," *Sahel Dimanche,* January 27, 2006.

143. Interview, June 25, 2008, Niamey.

144. Interview, November 20, 2007, Niamey.

145. "Au Conseil des ministres : adoption d'un Projet de décret portant création, attributions et composition du Comité . . ." *Le Sahel,* July 9, 2010.

146. Interview with a representative of the ANDDH, June 24, 2011, Niamey.

147. Interview with the president of the ANDDH, July 8, 2011, Niamey.

148. République du Niger, Ministère de la Population, de la Promotion de la Femme et de la Protection de l'Enfant, Avant projet du statut personnel au Niger (SPN) : Version amendée et validée par les foras régionaux.

149. Interview with a representative of the ANDDH, June 24, 2011, Niamey.

150. "Polémique autour du code de la famille."

151. Ibid.

152. Oumarou Moussa, "Le ministre Cissé Ousmane dément les rumeurs faisant état de l'imminence de l'adoption du code de la famille," Le Sahel, March 7, 2011; K.I., "Le Gouvernement multiplie les offensives en direction des leaders islamiques," La Griffe, March 7, 2011, 6; "Niger : Rejet de l'avant projet du code de la famille," Xinhua, March 9, 2011, http://french.news.cn/afrique/2011-03/09/c_13768296.htm.

153. "Polémique autour du code de la famille."

154. Nasser, "L'Association islamique rejette l'avant projet de code de la famille."

155. Ibid.

156. "Polémique autour du code de la famille."

157. Nasser, "L'Association islamique rejette l'avant projet de code de la famille"; "Polémique autour du code de la famille."

158. Interview, June 15, 2011, Niamey.

159. A letter by the Collectif des Associations Islamiques du Niger to the President of the CRN, August 19, 1999, as quoted in Zakari, L'islam dans l'espace nigérien, 141n136.

160. For example, Nasser, "L'Association islamique rejette l'avant projet de code de la famille"; "Polémique autour du code de la famille."

161. Galey, "Women Find a Place," 19; UN General Assembly, Universal Declaration of Human Rights, G.A. Res 217 (III) A, U.N. Doc. A/RES/217(III) (Dec. 10, 1948), Article 16.

162. Galey, "Women Find a Place," 20.

163. Nasser, "L'Association des femmes du Niger au débat national sur la santé."

164. UN Conference of the International Women's Year, Mexico City, Mexico, June 19–July 2, 1975, Report. U.N. Doc. E/CONF.66/34.

165. Interview, May 23, 2008, Niamey.

166. Farnsworth, "Law Reform in a Developing Country." The literature from this era is copious. See Alliott, "Problems of the Unification of African Laws"; Allott, "Towards the Unification of Laws in Africa"; articles published in the 1960s in the Journal of Law in Africa. For a critique of this line of scholarship, see Chanock, "Neither Customary nor Legal"; Griffiths, In the Shadow of Marriage; Trubek and Galanter, "Scholars in Self-Estrangement."

167. Chanock, Law, Custom and Social Order.

168. Cowen, "African Legal Studies," 560.

169. Allott, "Towards the Unification of Laws in Africa," 357.

170. Government of Canada, CIDA, Niger Funding Report.

171. Government of Canada, CIDA, "Divulgation proactive [. . .] : Rapports trimestriels, 2007–2008, 3e trimestre."

172. UN Development Program, "Recommendation by the Executive Director." I examined UNDP and UNFPA archives by using a keyword search for "Niger" on the website of the executive board of UNDP, http://www.undp.org/execbrd/, through Google's search engine.

173. African Development Fund, *Republic of Niger*. Approximately 2.7 million UA were disbursed to the Republic of Niger.

174. Martin and Hashi, "Gender."

175. World Bank, "World Bank Approves US$10 Million Grant."

176. World Bank, *Niger—Multi-Sector Demographic Project*.

177. World Bank, *Implementation Completion Report, Republic of Niger: Population Project*, Report No. 17762-NIR, May 1, 1998; World Bank, *Implementation Completion and Results Report*, Report No. ICR1949, September 30, 2013.

178. Charrad, *States and Women's Rights*.

179. Blofield and Haas, "Defining a Democracy"; Htun, *Sex and the State*.

180. République du Niger, Ministère de l'Agriculture et de l'Élevage, Principes d'orientation du code rural, Ordinance No. 93–15, Niamey, March 2, 1993.

181. République du Mali, *Code du Mariage et de la Tutelle*, Law No. 62–17/AN-RM, Bamako, February 3, 1962; Ndoye, *Code de la famille du Sénégal annoté*.

182. FAO Stat, "Niger."

183. Zakari, *L'islam dans l'espace nigérien*, 65.

3. Bargaining for Women's Representation

1. This sketch is based on "Niger Leader Mamadou Tandja Held after Military Coup," *BBC News*, February 18, 2010; http://news.bbc.co.uk/2/hi/africa/8522227.stm; "Military Coup Ousts Niger President Mamadou Tandja," *BBC News*, February 19, 2010, http://news.bbc.co.uk/2/hi/africa/8523196.stm; field notes June 30, 2011.

2. République du Niger, Law No. 2000–008 of June 7, 2000.

3. Hamani, *Les femmes et la politique au Niger*; Inter-Parliamentary Union (IPU), "Niger."

4. Hamani, *Les femmes et la politique au Niger*.

5. The scholarship on "first ladies syndrome," "wifeism," and "femocracy" examines how presidents' wives in authoritarian countries use women's rights discourse to attract foreign aid, which first wives then use to expand patronage networks and clamp down on women's associations. Abdullah, "Wifeism and Activism" ; Tsikata, "The First Lady Syndrome" ; Okeke, "First Lady Syndrome"; Ibrahim, "The First Lady Syndrome and the Marginalisation of Women from Power"; Mama, "Feminism or Femocracy?"; Messlant and Marchal, "Premières dames en Afrique."

6. Gaillard, *Foccart parle*, 134; Baulin, *Conseiller du Président Diori*, 129–31; Salifou, *Biographie politique de Diori Hamani*, 248.

7. For different accounts of the circumstances surrounding Aissa Diori's death, see Salifou, *Biographie politique de Diori Hamani*, 248.

8. Mariama Alzouma, "Maiga Amsou : Une femme de combat," *Aïcha* 11 (2009): 6.

9. Cooper, *Marriage in Maradi*; Hale, "Griottes"; Sidikou, *Recreating Words, Shaping Worlds*; Sidikou and Hale, eds., *Women's Voices from West Africa*; Alidou, *Engaging Modernity*.

10. Alidou *Engaging Modernity*, 24. See also Seydou Assane, "Habsou Garba continue à donner de la voix," *Aïcha* 21, (2011): 3.

11. Assane, "Habsou Garba continue"; Cooper, *Marriage in Maradi*.

12. Unless otherwise noted, the sources on women in politics in this section are Hamani, *Les femmes et la politique au Niger*; Chaïbou, *Répertoire biographique (Vol. 1)*.

13. Fatouma Djibo Annou was eventually replaced by a male MP, but Mamata Hamani Moussa of PNDS replaced a male MP, Gado Foumakoye, who became a minister. See Chaïbou, *Répertoire biographique,* 424.

14. Hamani, *Les femmes et la politique au Niger,* 52–54; Chaïbou, *Répertoire biographique,* 424.

15. Information on the distribution of seats across parties comes from Inter-Parliamentary Union (IPU), "Women in National Parliaments." Data on party affiliation are from "113 députés investis pour la 2e législature," *Le Républicain,* December 16, 2004, 6.

16. Ibid.; Amarou, "Moumouni Aïssata."

17. Seydou Assane, "Moumouni Aïssata : Une vie consacrée à l'enseignement," *Aïcha* 20 (January–February 2011): 5.

18. Hamani, *Les femmes et la politique au Niger,* 135.

19. Ibid., 135.

20. Conrad, "The Debate about Quota Systems," 135.

21. Celis, Krook, and Meier, "The Rise of Gender Quota Laws," 518. On the diffusion of quotas worldwide, see Dahlerup, ed. *Women, Quotas, and Politics*; Krook, *Quotas for Women in Politics.* On the adoption and impact of gender quotas in Africa, see Diop, "Les quotas en Africa francophone"; Tripp et al., *African Women's Movements*; Yoon, "Explaining Women's Legislative Representation in Sub-Saharan Africa."

22. See Dahlerup, ed., *Women, Quotas, and Politics*; Krook, *Quotas for Women in Politics*; International IDEA, "Global Database of Quotas for Women."

23. Childs and Krook, "Labels and Mandates in the United Kingdom."

24. James Chapman, "Labour to Enforce Quota System to Ensure Third of Shadow Cabinet Are Women," *Daily Mail,* September 9, 2010, http://www.dailymail.co.uk/news/article-1310312.

25. Tripp et al., *African Women's Movements,* 153–57. For an overview of the scholarship on women in parliament in Africa, see Bauer, " 'Let There Be a Balance,' " 370–84.

26. Tripp et al., *African Women's Movements,* 153–57; International IDEA, "Global Database of Quotas for Women."

27. In 2011, 112 seats were reserved for women. In addition, two representatives of the Uganda People's Defence Forces, one representative of the youth, one representative of persons with disabilities, and one representative of workers were required to be women. For the total number of representatives in Uganda's parliament, see International IDEA, "Global Database of Quotas for Women"; Muriaas and Wang, "Executive Dominance," 312.

28. Dahlerup, "Women in Arab Parliaments"; Howard-Merriam, "Guaranteed Seats for Political Representation of Women"; Tripp et al., *African Women's Movements,* 153–57; International IDEA, "Global Database of Quotas for Women."

29. Kingdom of Swaziland, *The Constitution of the Kingdom of Swaziland Act.*

30. République du Niger, Law No. 2000–008 of June 7, 2000, Article 3.

31. Ibid. Niger's quota is not a reserved seat because its quota is explicitly gender neutral; reserved seats are carved out specifically for women. Furthermore, during the 2000 quota debate, MPs differentiated the legal quota as proposed by the Nigérien government from the reserved seat system found in countries like Uganda.

32. République du Niger, Decree No. 2001-056/PRN/MDSP/PF/PE of February 28, 2001, Article 2.

33. République du Niger, Law No. 2000-008 of June 7, 2000, Article 4. This type of quota is rare. In 2011 in Ghana, the government followed a policy requiring that women make up one-third or more of cabinet ministers. See Bauer and Okpotor, " 'Her Excellency,' " 88.

34. Ibid., Articles 3, 4, and 6.

35. A.N.N., "Marche des femmes nigériennes," *Le Sahel*, May 14, 1991, 1, 3; "Pas question de créer un précédent !" *Le Sahel*, May 14, 1991, 3; " 'Thousands' Protest at Exclusion of Women from Conference Preparations," *Pan African News Agency*, May 13, 1991; interview with a protest organizer, November 26, 2007, Niamey.

36. A.N.N., "Marche des femmes nigériennes."

37. Interview, November 26, 2007, Niamey; Idrissa and Decalo, *Historical Dictionary of Niger*, 338.

38. Ibro Na Allah Amadou and Maïna Hassan, "Les femmes manifestent," *Le Sahel*, May 15, 1991, 3.

39. As reprinted in *Le Sahel*, May 14, 1991, 3.

40. Felstiner, Abel, and Sarat, "The Emergence and Transformation of Disputes."

41. Ibid., 635.

42. A.N.N., "Marche des femmes nigériennes."

43. Ibid.

44. Chaïbou, *Répertoire biographique (Vol. 2)*, 483. Note that there is a discrepancy in the final number of women that served on the CNPCN. For instance, according to Hamani, *Les femmes et la politique au Niger*, 35, six women served on the CNPCN.

45. Hamani, *Les femmes et la politique au Niger*.

46. Ibid.

47. The holiday was created in 1992. See Decree No. 92-370/PRN/MDS/P/PF/PE of November 25, 1992.

48. This observation is based on my interviews with women's activists and field notes from June 6, 2006, October 20, 2007, November 8, 2007, and February 8, 2008.

49. Kailou Youssouf, "Participation des femmes à la Conférence nationale : L'impasse," *Le Sahel*, May 1991.

50. Hamani, *Les femmes et la politique au Niger*, 50-53.

51. I am not aware of any systematic studies of this phenomenon.

52. Hamani, *Les femmes et la politique au Niger*.

53. Abdourhamane Harouna, "La femme face à la démocratie et la décentralisation : Nécessité d'une mobilisation générale," *Le Démocrate*, May 24, 1999.

54. Ibid.

55. République du Niger, Ministère du Développement Social, de la Population et de la Promotion de la Femme, Conférence mondiale sur les femmes et développement, 54.

56. "La femme face à la démocratie et la décentralisation."

57. République du Niger, Ministère du Développement Social, de la Population et de la Promotion de la Femme, Plan d'actions de la politique de promotion de la femme, 5.

58. Harouna, "La femme face à la decentralisation."

59. Hamani, *Les femmes et la politique au Niger*, 52.

60. République du Niger, Ministère du Développement Social, de la Population et de la Promotion de la Femme, Plan d'actions, Objective 5.6.

61. Ibid., Objective 5.7.

62. République du Niger, Ministère du Développement Social, de la Population, de la Promotion de la Femme et de la protection de l'enfant, Direction de la promotion de la femme, Politique de promotion de la femme, Mars 1996, Objective 5.5 and 5.6.

63. République du Niger, Ministère du Développement Social, de la Population et de la Promotion de la Femme, Conférence mondiale sur les femmes et développement, 66, 55.

64. République du Niger, Ministère du Développement Social, de la Population, de la Promotion de la Femme et de la protection de l'enfant, Direction de la promotion de la femme, Politique nationale du développement sociale, 3.4.3, Objective 3.2.

65. Chaïbou, *Répertoire biographique.*

66. Charlick and Ousseini, *The Participation of Women in Nigérien Political Life.* The report was prepared for USAID.

67. Ibid.

68. National Democratic Institute, *Niger Assessment Mission Final Report,* 14.

69. Ibid.

70. Written correspondence with a former president of CONGAFEN, June 30, 2012; interview, May 22, 2008, Niamey.

71. "Mme Foumakoye Aïchatou, Militante du CDS Rahama," *Haské,* October 7, 1991, 2.

72. Chaïbou, *Répertoire biographique,* 259.

73. Interview, December 31, 2012, Niamey.

74. Chaïbou, *Répertoire biographique,* 104–5.

75. Ibid., 260.

76. Zerbo, "Everyday Heroes." She was also known as *kalla yi cikin rarwuna*—"the fulard in the turban."

77. Interview with a former bureaucrat in the Ministry of Social Development, June 26, 2008, Niamey.

78. Interview, December 31, 2012, Niamey.

79. Interview with the first director of the Office on the Advancement of Women, December 6, 2008, Niamey.

80. Nathalie Prevost, "La loi sur le quota : Recit d'une bataille parlementaire dix ans après," *Aïcha* 21 (January 2011).

81. Ibid.

82. Mindaoudou, "Full Participation of Niger Women."

83. République du Niger, Ministère du Développement Social, de la Population et de la Promotion de la Femme, Conférence mondiale sur les femmes et développement, 47, 50.

84. Keita, "Niger Women and Politics."

85. République du Niger, Ministère du Développement Social, de la Population et de la Promotion de la Femme, Conférence mondiale sur les femmes et développement, 47.

86. Interview, December 31, 2012, Niamey.

87. Ibid.

88. République du Niger, Ministère du Développement Social, de la Population et de la Promotion de la Femme, Conférence mondiale sur les femmes et développement, 53, citing a study on "Le rôle de la femme nigérienne dans la vie économique, politique, et sociale" conducted by the Association des Femmes du Niger.

89. Aïchatou Arifa, "La promotion de la femme est-elle menacée par les préjuges sociaux?" *Haské,* March 2, 1992, 5.

90. Assemblée Nationale du Niger, Suite ex. et adoption projet de loi instituant le quota; Suite discussions générales; Declaration et representation de Mme Ministre; Adoption article par article, Cassette n° 8, 2000.

91. Ladoua, *Texte d'accompagnement à la communication de Ladoua Aï sur la loi sur le quota.*

92. Prevost, "La loi sur le quota."

93. Interview with a former bureaucrat in the Ministry of Social Development, June 26, 2008, Niamey.

94. Before the democratic transition, most laws were made by military decree.

95. République du Niger, Assemblée Nationale, Règlement intérieur de l'Assemblée Nationale, Résolution No. 2000-01/AN, January 2, 2000.

96. Note that women MPs in other African countries have proposed private member bills. The only MP to have proposed a bill in Botswana was a female MP who sponsored a bill on domestic violence. See Bauer, " 'Cows Will Lead the Herd into a Precipice.' " See also Powley, "Demonstrating Legislative Leadership"; Wang, "Women Changing Policy Outcomes."

97. The parliamentary committees at the time of the quota debates were Defense and Security, Finance, Foreign Affairs, General Affairs and Institutions, Economic Affairs and Planning, Rural Development and Environment, and Social and Cultural Affairs.

98. République du Niger, Assemblée Nationale, Règlement intérieur de l'Assemblée Nationale, Résolution No. 2000-01/AN, January 2, 2000, Article 18.

99. République du Niger, Assemblée Nationale, Rapport 020, March 4-June 1, 2000, CAG/I, CAE/P.

100. Ibid., CAS/C.

101. Ibid., CF.

102. Ibid., CDR/E.

103. Ibid., CD/S.

104. Ibid., CF.

105. Ibid., CDR/E.

106. Quotations of MPs speaking on the floor come from my transcription of Assemblée Nationale du Niger, Suite ex. et adoption projet de loi instituant le quota, Cassettes Nos. 6-8, May 11, 2000.

107. Ibid., CAE.

108. République du Niger, Constitution de la Vème République du Niger, Article 45.

109. Ibid.

110. Ibid., Articles 72, 95, 96, and 91.

111. Ibid., Article 53.

112. Ibid., Article 48.

113. Interview with a former head of legislation in the National Assembly, March 4, 2008, Niamey.

114. Idwal, "Adamou Moumouni Djermakoye a tiré sa révérence," *La Hache*, June 25, 2009, 4; Mamane, "La Belle Mort du Colonel Djermakoye !" *Notre Liberté*, June 19, 2009, 3.

115. Interview, March 21, 2008, Niamey.

116. Amnesty International, "Niger: Legal Concern/Fear of Ill-Treatment/Probable Prisoners of Conscience," AFR 43/01/97, January 17, 1997, http://www.amnesty.org/en/library /info/AFR43/001/1997/en.

117. Amnesty International, "Niger."

118. Interview, December 31, 2012.

119. Barkan, "African Legislatures and the 'Third Wave,'" 17–18.

120. Prevost, "La loi sur le quota."

121. Field notes, June 21, 2006, Niamey.

122. Alidou and Alidou, "Women, Religion, and the Discourses," 24–25.

123. Interview conducted by the author and Roukyatou Idrissa, April 1, 2008, Niamey.

124. Interview, March 10, 2008.

125. Interview, February 21, 2008.

126. Interview, February 21, 2008.

127. The survey may not have drawn on a representative sample of women. Djibo, *La participation des femmes africaines à la vie politique*.

128. Alidou, *Engaging Modernity*.

129. Htun and Jones, "Engendering the Right to Participate in Decision-Making"; Dahlerup, ed., *Women, Quotas, and Politics*; Krook, *Quotas for Women in Politics*; Tripp et al., *African Women's Movements*; Bush, "International Politics."

130. Interview with a former president of CONGAFEN, December 27, 2012, Niamey.

131. Interview, December 31, 2012, Niamey.

132. Howard-Merriam, "Guaranteed Seats for Political Representation of Women," 28.

133. Longman, "Rwanda," 140.

134. Caul, "Political Parties and the Adoption of Candidate Gender Quotas"; Bruhn, "Whores and Lesbians"; Opello, *Gender Quotas*.

135. Bauer, "'Cows Will Lead the Herd into a Precipice'"; Larserud and Taphorn, *Designing for Equality*.

136. Bauer and Britton, *Women in African Parliaments*; Tripp et al, *African Women's Movements*.

137. Bauer, "Update on the Women's Movement in Botswana."

138. Fish, *Are Muslims Distinctive?*, 181.

139. Ibid., 189.

140. Ibid., 193.

141. Afrobarometer, "Online Analysis."

142. Lax and Phillips, "Gay Rights in the States."

143. Cherif uses the term "core rights" to argue that women's education and employment are foundational for the protection of other kinds of women's rights. See Cherif, "Culture, Rights, and Norms."

144. IPU, "Niger."

145. M.Z., "Le système de quota et son décret d'application : De la théorie à la pratique," *Le Démocrate*, March 7, 2002, 4; Alidou and Alidou, "Women, Religion, and the Discourses," 23; Association des Femmes Juristes du Niger (AFJN), *Rapport d'activités 2006.*

146. Aghali Abdelkader, "Le quota des femmes dans l'Administration publique et les partis politiques," *Le Républicain*, March 27, 2003, 4.

147. AFJN, *Rapport d'activités.*

148. Interview with a former president of CONGAFEN, May 22, 2008, Niamey; interview with a former bureaucrat in the Ministry of Social Development, June 26, 2008, Niamey.

149. See also CONGAFEN et al., *English Executive Summary*, 24.

150. Institut PANOS, *Le piège du quota.*

151. Field notes, June 11, 2011, Niamey.

152. All eight special constituency seats went to men. Kang, "The Effect of Gender Quota Laws on the Election of Women," 97.

153. Inter-Parliamentary Union, "Niger: Last Elections"; Kang, "The Effect of Gender Quota Laws on the Election of Women." The election results for six seats were invalidated in March. The numbers refer to the results that followed the holding of the fresh elections in May.

154. Alidou and Alidou, "Women, Religion, and the Discourses."

155. Chaïbou, *Répertoire biographique*. A study of the qualifications of female and male MPs in Uganda finds that women elected through quotas are no more elite than are elected men. See O'Brien, "Quotas and Qualifications in Uganda."

156. Assane, "Moumouni Aïssata."

157. "La CONGAFEN interpelle les autorités politiques : Déclaration sur le non-respect du quota." *Matan Daga*, March 2003, 2.

158. "Les femmes réclament plus de place aux emplois supérieurs," *Pan African News Agency*, December 26, 2004.

159. CONGAFEN et al., *English Executive Summary*, 34–35.

160. Field notes, June 2011; "Assemblée générale des femmes Tarayya : Pour une présence plus marquée de la femme dans la vie publique," *Le Républicain*, January 23, 2003, 6.

161. June 14, 2011, Niamey.

162. Interview with a former minister of youth and sports, June 16, 2011, Niamey.

163. I compared chapter 3, section 1, in République du Niger, *Code électoral*, Ordinance No. 99-37 of September 4, 1999; Law No. 2004-56 of November 1, 2004; and Ordinance No. 2010-031 of May 27, 2010.

164. République du Niger, Constitution de la VIIème République du Niger, Titre VIII, Article 161. Note that the assistant rapporteur to the Conseil Constitutionnel National was a woman, Zeinabou Abdou Gourouza. The Constitution also called for the "equal representation in public institutions through a national policy and the respect of quotas" (Titre II, Article 22), but it does not call for a specific percentage or mode of application.

4. Bringing Rights Home

1. "Mise à jour du Mouvement de solidarité pour les droits des femmes africaines," *Pambazuka News*, July 20, 2006, http://www.pambazuka.org/fr/category/comment/47341; field notes, June 5, 2006. Sources vary on the official tally. The number of votes in favor of the bill is thirty-four in Mahamadou Diallo, "Protocole sur les droits de la femme : Un

texte incompris," *Le Républicain,* June 22, 2006, 3–4. The tally is forty-four against, thirty-one for, and three abstentions in Mahamane, Abdou, and Sidikou, *Etat de la gouvernance en Afrique de l'Ouest,* 66.

2. Liu and Boyle, "Making the Case"; Weiss, "Interpreting Islam and Women's Rights"; Gray, Kittilson, and Sandholtz, "Women and Globalization"; Hill Jr., "Estimating the Effects"; Cole, "Government Respect for Gendered Rights"; Lupu, "The Informative Power of Treaty Commitment."

3. Simmons, *Mobilizing for Human Rights.*

4. Wotipka and Tsutsui, "Global Human Rights and State Sovereignty"; Hafner-Burton, Tsutsui, and Meyer, "International Human Rights Law."

5. Wotipka and Ramirez, "World Society and Human Rights."

6. République du Niger, Constitution de la IVème République du Niger, 1996, Titre 11; Constitution de la Vème République du Niger, 1999, Titre 10; Constitution de la VIème République du Niger, 2009, Titre 14; Constitution de la VIIème République du Niger, 2010, Titre 10. The Constitutional Court may also be summoned by the president, the Speaker of the National Assembly, the prime minister, or one-tenth of the National Assembly, to review the constitutionality of the treaty.

7. Mansfield, Milner, and Pevehouse, "Vetoing Co-operation"; Haftel and Thompson, "Delayed Ratification." Lisa Baldez's book on why the United States has not ratified CEDAW, *Defying Convention,* came out after I completed revisions to this book. Baldez suggests that disagreements among women's organizations and the weakened commitment of the Republican Party to women's rights affected CEDAW's nonratification.

8. Evans, Jacobson, and Putnam, eds., *Double-edged Diplomacy.* Others have made a similar point about compliance with international women's rights treaties. See, for example, Simmons, *Mobilizing for Women's Rights,* chap. 6.

9. Twenty-two countries ratified the agreement by the end of 1981. As of the end of 2012, only six countries in the United Nations had not ratified CEDAW: Iran, Palau, Somalia, Sudan, Tonga, and the United States. UN Treaty Collection (TC), "Convention on the Elimination of All Forms of Discrimination against Women."

10. Neumayer, "Qualified Reservation"; Simmons, *Mobilizing for Human Rights,* 102.

11. The government of Algeria withdrew its reservation to Article 9 (2) in July 2009. For a list of countries that issued reservations to CEDAW, see UN TC, "Convention on the Elimination of All Forms of Discrimination against Women."

12. Interview with a member of the AFN, June 12, 2008, Niamey.

13. Neumayer, "Qualified Reservation"; Simmons, *Mobilizing for Human Rights,* 102.

14. Interview, May 23, 2008, Niamey.

15. Ibid.

16. M. Kaka, "Prochaine conférence régionale des femmes à Dakar : Les spécificités de la femme nigérienne," *Le Républicain,* November 10, 1994, 4.

17. Interview with a female member of a conservative Islamic association, April 1, 2008, Niamey; interview with a former president of CONGAFEN, May 22, 2008, Niamey.

18. Foumakoye, "Dix-huit mois de vie parlementaire," Annex A.

19. Interview, May 22, 2008, Niamey.

20. Cissé and Kämpf, *La situation des femmes,* 38.

21. Garçon, *Étude sur l'évolution*, 34.

22. Zeinabou Gaoh, "Les femmes hésitent à mettre en œuvre leurs droits pour préserver une certaine durabilité des rapports sociaux," *Le Sahel*, May 27, 1999, 4–5.

23. The speaker was the director of the Office on the Advancement of Women and Promotion of Children and president of CONGAFEN at the time.

24. "Niger's Military Junta Pledges Elections," *BBC News*, April 12, 1999, http://news.bbc.co.uk/2/hi/africa/317662.stm.

25. Interview, May 22, 2008, Niamey.

26. The past presidents of CONGAFEN corroborated this information when I presented my preliminary findings at the American Cultural Center, July 3, 2008, Niamey.

27. In 1989, an organization of women from political parties and civil society that opposed the military government in Chile wrote to the government inquiring why it had not ratified CEDAW. The following day, the government declared its intent to ratify the convention. In December of the same year, President Augusto Pinochet ratified CEDAW. See Baldez, *Why Women Protest*, 175–78.

28. Unless otherwise noted, this paragraph is based on information from an interview with the then minister of social development, December 31, 2012.

29. Abdoulaye Borka, "Réseau des femmes ministres et parlementaires Nigériennes," *Le Sahel*, May 1999, 4.

30. Decree No. 99–16/PCRN of April 16, 1999.

31. Ibid.

32. Maaroupi Elhadj Sani, "Fronde et divergence des associations islamiques," *Le Démocrate*, March 30, 1998, 5.

33. Gaoh, "Les femmes hésitent à mettre en œuvre leurs droits."

34. Interview, December 31, 2012.

35. Sani, "Fronde et divergence des associations islamiques."

36. The official got several facts wrong: Iran had not ratified CEDAW, and Mali, Morocco, Nigeria, and Senegal did not ratify CEDAW with reservations. Sani, "Fronde et divergence des associations islamiques."

37. République du Niger, Ministère de l'Intérieur et de la Decentralisation, Direction générale des affaires politiques et juridiques, Direction des libertés publiques, List of Recognized Islamic Associations.

38. Lawan Ousmane and Hamidou Julien, "L'Ordonnance signée comporte des réserves," *Le Sahel*, August 24, 1999, 4.

39. Ibid.

40. République du Niger, Ministère du Plan, Analyse de la situation des enfants et des femmes au Niger.

41. Sani, "Fronde et divergence des associations islamiques."

42. Ibid.

43. Zeinabou Gaoh, "Journée mondiale de la femme : Les sections féminines des associations islamiques en assemblée extraordinaire," *Le Sahel*, May 10, 1999, 4.

44. This is not limited to conservative religious activists in Niger. See Moustafa, "Islamic Law."

45. Sani, "Fronde et divergence des associations islamiques."

46. Ibid.

47. Ibid.
48. Interview with a member of ANASI, March 27, 2008, Niamey.
49. Interview with a female member of an Islamic association, April 19, 2008, Maradi.
50. Gaoh, "Journée mondiale de la femme."
51. Sani, "Fronde et divergence des associations islamiques." See also Masquelier, "Debating Muslims, Disputed Practices."
52. Ousmane and Julien, "L'Ordonnance signée comporte des reserves."
53. Interview, December 25, 2007, Kiota.
54. Issa Gorzo, "Les militaires, les marabouts et la Convention," *Le Démocrate,* September 27, 1999, 5.
55. République du Niger, Ordinance No. 99–30 of August 13, 1999. Niger acceded to the convention on October 8, 1999.
56. I am indebted to Pearl Robinson for bringing out this point.
57. Interview with a member of the AFN, June 12, 2008, Niamey.
58. "Le 'barreur' de Baré s'est barré," *L'Observateur* (Burkina Faso), September 19, 2004.
59. Interview, May 22, 2008, Niamey.
60. K. Idrissa, "Les régimes militaires entre 1974 et 1999 au Niger," 194.
61. République du Niger, Constitution de la Vème République du Niger, 1999; "Mallam-Wanké, 'un amnistié de moins,' " *Jeune Afrique,* September 20, 2004.
62. " 'L'adhésion à la Convention n'équivaut nullement à la mise en œuvre du code de la famille,' selon le Secrétaire Général du Gouvernment," *Le Sahel,* August 24, 1999, 3.
63. The government's spokesperson further noted that Niger's constitution already addresses many parts of CEDAW.
64. " 'L'adhésion à la Convention n'équivaut nullement à la mise en œuvre du code de la famille.' " The full text of the decree was published in "Le texte de l'Ordonnance du 13 Août 1999," *Le Sahel,* August 24, 1999, 3.
65. Ibid.
66. K. Idrissa, "Les régimes militaries entre 1974 et 1999 au Niger," 201.
67. Issa Gorzo, "Les associations islamiques persistent et signent," *Le Démocrate,* September 20, 1999, 3.
68. M. B. "Wanké rappelle les islamistes à l'ordre," *La Tribune du Peuple,* September 24, 1999, 3.
69. Ibid.
70. Issa Gorzo, "Les militaries, les marabouts et la Convention," *Le Démocrate,* September 27, 1999, 5.
71. The number of rioters differ across newspaper articles. Compare Joseph Seydou Allakaye, "Discriminations contre les femmes : Les intégristes montent au créneau à Maradi," *Le Républicain,* October 7, 1999, 4, and Issa Gorzo, "Violences religieuses à Maradi," *Le Démocrate,* October 11, 1999, 6.
72. Interview, December 31, 2012.
73. Gorzo, "Les militaries, les marabouts et la Convention."
74. Gorzo, "Les associations islamiques persistent et signent."
75. Gorzo, "Les militaries, les marabouts et la Convention." See also "Wanké rappelle les islamistes à l'ordre."

76. Gorzo, "Les militaires, les marabouts et la Convention"; Sani, "Fronde et divergence des associations islamiques."

77. Ibid.; Gorzo, *Le Démocrate,* September 27, 1999, 5.

78. Sani, "Fronde et divergence des associations islamiques."

79. For an analysis of the pan-African women's mobilization for the adoption of the Maputo Protocol, see Adams and Kang, "Regional Advocacy Networks."

80. See Articles 14.1 (c), 5, 14.2 (c), 24, 23, and 22.

81. Adams and Kang, "Regional Advocacy Networks."

82. Interview with a member of the pro-protocol lobby, October 29, 2007, Niamey.

83. République du Niger, Comité de Suivi du Projet de Protocole Additionnel à la Charte Africaine des Droits de l'Homme et des Peuples Relatif aux Droits des Femmes, Rapport de mission.

84. Field notes, June 13, 2006; SNV, Capitalisation des expériences genre 2006–2007, 32–33.

85. Association des Femmes Juristes du Niger (AFJN), *Rapport d'activités 2006.* The AFN helped lobby for CEDAW. Interview with a member, October 4, 2007, Niamey.

86. Diallo, "Protocole sur les droits de la femme."

87. Ibid.

88. Interview with a member of the pro-protocol lobby, October 29, 2007, Niamey.

89. Ibid.

90. République du Niger, Ministère des Affaires Etrangères, de la Coopération, et de l'Integration Africaine, Direction des Affaires Juriqidues et du Contentieux, Division Juridique Multilaterale, Exposé des motifs du projet de loi autorisant la ratification du Protocole à la Charte Africaine des droits de l'homme et des peuples relatif aux droits de la femme en Afrique. Niamey, October 18, 2005.

91. SNV, Capitalisation des expériences genre 2006–2007, 32.

92. Interview with a representative of the international community who was involved with the pro-protocol lobbying effort, May 9, 2008, Zinder.

93. Ibid.

94. République du Niger, Ministère de la Promotion de la Femme et de la Protection de l'Enfant, Direction de la Promotion de la Femme, Initiative Genre au Niger (IGN), Argumentaire pour la levée des reserves formulées sur la Cedef.

95. République du Niger, Assemblée Nationale, Journée d'information et de sensibilisation des parlementaires sur la Cedef.

96. Inter-Parliamentary Union (IPU), "Niger: Assemblée Nationale. Elections Held in 2004," http://www.ipu.org/parline-e/reports/arc/2237_04.htm.

97. The list of reservations comes from my reading of the lead committee's report: République du Niger, Assemblée Nationale, 1st Ordinary Sess., 2nd Legislature, Avis au nom de la Commission des Affaires Sociales et Culturelles sur le projet de loi autorisant la ratification du protocole additionnel.

98. This is based on my reading of the committee's report. See République du Niger, Assemblée Nationale, 1st Ordinary Sess., 2nd Legislature, Avis au nom de la Commission des Affaires Sociales et Culturelles sur le projet de loi autorisant la ratification du protocole additionnel. Niamey, March 3, 2006.

99. African Union, "Protocol to the African Charter on Human and Peoples' Rights on the Rights of Women in Africa."

100. Diallo, "Protocole sur les droits de la femme."

101. An observer gave me a copy of the version of the bill he had the day of the vote.

102. Interview, February 29, 2008.

103. Interview, March 21, 2008.

104. Diallo, "Protocole sur les droits de la femme."

105. Interview, February 29, 2008.

106. Interview, March 26, 2008.

107. Interview, February 28, 2008.

108. Interview, March 6, 2008.

109. Six female MPs and three male MPs attended the committee meeting. The remaining five male MPs were absent. République du Niger, Assemblée Nationale, 1st Ordinary Sess., 2nd Legislature, Avis au nom de la Commission des Affaires Sociales et Culturelles sur le projet de loi autorisant la ratification du protocole additionnel.

110. Field notes, June 5, 2006.

111. "Déclaration des associations islamiques : Les islamistes invitent les députés à rejeter 'le complot diabolique,'" Le Républicain, November 2, 2006, 10.

112. "'C'est en fait avec le Protocole que la vraie discrimination à l'égard de la femme va commencer,'" As-Salam, December 12, 2006, 5.

113. "Un député nigérien juge irrecevable le protocole sur les droits de la femme africaine," Agence de Presse Africaine, March 10, 2007, http://www.nigerdiaspora.info/index.php /les-infos-du-pays/politique-niger/politique-niger/item/381-un-d%C3%A9put%C3%A9 -nig%C3%A9rien-juge-irrecevable-le-protocole-sur-les-droits-de-la-femme-africaine.

114. Gorel Harouna, "Code de la famille : Ces textes qui divisent les femmes," Le Républicain, October 5, 2006, 7.

115. Interview with a conservative female activist, May 5, 2008, Zinder.

116. "Déclaration des femmes musulmanes de Dosso" and "Déclaration des femmes musulmanes de Zinder," As-Salam, December 12, 2006, 9.

117. Boubacar Guede, "Les femmes musulmanes appellent au rejet du protocole à la charte africaine sur leurs droits," Agence de Presse Africaine, March 7, 2007, http://www.niger diaspora.info/index.php/les-infos-du-pays/sport/item/48882-les-femmes-musulmanes -appellent-au-rejet-du-protocole-%C3%A0-la-charte-africaine-sur-leurs-droits.

118. "Les femmes des organisations islamiques rejettent le protocole," Le Républicain, May 18, 2007, http://www.republicain-niger.com/Index.asp?affiche=News_display.asp&Arti cleID=3689&rub=Actualit%C3%A9s.

119. "Le gouvernement a-t-il renoncé au protocole sur les droits de la femme ?" La Griffe, May 28, 2007, http://nigerdiaspora.info/index.php/les-nouvelles-du-pays/environnement -niger/item/59773-le-gouvernement-a-t-il-renonc%C3%A9-au-protocole-sur-les-droits -de-la-femme.

120. "'C'est en fait avec le Protocole que la vraie discrimination à l'égard de la femme va commencer,'"

121. République du Niger, Argumentaires islamiques sur le Protocole additionnel à la Charte Africaine des droits de l'homme et des peuples relatif aux droits des femmes en Afrique.

122. Harouna, "Code de la famille."

123. Interview with a conservative female activist, May 5, 2008.

124. Ibid.

125. Interview with a female member of ANASI, March 27, 2008, Niamey.

126. Comité des associations islamiques nigériennes opposées au Protocole à la Charte Africaine sur les Droits de l'Homme et des Peuples, relatif à la Femme, *Examen critique du Protocole,* 5.

127. Harouna, "Code de la famille."

128. "Déclaration des associations islamiques : Les islamistes invitent les députés à rejeter 'le complot diabolique'" *Le Républicain,* November 2, 2006, 10.

129. "Déclaration des femmes musulmanes de Dosso" and "Déclaration des femmes musulmanes de Zinder," *As-Salam,* December 12, 2006, 9.

130. "Protocole lesbien : Ali Zada adresse une letter ouverte aux Députés Nationaux," dated December 6, 2006, from the personal archives of Zada Ali, 6.

131. "Les femmes des organisations islamiques rejettent le protocole."

132. Guede, "Les femmes musulmanes appellent au rejet du protocole à la charte africaine sur leurs droits."

133. Mahamane Souleymane, "Regards croisés sur le protocole de Maputo et le Hadj 2007," *As-Salam,* October 2007.

134. Ibid.

135. Ali, "Protocole lesbien," 5.

136. Association des Femmes Juristes du Niger (AFJN), *Rapport d'activités 2006.*

137. Ibid.

138. "The Parliament of Niger Asked to Adopt Additional Protocol to Women's Charter," *Agence de Presse Africaine,* March 2, 2007, http://africanpress.me/2007/03/02/the -parliament-of-niger-asked-to-adopt-additional-protocol-to-womens-charter/.

139. "Le gouvernement a-t-il renoncé au protocole sur les droits de la femme ?"

140. République du Niger, Argumentaires islamiques sur le Protocole additionnel à la Charte Africaine.

141. Interview, June 5, 2006.

142. Republique du Niger, Ministère des Affaires Étrangeres, de la Coopération, et de l'Integration Africaine, Direction des Affaires Juridiques et du Contentieux, Exposé des motifs du projet de loi autorisant la ratification du Protocole à la charte africaine des droits de l'homme et des peuples relatif aux droits de la femme en Afrique, adopté à Maputo (Mozambique), le 11 juillet 2003. A possible third attempt at sending a bill of ratification occurred at the end of 2007.

143. "Le gouvernement a-t-il renoncé au protocole sur les droits de la femme ?"

144. Idrissa and Decalo, *Historical Dictionary of Niger,* xliii.

145. Ibid. See, for example, "Rebels Attack Army Base in Niger," *BBC News,* June 22, 2007, http://news.bbc.co.uk/2/hi/africa/6232390.stm.

146. Field notes, June 27, 2006.

147. "Mise à jour du Mouvement de solidarité pour les femmes africaines," *Pambazuka* 10, July 20, 2006, http://pambazuka.org/fr/category/comment/47341.

148. Alio, "L'islam et la femme dans l'espace public au Niger," 124.

149. International Federation for Human Rights (FIDH), "La FIDH appelle les députés à adopter à la session parlementaire de mars le Protocole à la Charte africaine des droits de l'Homme et des peuples relatif aux droits des femmes."

150. "Protocole de Maputo relatif aux droits humains de la femme," *Media Niger,* December 27, 2011, http://www.medianiger.info/news_print.asp?pcmd=articleprint&article id=2614.

151. Alio, "L'islam et la femme." E.g., cassette recording of Abdallah Omar "La femme en Islam"; Souleymane, "Seconde lecture du procotole relatif aux droits de la femme," *As-Salam,* May 2007.

152. Moravcsik, "The Origins of Human Rights Regimes."

153. Hafner-Burton, Mansfield, and Pevehouse, "Human Rights Institutions, Sovereignty Costs, and Democratization."

154. Hathaway, "Why Do Countries Commit to Human Rights Treaties?," 613; Vreeland, "Political Institutions and Human Rights," 94.

155. Contrast Part V of CEDAW with Article 26 of the Maputo Protocol.

156. A. Idrissa, "Modèle islamique et modèle occidental," 364.

157. Field notes, September 27, 2007. The same source repeated this sentiment in December 2007.

158. Interview with a member of AFJN, October 4, 2007, Niamey.

159. UN Committee on the Elimination of Discrimination against Women (CEDAW). "Initial et deuxième rapports du Niger sur la Convention sur l'élimination de toutes les formes de discrimination à l'égard des femmes."

160. UN Committee on the Elimination of Discrimination against Women (CEDAW), "Concluding comments of the Committee on the Elimination of Discrimination against Women: Niger," point 10.

161. Ibid, point 12.

Conclusion

1. Abu-Lughod, *Veiled Sentiments,* 159, 167.

2. For more recent examples, see Alidou, *Engaging Modernity;* Badran, *Gender and Islam in Africa;* Rinaldo, *Mobilizing Piety;* Shehabuddin, *Reshaping the Holy;* Tadros, *Women in Politics.*

3. Abu-Lughod, "Do Muslim Women Really Need Saving?" See also her book-length treatise on the subject, *Do Muslim Women Need Saving?*

4. Blofield, *The Politics of Moral Sin,* 3.

5. E.g., Hassim, *Women's Organizations and Democracy;* Viterna and Fallon, "Democratization, Women's Movements, and Gender-Equitable States"; Waylen, *Engendering Transitions.*

6. Boko-Nadjo, "Le code des personnes et de la famille béninois."

7. Interview with a female judge, June 4, 2008, Cotonou, Benin. See also "Minorité féminine à l'assemblée nationale: L'honorable Justine Achadé propose le quota de 50%," *Quotidien Nokoué,* October 9, 2004, 3.

8. Merry, *Human Rights and Gender Violence,* 1.

9. Barkan, "Can Established Democracies Nurture Democracy Abroad?," 395.

10. Bush, "International Politics and the Spread of Quotas"; Krook, O'Brien, and Swip, "Military Invasion and Women's Political Representation."
11. Stepan, "Religion, Democracy, and the 'Twin Tolerations.' "
12. Walsh, *Women's Rights in Democratizing States.*
13. Ibid., 3.
14. Ashforth, *Witchcraft, Violence, and Democracy,* xii.
15. Ibid., 15.
16. For example, Mottl, "The Analysis of Countermovements"; Zald and Useem, "Movement and Countermovement Interaction"; Meyer and Staggenborg, "Movements, Countermovements, and the Structure of Political Opportunity."
17. Andrews, "Movement-Countermovement Dynamics and the Emergence of New Institutions."
18. Kampwirth, "Resisting the Feminist Threat." Bob's analysis in *The Global Right Wing* supports her argument.
19. Research conducted in postwar Liberia finds that the local women's movement helped enforce rape law there. See Medie, "Fighting Gender-Based Violence." Enforcement of the rape law, however, has been particularly limited for returning refugee women. See Yacob-Haliso, "Investigating the Role of Government Legislation."
20. Olivier de Sardan and Tidjani Alou, *Les pouvoirs locaux au Niger.*
21. Hirsch, *Pronouncing and Persevering.* Roberta Ann Dunbar collected minutes of the clerk for cases concerning divorce, alimony, and child custody from a court in Zinder, but to my knowledge, Dunbar had not published an analysis of the minutes. See Dunbar, "Contribution à l'étude de la jurisprudence nigérienne."

Appendix

1. Charlick and Ousseini, *The Participation of Women in Nigérien Political Life*; Villalón, "The Moral and the Political in African Democratization"; Cooper, *Marriage in Maradi*; Alidou, *Engaging Modernity.*
2. Organization for Economic Cooperation and Development, "Creditor Reporting System," http://stats.oecd.org/Index.aspx?datasetcode=CRS1#. Note: All monetary amounts are in U.S. dollars.

BIBLIOGRAPHY

Magazines and Newspapers

Full citations for magazine and newspaper articles are provided in the endnotes.

Africa Confidential, London
Agence de Presse Africaine, Dakar
Aïcha, Niamey
Amina, Paris
As-Salam, Niamey
Le Démocrate, Niamey
La Griffe, Niamey
La Hache, Niamey
Haské, Niamey
Jeune Afrique, Paris
Matan Daga, Niamey
Matan Niger, Niamey
Media Niger
Notre Liberté, Niamey
Pan African News Agency, Dakar
Le Républicain, Niamey
Le Sahel, Niamey
La Tribune du Peuple, Niamey

Republic of Niger Government Documents

Argumentaires islamiques sur le Protocole additionnel à la Charte Africaine des droits de l'homme et des peuples relatif aux droits des femmes en Afrique. Niamey [by 2008].

Assemblée Nationale. Règlement intérieur de l'Assemblée Nationale, Résolution No. 2000–01 /AN, January 2, 2000.

———. 1st Ordinary Sess., 2nd Legislature, Avis au nom de la Commission des Affaires Sociales et Culturelles sur le projet de loi autorisant la ratification du protocole additionnel. Niamey, March 3, 2006.

———. Journée d'information et de sensibilisation des parlementaires sur la Cedef. Niamey: UNDP and Coopération Belge Projet d'appui au renforcement des capacités du parlement (GPPS II), November 2005.

———. Rapport 020, March 4–June 1, 2000.

———. Suite ex. et adoption projet de loi instituant le quota; Suite discussions générales; Declaration et representation de Mme Ministre; Adoption article par article. 1ere Session Ordinaire. Cassettes Nos. 6–8, May 11, 2000.

Code électoral. Ordinance No. 99–37 of September 4, 1999.

Comité de Suivi du Projet de Protocole Additionnel à la Charte Africaine des Droits de l'Homme et des Peuples Relatif aux Droits des Femmes. Rapport de mission: Atelier sur le formation en lobbying et plaidoyer sur le Protocole additionnel à la Charte Africaine des droits de l'homme et des peuples, Lomé du 04 au 09 décembre. Niamey, 2000.

Constitution de la IIème République du Niger, 1992.

Constitution de la IVème République du Niger, 1996.

Constitution de la Vème République du Niger, 1999.

Constitution de la VIème République du Niger, 2009.

Constitution de la VIIème République du Niger, 2010.

Decree No. 89–50/PCSON/MAS/CF of September 1, 1989.

Decree No. 88–390/PCMS/MSP/AS/CF of November 24, 1989.

Decree No. 92–370/PRN/MDS/P/PF/PE of November 25, 1992.

Decree No. 99–16/PCRN of April 16, 1999.

Decree No. 2001–056/PRN/MDSP/PF/PE of February 28, 2001.

Law No. 62–11 of March 16, 1962.

Law No. 2000–008 of June 7, 2000.

Law No. 2004–56 of November 1, 2004.

Ministère de l'Agriculture et de l'Élevage. Principes d'orientation du code rural. Ordinance No. 93–15. Niamey, March 2, 1993.

Ministère de l'Economie et des Finances. Enquête démographique et de santé et à indicateurs multiples 2006. Niamey: Institut National de la Statistique/Calverton, Md: Macro International, 2007.

Ministère de l'Intérieur et de la Decentralisation, Direction générale des affaires politiques et juridiques, Direction des libertés publiques. List of Recognized Islamic Associations. Niamey [by 2006].

Ministère de la Promotion de la Femme et de la Protection de l'Enfant. Direction de la Promotion de la Femme. Initiative Genre au Niger (IGN). Argumentaire pour la levée des reserves formulées sur la Cedef. Niamey, November 2005.

Ministère des Affaires Étrangères, de la Coopération, et de l'Integration Africaine. Direction des Affaires Juridiques et du Contentieux, Division Juridique Multilaterale. Exposé des motifs du projet de loi autorisant la ratification du Protocole à la Charte Africaine des droits de l'homme et des peuples relatif aux droits de la femme en Afrique. Niamey, October 18, 2005.

——. Exposé des motifs du projet de loi autorisant la ratification du Protocole à la Charte Africaine des droits de l'homme et des peuples relatif aux droits de la femme en Afrique, adopté à Maputo (Mozambique), le 11 juillet 2003. Niamey, April 2, 2007.

Ministère du Développement Social, de la Population, de la Promotion de la Femme et de la protection de l'enfant, Direction de la promotion de la femme. Politique de promotion de la femme, Mars 1996. Niamey, 1996.

——. Direction de la promotion de la femme. Politique nationale du développement sociale : Promotion de la Femme. Niamey, 1998.

Ministère du Développement Social, de la Population et de la Promotion de la Femme. Avant projet du statut personnel au Niger (SPN): Version amendée et validée par les foras régionaux. Niamey, January 2011.

——. Conférence mondiale sur les femmes et développement: Rapport national. Niamey, 1994.

——. Direction de la promotion de la femme. La politique de promotion de la femme au Niger. Niamey, January 1993.

——. Direction de la promotion de la femme. Synthèses du projet de code de la famille. Niamey, September 1993.

——. Plan d'actions de la politique de promotion de la femme: Version préliminaire pour observations. Niamey, 1994.

Ministère du Plan. Analyse de la situation des enfants et des femmes au Niger: Rapport provisoire. Niamey: UNICEF, 1998.

Ordinance No. 99-30 of August 13, 1999.

Ordinance No. 2010-031 of May 27, 2010.

Articles, Books, Chapters, Reports, and Databases

Abadie, Maurice. *Afrique centrale: La colonie du Niger.* Paris: Adrien Maisonneuve, 1927.

Abba, Souleymane. "La chefferie traditionnelle en question." *Politique Africaine* 38 (1990): 51–60.

Abdullah, Hussaina. "Wifeism and Activism: The Nigerian Women's Movement." In *The Challenge of Local Feminisms: Women's Movements in Global Perspectives,* edited by Amrita Basu, 209–25. Boulder, Colo.: Westview, 1995.

Abdourhaman, Amina Moussa. "Le code de la famille au Niger: Historique et perspectives." In *Quel droit de la famille pour le Niger?* Niamey: Université Abdou Moumouni, 2005.

Abu-Lughod, Lila. *Do Muslim Women Need Saving?* Cambridge, Mass.: Harvard University Press, 2013.

——. "Do Muslim Women Really Need Saving? Anthropological Reflections on Cultural Relativism and Its Others." *American Anthropologist* 104, no. 3 (2002): 783–90.

——. *Veiled Sentiments: Honor and Poetry in a Bedouin Society.* Berkeley: University of California Press, 1986.

Adamou, Aboubacar. *Agadez et sa région: Contribution à l'étude du Sahel et du Sahara nigériens.* Niamey: Institut de recherche en sciences humaines, 1979.

Adams, Melinda. "'National Machineries' and Authoritarian Politics: The Case of Cameroon." *International Feminist Journal of Politics* 9, no. 2 (2007): 176–97.

Adams, Melinda, and Alice Kang. "Regional Advocacy Networks and the Protocol on the Rights of Women in Africa." *Politics & Gender* 3, no. 3 (2007): 451–74.

Adamu, Fatima. "A Double-Edged Sword: Challenging Women's Oppression within Muslim Society in Northern Nigeria." *Gender & Development* 7, no. 1 (1999): 56–61.

African Development Fund. *Republic of Niger: Gender Equity Reinforcement Project Completion Report.* P-NE-IB0-006, 2012. African Development Bank Group. http://www.afdb.org/en/documents/document/niger-gender-equity-reinforcement-project-porject-completion-report-pcr-22708/.

African Union. "List of Countries which have Signed, Ratified, Acceded to the Protocol to the African Charter on Human and Peoples' Rights on the Rights of Women in Africa." September 19, 2012, http://www.au.int/en/sites/default/files/Rights%20of%20Women.pdf.

———. "Protocol to the African Charter on Human and Peoples' Rights on the Rights of Women in Africa." July 11, 2003, http://www.africaunion.org/root/au/ Documents/Treaties/Text/Protocol%20on%20the%20Rights%20of%20Women.pdf.

Afrobarometer. "Online Analysis: Afrobarometer Round 5 (2010–2012)." http://www.afrobarometer-online-analysis.com/aj/AJBrowserAB.jsp.

Alidou, Ousseina. *Engaging Modernity: Muslim Women and the Politics of Agency in Postcolonial Niger.* Madison: University of Wisconsin Press, 2005.

Alidou, Ousseina, and Hassana Alidou. "Women, Religion, and the Discourses of Legal Ideology in Niger Republic." *Africa Today* 54, no. 3 (2008): 21–36.

Alio, Mahaman. "L'islam et la femme dans l'espace public au Niger." *Afrique et développement* 34, nos. 3–4 (2009): 111–28.

———. "L'islam et la femme dans l'espace public nigérien." Paper presented at the 12th General Assembly of CODESRIA: Governing the African Public Sphere, Yaoundé, Cameroun, December 7–11, 2008.

———. "Une révolution avortée: Le code de la famille au Niger." In *Quel droit de la famille pour le Niger?* Niamey: Université Abdou Moumouni, 2005.

Alliott, Michel. "Problems of the Unification of African Laws." *Journal of African Law* 11, no. 2 (1967): 86–98.

Allott, Antony. "Towards the Unification of Laws in Africa." *International and Comparative Law Quarterly* 14, no. 2 (1965): 366–89.

Amarou, Bisso. "Female Organizations: The Strength of Unity." In *Niger Women: Myth and Reality,* 15. Niamey: Ministère du développement social, de la population et de la promotion de la femme/Women advancement directorate, 1995.

———. "Moumouni Aïssata: Wisdom and Strictness." In *Niger Women: Myth and Reality,* 13–14. Niamey: Ministère du développement social, de la population et de la promotion de la femme/Women advancement directorate, 1995.

Amnesty International. "Niger: Harassment of Government Opponents Has Become Systematic," AFR/43/03/97, 1997. http://www.amnesty.org/en/library/info/AFR43/003/1997/en.

Andrews, Kenneth. "Movement-Countermovement Dynamics and the Emergence of New Institutions: The Case of 'White Flight' Schools in Mississippi." *Social Forces* 80, no. 3 (2002): 911–36.

An-Na'im, Abdullahi. *African Constitutionalism and the Role of Islam.* Philadelphia: University of Pennsylvania Press, 2006.

Apodaca, Clair. "The Effects of Foreign Aid on Women's Attainment of Their Economic and Social Human Rights." *Journal of Third World Studies* 17, no. 2 (2000): 205–19.

Arzika, Mahamadou. "Droit et société au Niger : L'évolution du droit coutumier." Thèse doctorale, Université de Strasbourg, 1987.

Ashforth, Adam. *Witchcraft, Violence, and Democracy.* Chicago: University of Chicago Press, 2005.

Association des Femmes Juristes du Niger (AFJN). *Rapport d'activités 2006.* Niamey: AFJN, 2006.

Badran, Margot, ed. *Gender and Islam in Africa: Rights, Sexuality, and Law.* Washington, D.C.: Woodrow Wilson Center Press, 2011.

Baldez, Lisa. *Defying Convention: U.S. Resistance to the UN Treaty on Women's Rights.* New York: Cambridge University Press, 2014.

———. *Why Women Protest: Women's Movements in Chile.* Cambridge: Cambridge University Press, 2002.

Banaszak, Lee Ann. *The Women's Movement Inside and Outside the State.* Cambridge: Cambridge University Press, 2010.

Barkan, Joel. "African Legislatures and the 'Third Wave' of Democratization." In *Legislative Power in Emerging African Democracies,* edited by Joel Barkan, 1–32. Boulder, Colo.: Lynne Rienner, 2009.

———. "Can Established Democracies Nurture Democracy Abroad? Some Lessons from Africa." In *Democracy's Victory and Crisis,* edited by Axel Hadennius, 371–403. Cambridge: Cambridge University Press, 1997.

Bashevkin, Sylvia. *Women on the Defensive: Living through Conservative Times.* Toronto: University of Toronto Press, 1998.

Bauer, Gretchen. "'Cows Will Lead the Herd into a Precipice': Where Are the Women MPs in Botswana?" *Botswana Notes and Records* 42 (2010): 56–70.

———. "'Let There Be a Balance': Women in African Parliaments." *Political Studies Review* 10, no. 3 (2012): 370–84.

———. "Update on the Women's Movement in Botswana: Have Women Stopped Talking?" *African Studies Review* 54, no. 2 (2011): 23–26.

Bauer, Gretchen, and Hannah Britton, eds. *Women in African Parliaments.* Boulder, Colo.: Lynne Rienner, 2006.

Bauer, Gretchen, and Faith Okpotor. "'Her Excellency': An Exploratory Overview of Women Cabinet Ministers in Africa." *Africa Today* 60, no. 1 (2013): 76–97.

Baulin, Jacques. *Conseiller du Président Diori.* Paris: Éditions Euraforpress, 1986.

Bayart, Jean-François. *The State in Africa: The Politics of the Belly.* Translated by Christopher Harrison, Elizabeth Harrison, and Mary Harper. London: Longman, 1993.

Beck, Linda. "Democratization and the Hidden Public: The Impact of Patronage Networks on Senegalese Women." *Comparative Politics* 35, no. 2 (2003): 147–69.

Beckwith, Karen. "Women's Movements at Century's End: Excavation and Advances in Political Science." *Annual Review of Political Science* 4 (2001): 371–90.

Berk, Richard. "An Introduction to Sample Selection Bias in Sociological Data." *American Sociological Review* 48, no. 3 (1983): 386–98.

Bivins, Mary Wren. "Daura and Gender in the Creation of a Hausa National Epic." *African Languages and Cultures* 10, no. 1 (1997): 1–28.

Blofield, Merike. *The Politics of Moral Sin: Abortion and Divorce in Spain, Chile, and Argentina.* New York: Routledge, 2006.

Blofield, Merike, and Liesl Haas. "Defining a Democracy: Reforming the Laws on Women's Rights in Chile, 1990–2002." *Latin American Politics and Society* 47, no. 3 (2005): 35–68.

Bob, Clifford. *The Global Right Wing and the Clash of World Politics.* Cambridge: Cambridge University Press, 2012.

Boko-Nadjo, Geneviève. "Le code des personnes et de la famille béninois." Paper presented at the NGO Forum, Addis Ababa, Ethiopia, October 6–7, 2004.

Bonte, Pierre. *Production et échanges chez les Touareg Kel Gress du Niger.* Paris: Institut d'ethnologie, 1971.

Bop, Codou. "Roles and the Position of Women in Sufi Brotherhoods in Senegal." *Journal of the American Academy of Religion* 73, no. 4 (2005): 1099–1119.

Boye, Abd-el Kader, Kathleen Hill, Stephen Isaacs, and Deborah Gordis. "Marriage Law and Practice in the Sahel." *Studies in Family Planning* 22, no. 6 (1991): 343–49.

Brand, Laurie. *Women, the State, and Political Liberalization: Middle Eastern and North African Experience.* New York: Columbia University Press, 1998.

Bruhn, Kathleen. "Whores and Lesbians: Political Activism, Party Strategies, and Gender Quotas in Mexico." *Electoral Studies* 22, no. 1 (2003): 101–19.

Burrell, Barbara. *A Woman's Place Is in the House: Campaigning for Congress in the Feminist Era.* Ann Arbor: University of Michigan Press, 1994.

Bush, Sarah Sunn. "International Politics and the Spread of Quotas for Women in Legislatures." *International Organization* 65, no. 1 (2011): 103–37.

Caul, Miki. "Political Parties and the Adoption of Candidate Gender Quotas: A Cross-National Analysis." *Journal of Politics* 63, no. 4 (2001): 1214–29.

Celis, Karen, Mona Lena Krook, and Petra Meier. "The Rise of Gender Quota Laws: Expanding the Spectrum of Determinants for Electoral Reform." *West European Politics* 34, no. 3 (2011): 514–30.

Central Intelligence Agency. "'World Factbook: Niger." October 28, 2013. https://www.cia .gov/library/publications/the-world-factbook/geos/ng.html.

Chaïbou, Maman. *Répertoire biographique des personnalités de la classe et des leaders d'opinion du Niger de 1945 à nos jours, Vol. 1. Les parlementaires.* Niamey: Edition Democratie, 1999.

———. *Répertoire biographique des personnalités de la classe politique et leaders d'opinion du Niger de 1945 à nos jours, Vol. 2.* Niamey: Edition Democratie, 1999.

Chanock, Martin. *Law, Custom and Social Order: The Colonial Experience in Malawi and Zambia.* Cambridge: Cambridge University Press, 1985.

———. "Neither Customary nor Legal: African Customary Law in an Era of Family Law Reform." *International Journal of Law and the Family* 3, no. 1 (1989): 72–88.

Chan-Tiberghien, Jennifer. *Gender and Human Rights Politics in Japan: Global Norms and Domestic Networks.* Stanford, Calif.: Stanford University Press, 2004.

Charlick, Robert. *Niger: Personal Rule and Survival in the Sahel.* Boulder, Colo.: Westview Press, 1991.

Charlick, Robert, and Hadiza Ousseini. *The Participation of Women in Nigérien Political Life.* Report prepared for USAID, Niamey, December 13–28, 1996.

Charrad, Mounira. *States and Women's Rights: The Making of Postcolonial Tunisia, Algeria, and Morocco*. Berkeley: University of California Press, 2001.

Cheibub, José Antonio, Jennifer Gandhi, and James Raymond Vreeland. "Democracy and Dictatorship Revisited." *Public Choice* 143, no. 2–1 (2010): 67–101.

Cherif, Feryal. "Culture, Rights, and Norms: Women's Rights Reform in Muslim Countries." *Journal of Politics* 72, no. 4 (2010): 1144–60.

Childs, Sarah, and Mona Lena Krook. "Labels and Mandates in the United Kingdom." In *The Impact of Gender Quotas,* edited by Susan Franceschet, Mona Lena Krook, and Jennifer M. Piscopo, 89–102. Oxford: Oxford University Press, 2012.

Cichowski, Rachel. *The European Court and Civil Society: Litigation, Mobilization, and Governance*. Cambridge: Cambridge University Press, 2007.

Cissé, Mariama, and Henriette Kämpf. *La situation des femmes devant les juridictions nigériennes*. Niamey: Coopération Suisse, 1997.

Clair, Andrée. *Le Niger, pays à découvrir*. Paris: Hachette, 1965.

Cole, Wade. "Government Respect for Gendered Rights: The Effect of the Convention on the Elimination of Discrimination against Women on Women's Rights Outcomes, 1981–2004." *International Studies Quarterly* 57, no. 2 (2013): 233–49.

Coles, Catherine, and Beverly Mack, eds. *Hausa Women in the Twentieth Century*. Madison: University of Wisconsin Press, 1991.

Collier, Ruth, and David Collier. *Shaping the Political Arena*. Princeton, N.J.: Princeton University Press, 1991.

Collion, Marie-Hélène. "Colonial Rule and Changing Peasant Economy in Damagherim, Niger Republic." PhD diss., Cornell University, 1982.

Comité des associations islamiques nigériennes opposées au Protocole à la Charte Africaine sur les Droits de l'Homme et des Peuples, relatif à la Femme. *Examen critique du Protocole*. Niamey, 2007.

CONGAFEN. *Compte rendu de l'atelier sur le thème: La femme nigérienne et les droits de la famille*. Niamey: CONGAFEN, 2001.

CONGAFEN, ONG Dimol, SOS FEVVF, AFJN, ANDDH, MAPADEV, and LUCOFVEM. *English Executive Summary of Nigérien NGO Report on the Status of the Convention on the Elimination of Discrimination Against Women (CEDAW/CEDEF)*. Niamey, 2007.

Conrad, Thomas. "The Debate about Quota Systems: An Analysis." *American Journal of Political Science* 20, no. 1 (1976), 135–49.

Cooper, Barbara. "The Politics of Difference and Women's Associations in Niger: Of 'Prostitutes,' the Public, and Politics." *Signs* 20, no. 4 (1995): 851–82.

———. *Marriage in Maradi: Gender and Culture in a Hausa Society in Niger*. Portsmouth, N.H.: Heinemann, 1997.

———. "Gender and Religion in Hausaland: Variations in Islamic Practice in Niger and Nigeria." In *Women in Muslim Societies: Diversity within Unity,* edited by Herbert Bodman and Nayereh Tohidi, 21–37. Boulder, Colo.: Lynne Rienner, 1998.

———. *Evangelical Christians in the Muslim Sahel*. Bloomington: Indiana University Press, 2006.

———. "Injudicious Intrusions: Chiefly Authority and Islamic Judicial Practice in Maradi, Niger." In *Muslim Family Law in Sub-Saharan Africa: Colonial Legacies and Post-Colonial*

Challenges, edited by Shamil Jeppie, Ebrahim Moosa, and Richard Roberts, 183–218. Amsterdam: Amsterdam University Press, 2010.

———. "Secular States, Muslim Law, and Islamic Religious Culture: Gender Implications of Legal Struggles in Hybrid Legal Systems in Contemporary West Africa." *Droits et Culture* 59, no. 1 (2010): 97–120.

Coquery-Vidrovitch, Catherine. *Les Africaines : Histoire des femmes d'Afrique Noire du XIXe au XXe siècle.* Paris: Éditions Desjonquères, 1994.

Cowen, Denis. "African Legal Studies: A Survey of the Field and the Role of the United States." *Law and Contemporary Problems* 27, no. 4 (1962): 545–75.

Creevey, Lucy. "Senegal: Contending with Religious Constraints." In *Women in African Parliaments,* edited by Gretchen Bauer and Hannah Britton. Boulder, Colo.: Lynne Rienner, 2006.

Dahlerup, Drude. "Women in Arab Parliaments: Can Gender Quotas Contribute to Democratization?" *al-raida* 126–127 (Summer/Fall 2009): 28–38.

———, ed. *Women, Quotas, and Politics.* New York: Routledge, 2006.

Dahlerup, Drude, and Lenita Freidenvall. "Quotas as a 'Fast Track' to Equal Political Representation for Women: Why Scandinavia Is No Longer the Model." *International Feminist Journal of Politics* 7, no. 1 (2005): 26–48.

Daloz, Jean-Pascal. " 'Big Men' in Sub-Saharan Africa: How Elites Accumulate Positions and Resources." *Comparative Sociology* 2, no. 1 (2003): 271–85.

Diop, Aissata De. "Les quotas en Africa francophone : Des débuts modestes." In *Les Femmes au parlement: Au-delà du nombre,* edited by Julie Ballington and Marie-José Protais, 133–42. Stockholm: International IDEA, 2002.

Disney, Jennifer Leigh. *Women's Activism and Feminist Agency in Mozambique and Nicaragua.* Philadelphia: Temple University Press, 2008.

Djibo, Hadiza. *La participation des femmes africaines a la vie politique: Les exemples du Sénégal et du Niger.* Paris: L'Harmattan, 2001.

Donno, Daniela, and Bruce Russett. "Islam, Authoritarianism, and Female Empowerment: What Are the Linkages?" *World Politics* 56, no. 4 (2004): 582–607.

Duffy, Helen. "*Hadijatou Mani Koroua v Niger:* Slavery Unveiled by the ECOWAS Court." *Human Rights Law Review* 9, no. 1 (2009): 151–70.

Dunbar, Roberta Ann. "Contribution à l'étude de la jurisprudence nigérienne: Extraits des jugements civils et coutumiers concernant les femmes, Le tribunal de première instance, Zinder 1957–1981." Unpublished manuscript, Niamey, Niger, 1982.

———. "Damagaram (Zinder, Niger), 1812–1906: The History of a Central Sudanic Kingdom." PhD diss., University of California–Los Angeles, 1970.

———. "Islamic Values, the State, and 'the Development of Women': The Case of Niger." In *Hausa Women in the Twentieth Century,* edited by Catherine Coles and Beverly Mack, 69–89. Madison: University of Wisconsin Press, 1991.

Dunbar, Roberta Ann, and Hadiza Djibo. *Islam, Public Policy, and the Legal Status of Women in Niger.* Report prepared for USAID-Niamey, March 1992.

Esposito, John. *Women in Muslim Family Law.* 2nd ed. With Natana DeLong-Bas. Syracuse, N.Y.: Syracuse University Press, 2001.

Evans, Peter, Harold Jacobson, and Robert Putnam, eds. *Double-Edged Diplomacy: International Bargaining and Domestic Politics.* Berkeley: University of California Press, 1993.

Ewig, Christina. "Hijacking Global Feminism: Feminists, the Catholic Church, and the Family Planning Debacle in Peru." *Feminist Studies* 32, no. 3 (2006): 632–59.

Fallon, Kathleen. *Democracy and the Rise of Women's Movements in Sub-Saharan Africa.* Baltimore, Md.: Johns Hopkins University Press, 2008.

FAO Stat. "Niger: Economic Indicators." http://faostat.fao.org/CountryProfiles/Country_Profile/Direct.aspx?lang=en&area=158.

Farnsworth, E. Allan. "Law Reform in a Developing Country: A New Code of Obligations for Senegal." *Journal of African Law* 8, no. 1 (1964): 6–19.

Felstiner, William, Richard Abel, and Austin Sarat. "The Emergence and Transformation of Disputes: Naming, Blaming, Claiming . . ." *Law & Society Review* 15 (1980): 630–49.

Fish, M. Steven. *Are Muslims Distinctive? A Look at the Evidence.* Oxford: Oxford University Press, 2011.

———. "Islam and Authoritarianism." *World Politics* 55, no. 1 (2002): 4–37.

Foumakoye, Aïchatou Nana. "Dix-huit mois de vie parlementaire: 09 Février 1993–17 Octobre 1994." Unpublished.

Franceschet, Susan. "'State Feminism' and Women's Movements: The Impact of Chile's Servicio Nacional de la Mujer on Women's Activism." *Latin American Research Review* 38, no. 1 (2003): 9–40.

Freedom House. "Country Ratings and Status, FIW 1973–2014 (Excel)." http://www.freedomhouse.org/report-types/freedom-world#.UxJH-fRdXk0.

Fuglestad, Finn. *A History of Niger, 1850–1960.* Cambridge: Cambridge University Press, 1983.

———. "Djibo Bakary, the French, and the Referendum of 1958 in Niger." *Journal of African History* 14, no. 2 (1973): 313–30.

Gado, Boureima Alpha. *Miroir du passé. Tome 1, Grandes figures de l'histoire du Niger.* Niamey: Imprimerie Nigérienne, 1993.

Gaillard, Phillippe. *Foccart parle, Entretiens avec Philippe Gaillard, Tome II.* Paris: Fayard /Jeune Afrique, 1997.

Gal, Susan, and Gail Kligman. *The Politics of Gender after Socialism: A Comparative-Historical Essay.* Princeton, N.J.: Princeton University Press, 2000.

Galey, Margaret. "Women Find a Place." In *Women, Politics, and the United Nations,* edited by Anne Winslow, 11–27. Westport, Conn.: Greenwood Press, 1994.

Garçon, Loïc. *Étude sur l'évolution de l'islam au Niger.* Niamey: Embassy of Canada to Niger, 1997.

Gazibo, Mamoudou. "Foreign Aid and Democratization: Benin and Niger Compared." *African Studies Review* 48, no. 3 (2005): 67–87.

Geisler, Gisela. "'Parliament Is Another Terrain of Struggle': Women, Men and Politics in South Africa." *Journal of Modern African Studies* 38, no. 4 (2000): 605–30.

Gelb, Joyce, and Marian Lief Palley. *Women and Public Policies.* Princeton, N.J.: Princeton University Press, 1987.

Goodliffe, Jay, and Darren Hawkins. "Explaining Commitment: States and the Convention against Torture." *Journal of Politics* 68, no. 2 (2006): 358–71.

Government of Canada, Canadian International Development Agency (CIDA). "Divulgation proactive [. . .] : Rapports trimestriels, 2007-2008, 3e trimestre, Coordination des

organisations non gouvernementales et associations féminines nigériennes." http://www
.acdi-cida.gc.ca/acdi-cida/contributions.nsf/Fra/D9D308F45ED850978525798B0056439D.

———. *Niger Funding Report.* 1987.

Gray, Mark, Miki Caul Kittilson, and Wayne Sandholtz. "Women and Globalization: A Study of 180 Countries, 1975–2000." *International Organization* 60, no. 2 (2006): 293–333.

Grégoire, Emmanuel. "Quelques aspects des échanges entre le Niger et le Nigeria." In *Les terrains du développement: Approche plurisdisciplinaire des économies du Sud,* edited by Claude Robineau, 153–59. Paris: ORSTOM, 1992.

Griffiths, Anne. *In the Shadow of Marriage: Gender and Justice in an African Community.* Chicago: University of Chicago Press, 1997.

Haas, Liesl. *Feminist Policymaking in Chile.* University Park: Pennsylvania State University Press, 2010.

Hafner-Burton, Emilie, Edward Mansfield, and Jon Pevehouse. "Human Rights Institutions, Sovereignty Costs, and Democratization." *British Journal of Political Science* 45, no. 1 (2015): 1–27.

Hafner-Burton, Emilie, Kiyoteru Tsutsui, and John Meyer. "International Human Rights Law and the Politics of Legitimation: Repressive States and Human Rights Treaties." *International Sociology* 23, no. 1 (2008): 115–41.

Haftel, Yoram, and Alexander Thompson. "Delayed Ratification: The Domestic Fate of Bilateral Investment Treaties." *International Organization* 67, no. 2 (2013): 355–87.

Hale, Sondra. *Gender Politics in Sudan: Islamism, Socialism, and the State.* Boulder, Colo.: Westview Press, 1996.

Hale, Thomas. "Griottes: Female Voices from West Africa." *Research in African Literatures* 25, no. 3 (1994): 71–91.

Hallaq, Wael. *Shari'a: Theory, Practice, Transformations.* Cambridge: Cambridge University Press, 2009.

Hamani, Abdou. *Les femmes et la politique au Niger.* Paris: L'Harmattan, 2001.

Hamani, Djibo. *L'Adar précolonial (République du Niger): Contribution à l'étude de l'histoire des états Hausa.* Paris: L'Harmattan, 2006.

Hanretta, Sean. "Gender and Agency in the History of a West African Sufi Community: The Followers of Yacouba Sylla." *Comparative Studies in Society and History* 50, no. 2 (2008): 478–508.

Hanson, Holly. "Queen Mothers and Good Government in Buganda: The Loss of Women's Political Power in Nineteenth-Century East Africa." In *Women in African Colonial Histories,* edited by Jean Allman, Susan Geiger, and Nakanyike Musisi, 219–36. Bloomington: Indiana University Press, 2002.

Hassane, Moulaye. "Contribution des associations islamiques à la dynamique de l'islam au Niger." Working Paper 72, Institut für Ethnologie und Afrikastudien, 2006.

Hassim, Shireen. *Women's Organizations and Democracy in South Africa.* Madison: University of Wisconsin Press, 2005.

Hathaway, Oona. "Do Human Rights Treaties Make a Difference?" *Yale Law Journal* 111, no. 8 (2002): 1935–2042.

———. "Why Do Countries Commit to Human Rights Treaties?" *Journal of Conflict Resolution* 51, no. 4 (2007): 588–621.

Hayter, Teresa. "French Aid to Africa—Its Scope and Achievements." *International Affairs* 41, no. 2 (1965): 236–51.

Heckman, James. "Sample Selection Bias as a Specification Error." *Econometrica* 47, no. 1 (1979): 153–61.

Hill, Daniel, Jr. "Estimating the Effects of Human Rights Treaties on State Behavior." *Journal of Politics* 72, no. 4 (2010): 1161–74.

Hirsch, Susan. *Pronouncing and Persevering: Gender and the Discourses of Disputing in an African Islamic Court.* Chicago: University of Chicago Press, 1998.

Howard-Merriam, Kathleen. "Guaranteed Seats for Political Representation of Women: The Egyptian Example." *Women & Politics* 10, no. 1 (1990): 17–42.

Htun, Mala. *Sex and the State: Abortion, Divorce, and the Family under Latin American Dictatorships and Democracies.* Cambridge: Cambridge University Press, 2003.

Htun, Mala, and Mark Jones. "Engendering the Right to Participate in Decision-Making: Electoral Quotas and Women's Leadership in Latin America." In *Gender and the Politics of Rights and Democracy in Latin America,* edited by Nikki Craske and Maxine Molyneux, 32–56. New York: Palgrave, 2002.

Htun, Mala, and Timothy Power. "Gender, Parties, and Support for Equal Rights in the Brazilian Congress." *Latin American Politics & Society* 48, no. 4 (2006): 83–104.

Htun, Mala, and S. Laurel Weldon. "When Do Governments Promote Women's Rights? A Framework for the Comparative Analysis of Sex Equality Policy." *Perspectives on Politics* 8, no. 1 (2010): 207–16.

Hughes, Melanie, Mona Lena Krook, and Pamela Paxton. "Transnational Women's Activism and the Global Diffusion of Gender Quotas." *International Studies Quarterly* (forthcoming).

Hughes, Melanie. "Armed Conflict, International Linkages, and Women's Parliamentary Representation in Developing Nations." *Social Problems* 56, no. 1 (2009): 174–204.

Hyden, Goran. *African Politics in Comparative Perspective.* Cambridge: Cambridge University Press, 2006.

Ibrahim, Jibrin. "The First Lady Syndrome and the Marginalisation of Women from Power: Opportunities or Compromises for Gender Equality?" *Feminist Africa* 3 (2004). http://agi.ac.za/journal/feminist-africa-issue-3-2004-national-politricks.

Idrissa, Abdourahmane. "The Invention of Order: Republican Codes and Islamic Law in Niger." PhD diss., University of Florida, 2009.

———. "Modèle islamique et modèle occidental: Le conflit des élites au Niger." In *L'islam politique au sud du Sahara: Identités, discours et enjeux,* edited by Muriel Gomez-Perez, 347–72. Paris: Karthala, 2005.

Idrissa, Abdourahmane, and Samuel Decalo. *Historical Dictionary of Niger.* 4th ed. Lanham, Md.: Scarecrow Press, 2012.

Idrissa, Kimba. *Guerres et sociétés: Les populations du "Niger" occidental au XIXe siècle et leurs réactions face à la colonisation (1896–1906).* Niamey: Institut de recherches en sciences humaines, 1981.

———. "La dynamique de la gouvernance: Administration, politique et ethnicité au Niger." In *Le Niger: État et Démocratie,* edited by Kimba Idrissa, 15–84. Paris: L'Harmattan, 2001.

———. "Les régimes militaires entre 1974 et 1999 au Niger." In *Armée et politique au Niger,* edited by Kimba Idrissa, 163–206. Dakar: CODESRIA, 2008.

Illiassou, Ali, and Mahaman Tidjani Alou. "Processus électoral et démocratisation au Niger." *Politique Africaine* 53 (1994): 128–32.

Illou, Aichatou. "Le rôle de l'information et de la communication dans les actions de l'association des femmes du Niger (AFN)." Mémoire, diplôme du niveau superieur de l'Institut de formation aux techniques de l'information et de la communication, 1990.

Inglehart, Ronald, and Pippa Norris. *Rising Tide: Gender Equality and Cultural Change around the World.* Cambridge: Cambridge University Press, 2003.

Institut PANOS. *Le piège du quota se referme sur les femmes.* 2005. http://www.panos-ao.org /ipao/spip.php?article3491#.

International Federation for Human Rights (FIDH). "La FIDH appelle les députés à adopter à la session parlementaire de mars le Protocole à la Charte africaine des droits de l'Homme et des peoples relatif aux droits des femmes." http://www.fidh.org/La-FIDH-appelle -les-deputes-a.

International IDEA. "Global Database of Quotas for Women." http://www.quotaproject.org/.

Inter-Parliamentary Union (IPU). "Niger: Assemblée Nationale. Elections Held in 2004." http://www.ipu.org/parline-e/reports/arc/2237_04.htm.

———. "Niger: Election Archives." http://www.ipu.org/parline-e/reports/2237_arc.htm.

———. "Niger: Last Elections, 2011." http://www.ipu.org/parline-e/reports/2237_E.htm.

———. "PARLINE Database on National Parliaments." http://www.ipu.org/parline/parline search.asp.

———. "Women in National Parliaments, Situation as of 31 December 2012." http://www.ipu .org/wmn-e/arc/classif311212.htm.

Jeppie, Shamil, Ebrahim Moosa, and Richard Roberts, eds. Introduction to *Muslim Family Law in Colonial and Postcolonial Africa,* 13–60. Amsterdam: Amsterdam University Press, 2010.

Jones, Mark. "Gender Quotas, Electoral Laws, and the Election of Women: Lessons from the Argentine Provinces." *Comparative Political Studies* 31, no. 1 (1998): 3–21.

Kang, Alice. "The Effect of Gender Quota Laws on the Election of Women: Lessons from Niger." *Women's Studies International Forum* 41, no. 2 (2013): 94–102.

Kampwirth, Karen. "Resisting the Feminist Threat: Antifeminist Politics in Post-Sandinista Nicaragua." *NWSA Journal* 18, no. 2 (2006): 73–100.

Katzenstein, Mary. *Faithful and Fearless: Moving Feminist Protest inside the Church and Military.* Princeton, N.J.: Princeton University, 1999.

Katzenstein, Mary, and Carol McClurg Mueller, eds. *The Women's Movements of the United States and Western Europe: Consciousness, Political Opportunity, and Public Policy.* Philadelphia: Temple University Press, 1987.

Keck, Margaret, and Kathryn Sikkink. *Activists beyond Borders: Advocacy Networks in International Politics.* Ithaca, N.Y.: Cornell University Press, 1998.

Keita, Mariama Diallo. "Niger Women and Politics: Women Political Atavism [*sic*]." In *Niger Women: Myth and Reality,* 12. Niamey: Ministère du développement social, de la population et de la promotion de la femme/Women advancement directorate, 1995.

Kelley, Thomas. "Exporting Western Law to the Developing World: The Troubling Case of Niger." *Global Jurist* 7, no. 3 (2007): Article 8.

Kendhammer, Brandon. "The *Sharia* Controversy in Northern Nigeria and the Politics of Islamic Law in New and Uncertain Democracies." *Comparative Politics* 45, no. 3 (2013): 291–311.

Kenworthy, Lane, and Melissa Malami. "Gender Inequality in Political Representation: A Worldwide Comparative Analysis." *Social Forces* 78, no. 1 (1999): 235–68.

Kingdom of Swaziland. *The Constitution of the Kingdom of Swaziland Act,* 2005. http://www .gov.sz/images/stories/Constitution%20of%20%20SD-2005A001.pdf.

Kondo, Dorinne. *Crafting Selves: Power, Gender and Discourses of Identity in a Japanese Workplace.* Chicago: University of Chicago Press, 1990.

Krook, Mona Lena. *Quotas for Women in Politics.* Oxford: Oxford University Press, 2010.

Krook, Mona Lena, Diana Z. O'Brien, and Krista Swip. "Military Invasion and Women's Political Representation: Gender Quotas in Post-Conflict Afghanistan and Iraq." *International Feminist Journal of Politics* 12, no. 1 (2010): 66–79.

Kuru, Ahmet. *Secularism and State Policies toward Religion: The United States, France, and Turkey.* Cambridge: Cambridge University Press, 2009.

Ladoua, Aï. *Texte d'accompagnement à la communication de Ladoua Aï sur la loi sur le quota.* Prepared for an SNV conference on "Partegeons, nous savoir," 2005.

Larserud, Stina, and Rita Taphorn. *Designing for Equality: Best-Fit, Medium-Fit, and Nonfavourable Combinations of Electoral Systems and Gender Quotas.* Stockholm: International IDEA, 2007.

Lax, Jeffrey, and Justin Phillips. "Gay Rights in the States: Public Opinion and Policy Responsiveness." *American Political Science Review* 103, no. 3 (2009): 367–86.

Levi, Margaret. *Of Rule and Revenue.* Berkeley: University of California Press, 1989.

Lindberg, Staffan. "What Accountability Pressures Do MPs in Africa Face and How Do They Respond? Evidence from Ghana." *Journal of Modern African Studies* 48, no. 1 (2010): 117–42.

Liu, Dongxiao, and Elizabeth Heger Boyle. "Making the Case: The Women's Convention and Equal Employment Opportunity in Japan." *International Journal of Comparative Sociology* 42, no. 4 (2001): 389–404.

Longman, Timothy. "Rwanda: Achieving Equality or Serving an Authoritarian State?" In *Women in African Parliaments,* edited by Hannah Britton and Gretchen Bauer, 133–50. Boulder, Colo.: Lynne Rienner, 2006.

Lovejoy, Paul. *Salt of the Desert Sun: A History of Salt Production and Trade in the Central Sudan.* Cambridge: Cambridge University Press, 1986.

Lovejoy, Paul, and J. S. Hogendorn. "Revolutionary Mahdism and Resistance to Colonial Rule in the Sokoto Caliphate, 1905–6." *Journal of African History* 31, no. 2 (1990): 217–44.

Lund, Christian. "Legitimacy, Land, and Democracy in Niger." *Review of African Political Economy* 24, no. 71 (1997): 99–112.

———. "Precarious Democratization and Local Dynamics in Niger: Micro-Politics in Zinder." *Development and Change* 32, no. 5 (2001): 845–69.

Lupu, Yonatan. "The Informative Power of Treaty Commitment: Using the Spatial Model to Address Selection Effects." *American Journal of Political Science* 57, no. 4 (2013): 912–25.

Lycklama à Nijeholt, Geertje, Virginia Vargas, and Saskia Wieringa, eds. *Women's Movements and Public Policy in Europe, Latin America, and the Caribbean.* New York: Garland, 1998.

Lydon, Ghislaine. "The Unraveling of a Neglected Source: A Report on Women in Franco-phone West Africa in the 1930s." *Cahiers d'Études Africaines* 37, no. 147 (1997): 575.

MacLeod, Arlene Elowe. *Accommodating Protest: Working Women, the New Veiling, and Change in Cairo.* New York: Columbia University Press, 1991.

Mahamane, Addo, Ibro Abdou, and Fatimata Sidikou. *État de la gouvernance en Afrique de l'Ouest: Le cas du Niger 2011.* Report prepared for CODESRIA/OSIWA, 2011.

Mama, Amina. "Feminism or Femocracy? State Feminism and Democratisation in Nigeria." *Africa Development* 20, no. 1 (1995): 37–58.

Mann, Gregory. "What Was the *Indigénat?* The 'Empire of Law' in French West Africa." *Journal of African History* 50 (2009): 331–53.

Mansbridge, Jane. *Why We Lost the ERA.* Chicago: University of Chicago, 1986.

Mansfield, Edward, Helen Milner, and Jon Pevehouse. "Vetoing Co-operation: The Impact of Veto Players on Preferential Trading Arrangements." *British Journal of Political Science* 37, no. 3 (2007): 403–32.

Marshall, Susan. "Development, Dependence, and Gender Inequality in the Third World." *International Studies Quarterly* 29, no. 2 (1985): 217–40.

Martin, Doris, and Fatuma Omar Hashi. "Gender, the Evolution of Legal Institutions and Economic Development in Sub-Saharan Africa." World Bank Working Paper 3, Poverty and Social Policy Division, Technical Department, Africa Region, 19311, June 1992.

Masquelier, Adeline. "Debating Muslims, Disputed Practices: Struggles for the Realization of an Alternative Moral Order in Niger." In *Civil Society and the Political Imagination in Africa: Critical Perspectives,* edited by John Comaroff and Jean Comaroff, 219–50. Chicago: University of Chicago Press, 1999.

———. *Prayer Has Spoiled Everything: Possession, Power, and Identity in an Islamic Town of Niger.* Durham, N.C.: Duke University Press, 2001.

———. *Women and Islamic Revival in a West African Town.* Bloomington: Indiana University Press, 2009.

Matland, Richard. "Institutional Variables Affecting Female Representation in National Legislatures: The Case of Norway." *Journal of Politics* 55, no. 3 (1993): 737–55.

Mazur, Amy. *Theorizing Feminist Policy.* Oxford: Oxford University Press, 2002.

Mbow, Penda. "Les femmes, l'Islam et les associations religieuses au Sénégal." In *Transforming Female Identities: Women's Organizational Forms in West Africa,* edited by Eva Evers Rosander, 148–63. Uppsala: Nordiska Afrikainstitutet, 1997.

McCammon, Holly. *The U.S. Women's Jury Movements and Strategic Adaptation: A More Just Verdict.* Cambridge: Cambridge University Press, 2012.

McCauley, John. "Africa's New Big Man Rule? Pentecostalism and Patronage in Ghana." *African Affairs* 112, no. 446 (2013): 1–21.

McIntosh, Marjorie Keniston. *Yoruba Women, Work, and Social Change.* Bloomington: Indiana University Press, 2009.

Medie, Peace. "Fighting Gender-Based Violence: The Women's Movement and the Enforcement of Rape Law in Liberia." *African Affairs* 112, no. 448 (2013): 377–97.

Meintjes, Sheila. "The Politics of Engagement: Women Transforming the Policy Process—Domestic Violence Legislation in South Africa." In *No Shortcuts to Power: African*

Women in Politics and Policy Making, edited by Anne Marie Goetz and Shireen Hassim, 140–59. London: Zed Books, 2003.

Merry, Sally Engle. *Human Rights and Gender Violence: Translating International Law into Local Justice.* Chicago: University of Chicago Press, 2006.

Messiant, Christine, and Roland Marchal. "Premières dames en Afrique: Entre bonnes œuvres, promotion de la femme et politiques de la compassion." *Politique Africaine* 95 (2004): 5–17.

Meunier, Olivier. *Dynamique de l'enseignement islamique du Niger.* Paris: L'Harmattan, 1997.

Meyer, David, and Suzanne Staggenborg. "Movements, Countermovements, and the Structure of Political Opportunity." *American Journal of Sociology* 101, no. 6 (1996): 1628–60.

Mezey, Michael. "The Functions of Legislatures in the Third World." *Legislative Studies Quarterly* 8, no. 4 (1983): 511–50.

Miles, William. *Hausaland Divided: Colonialism and Independence in Nigeria and Niger.* Ithaca, N.Y.: Cornell University Press, 1994.

———. "Partitioned Royalty: The Evolution of Hausa Chiefs in Nigeria and Niger." *Journal of Modern African Studies* 25, no. 2 (1987): 233–58.

———. "Shari'a as De-Africanization: Evidence from Hausaland." *Africa Today* 50, no. 1 (2003): 51–75.

———. "Traditional Rulers and Development Administration: Chieftaincy in Niger, Nigeria, and Vanuatu." *Studies in Comparative International Development* 28, no. 3 (1993): 31–50.

Mills, David, and Richard Ssewakiryanga. "'That Beijing Thing': Challenging Transnational Feminisms in Kampala." *Gender, Place & Culture* 9, no. 4 (2002): 385–98.

Mindaoudou, Aïchatou. "Full Participation of Niger Women." In *Niger Women: Myth and Reality,* 9. Niamey: Ministère du développement social, de la population et de la promotion de la femme/Women advancement directorate, 1995.

Minkenberg, Michael. "The Policy Impact of Church-State Relations: Family Policy and Abortion in Britain, France, and Germany." *West European Politics* 26, no. 1 (2003): 195–217.

Mir-Hosseini, Ziba. *Islam and Gender: The Religious Debate in Contemporary Iran.* Princeton, N.J.: Princeton University Press, 1999.

Mohanty, Chandra Talpade. "'Under Western Eyes' Revisited: Feminist Solidarity through Anticapitalist Struggles." *Signs* 28, no. 2 (2003): 499–535.

Moravcsik, Andrew. "The Origins of Human Rights Regimes: Democratic Delegation in Postwar Europe." *International Organization* 54, no. 2 (2000): 217–52.

Morgan, Kimberly. *Working Mothers and the Welfare State: Religion and the Politics of Work-Family Policies in Western Europe and the United States.* Stanford, Calif.: Stanford University Press, 2006.

Mottl, Tahi. "The Analysis of Countermovements." *Social Problems* 27, no. 5 (1980): 620–35.

Mounier, Pierre. "La dynamique des interrelations politiques: Le cas du sultanat de Zinder (Niger)." *Cahiers d'Études Africaines* 39, no. 154 (1999): 367–86.

Mounkaïla, Aïchatou. "Les obstacles à la participation de la femme à la vie politique au Niger." Mémoire, Ecole Normale d'Administration, Niger, 1992.

Mounkaïla, Fatimata. "Femmes et politique au Niger: Présence et représentations." In *Le Niger: État et démocratie,* edited by Kimba Idrissa, 384–86. Paris: L'Harmattan, 2001.

————. *Le mythe et l'histoire dans la geste de Zabarkâne.* Niamey: Centre d'Études Linguistiques et Historiques par Tradition Orale, 1988.

Moustafa, Tamir. "Islamic Law, Women's Rights, and Popular Legal Consciousness in Malaysia." *Law & Social Inquiry* 38, no. 1 (2013): 168–88.

————. "Liberal Rights versus Islamic Law? The Construction of a Binary in Malaysian Politics." *Law & Society Review* 47, no. 4 (2013): 771–802.

Muriaas, Ragnhild, and Vibeke Wang. "Executive Dominance and the Politics of Quota Representation in Uganda." *Journal of Modern African Studies* 50, no. 2 (2012): 309–38.

Nast, Heidi. *Concubines and Power: Five Hundred Years in a Northern Nigerian Palace.* Minneapolis: University of Minnesota Press, 2005.

National Democratic Institute. *Niger Assessment Mission Final Report.* Washington, D.C.: NDI, February 1998.

Ndoye, Doudou. *Code de la famille du Sénégal annoté: Textes et la jurisprudence.* Dakar: Cabinet Doudou Ndoye, 1996.

Neumayer, Eric. "Qualified Reservation: Explaining Reservations to International Human Rights Treaties." *Journal of Legal Studies* 36, no. 2 (2007): 397–429.

Niandou-Souley, Abdoulaye. "L'armée et le pouvoir." *Politique Africaine* 38 (1990): 40–50.

Niandou-Souley, Abdoulaye, and Gado Alzouma. "Islamic Renewal in Niger: From Monolith to Plurality." *Social Compass* 43, no. 2 (1996): 249–65.

Nicolas, Guy. "Détours d'une conversion collective : Ouverture à l'islam d'un bastion soudanais de résistance à une guerre sainte." *Archives des sciences sociales des religions* 48, no. 1 (1979): 83–105.

————. *Don rituel et échange marchand dans une société sahéliénne.* Paris: Institut d'éthnologie, 1986, 108.

————. *Dynamique sociale et appréhension du monde au sein d'une société hausa.* Paris: Institut d'ethnologie, 1975.

Norris, Pippa. "Petroleum Patriarchy? A Response to Ross." *Politics & Gender* 5, no. 4 (2009): 553–60.

O'Brien, Diana. "Quotas and Qualifications in Uganda." In *The Impact of Gender Quotas,* edited by Susan Franceschet, Mona Lena Krook, and Jennifer Piscopo, 57–71. Oxford: Oxford University Press, 2012.

Okeke, Phil. "First Lady Syndrome: The (En)Gendering of Bureaucratic Corruption in Nigeria." *CODESRIA Bulletin* 3–4 (1998).

Olivier de Sardan, Jean-Pierre. *Les sociétés songhay-zarma (Niger-Mali): Chefs, guerries, esclaves, paysans.* Paris: Karthala, 1984.

Olivier de Sardan, Jean-Pierre, and Mahmane Tidjani Alou, eds. *Les pouvoirs locaux au Niger, Tome 1 : À la veille de la décentralisation.* Dakar: Codesria, 2009.

Opello, Katherine. *Gender Quotas, Parity Reform, and Political Parties in France.* New York: Lexington, 2006.

Organization for Economic Cooperation and Development. "Creditor Reporting System." http://stats.oecd.org/Index.aspx?datasetcode=CRS1#.

Osborn, Emily Lynn. " 'Circle of Iron': African Colonial Employees and the Interpretation of Colonial Rule in French West Africa." *Journal of African History* 44, no. 1 (2003): 29–50.

Paxton, Pamela. "Women in National Legislatures: A Cross-National Analysis." *Social Science Research* 26, no. 4 (1997): 442–64.

Paxton, Pamela, Melanie Hughes, and Jennifer Green. "The International Women's Movement and Women's Political Representation, 1893–2003." *American Sociological Review* 71, no. 6 (2006): 898–920.

Pew Forum on Religion and Public Life. *Mapping the Global Muslim Population: A Report on the Size and Distribution of the World's Muslim Population.* Washington, D.C.: Pew Research Center, 2009.

Piault, Colette. *Contribution à l'étude de la vie quotidienne de la femme mawri.* Niamey: Études Nigériennes no. 10, 1965.

Poe, Steven, Dierdre Wendel-Blunt, and Karl Ho. "Global Patterns in the Achievement of Women's Human Rights to Equality." *Human Rights Quarterly* 19, no. 4 (1997): 813–35.

Polity IV. "Authority Trends, 1960–2010: Niger." http://www.systemicpeace.org/polity/nir2.htm.

Pearson, Elizabeth. *Demonstrating Legislative Leadership: The Introduction of Rwanda's Gender-Based Violence Bill.* Edited by Elizabeth Powley. Washington, D.C.: Institute for Inclusive Security, 2008. http://iis.niceandserious.com/explore-resources/research-and-publications-library/page/7/.

Razavi, Shahra, and Anne Jenichen. "The Unhappy Marriage of Religion and Politics: Problems and Pitfalls for Gender Equality." *Third World Quarterly* 31, no. 6 (2010): 833–50.

Reingold, Beth. *Representing Women: Sex, Gender, and Legislative Behavior in Arizona and California.* Chapel Hill: University of North Carolina Press, 2000.

République du Mali. *Code du Mariage et de la Tutelle.* Law No. 62-17/AN-RM. Bamako, February 3, 1962.

Reynolds, Andrew. "Women in the Legislatures and Executives of the World: Knocking at the Highest Glass Ceiling." *World Politics* 51, no. 4 (1999): 547–72.

Rinaldo, Rachel. *Mobilizing Piety: Islam and Feminism in Indonesia.* Oxford: Oxford University Press, 2013.

Risse-Kappen, Thomas, Stephen Ropp, and Kathryn Sikkink. *The Power of Human Rights: International Norms and Domestic Change.* Cambridge: Cambridge University Press, 1999.

Rizzo, Helen, Abdel-Hamid Abdel-Latif, and Katherine Meyer. "The Relationship between Gender Equality and Democracy: A Comparison of Arab Versus Non-Arab Muslim Societies." *Sociology* 41, no. 6 (2007): 1151–70.

Roberts, Richard. "Custom and Muslim Family Law in the Native Courts of the French Soudan, 1905–1912." In *Muslim Family Law in Sub-Saharan Africa: Colonial Legacies and Post-Colonial Challenges,* edited by Shamil Jeppie, Ebrahim Moosa, and Richard Roberts, 85–108. Amsterdam: Amsterdam University Press, 2010.

———. "Representation, Structure and Agency: Divorce in the French Soudan during the Early Twentieth Century." *Journal of African History* 40, no. 3 (1999): 389–410.

Robinson, David. *Muslim Societies in African History.* Cambridge: Cambridge University Press, 2004.

———. "Sénégal: Tribunal Musulman de Saint-Louis, City Hall, Quartier Nord." In "Court Records in Africana Research," special issue, *History in Africa* 17 (1990): 313.

Robinson, Pearl. "Niger: Anatomy of a Neotraditional Corporatist State." *Comparative Politics* 24, no. 1 (1991): 1–20.

Ross, Michael. "Oil, Islam, and Women." *American Political Science Review* 102, no. 1 (2008): 107–23.

Rouch, Jean. *Les Songhay*. Paris: Presses Universitaires de France, 1954.

Rule, Wilma. "Electoral Systems, Contextual Factors, and Women's Opportunity for Election to Parliament in Twenty-Three Democracies." *Western Political Quarterly* 40, no. 3 (1987): 477–98.

Rule, Wilma, and Joseph Zimmerman, eds. *Electoral Systems in Comparative Perspective: Their Impact on Women and Minorities*. Westport, Conn.: Greenwood, 1994.

Salacuse, Jeswald. *An Introduction to Law in French-Speaking Africa, Vol. 1, Africa South of the Sahara*. Charlottesville, Va.: Michi, 1969.

Salifou, André. *Biographie politique de Diori Hamani: Premier président de la République du Niger*. Paris: Karthala, 2010.

———. *Histoire du Niger*. Paris: Nathan, 1989.

———. *Le Damagaram ou le sultanat de Zinder au XIX siècle*. Niamey: Études Nigériennes no. 27, 1979.

Salime, Zakia. *Between Feminism and Islam: Human Rights and Sharia Law in Morocco*. Minneapolis: University of Minnesota Press, 2011.

Schatzberg, Michael. *Political Legitimacy in Middle Africa: Father, Family, Food*. Bloomington: Indiana University Press, 2001.

Séré de Rivières, Edmond. *Histoire du Niger*. Paris: Berger-Levrault, 1965.

Shehabuddin, Elora. *Reshaping the Holy: Democracy, Development, and Muslim Women in Bangladesh*. New York: Columbia University Press, 2008.

Shereikis, Rebecca. "Customized Courts: French Colonial Legal Institutions in Kayes, French Soudan, c. 1880–c. 1913 (Mali)." PhD diss., Northwestern University, 2003.

Sidikou, Aissata. *Recreating Words, Shaping Worlds: The Verbal Art of Women from Niger, Mali, and Senegal*. Trenton, N.J.: Africa World Press, 2001.

Sidikou, Aissata, and Thomas Hale, eds. *Women's Voices from West Africa: An Anthology of Songs from the Sahel*. Bloomington: Indiana University Press, 2012.

Simmons, Beth. *Mobilizing for Human Rights: International Law in Domestic Politics*. Cambridge: Cambridge University Press, 2009.

Skocpol, Theda. *Protecting Soldiers and Mothers: The Political Origins of Social Policy in the United States*. Cambridge, Mass.: Harvard University Press, 1992.

SNV. Capitalisation des expériences genre 2006–2007. Niamey: SNV, December 2007.

Solivetti, Luigi. "Family, Marriage and Divorce in a Hausa Community: A Sociological Model." *Africa: Journal of the International African Institute* 64, no. 2 (1994): 252–71.

Solus, Henry. *Traité de la condition des indigènes en droit privé, colonies et pays de protectorat et pays sous mandat*. Paris: Recueil Sirey, 1927.

Sounaye, Abdoulaye. "God Made Me a Preacher: Youth and Their Appropriation of the Islamic Sermon in Niamey, Niger." PhD diss., Northwestern University, 2012.

Spierings, Niels, Jeroen Smits, and Mieke Verloo. "On the Compatibility of Islam and Gender Equality: Effects of Modernization, State Islamization, and Democracy on Women's

Labor Market Participation in 45 Muslim Countries." *Social Indicators Research* 90, no. 3 (2009): 503–22.

Stepan, Alfred. "Religion, Democracy, and the 'Twin Tolerations.'" *Journal of Democracy* 11, no. 4 (2000): 37–57.

Stepan, Alfred, and Graeme Robertson. "An 'Arab' More Than 'Muslim' Electoral Gap." *Journal of Democracy* 14, no. 3 (2003): 30–44.

———. "Arab, Not Muslim, Exceptionalism." *Journal of Democracy* 15, no. 4 (2004): 140–46.

Stetson, Dorothy McBride. "Human Rights for Women—International Compliance with a Feminist Standard." *Women & Politics* 15, no. 3 (1995): 71–95.

Stoller, Paul. *Fusion of the Worlds: An Ethnography of Possession among the Songhay of Niger.* Chicago: University of Chicago Press, 1989.

Streicker, Allen. "On Being Zarma: Scarcity and Stress in the Nigérien Sahel." PhD diss., Northwestern University, 1980.

Swers, Michele. *The Difference Women Make: The Policy Impact of Women in Congress.* Chicago: University of Chicago Press, 2002.

Tadros, Mariz, ed. *Women in Politics: Gender, Power, and Development.* London: Zed Books, 2014.

Talfi, Bachir. *Quel droit applicable à la famille au Niger? Le pluralisme juridique en question.* Copenhagen, Denmark: Danish Institute for Human Rights, 2008.

Tarrow, Sidney. *Power in Movement: Social Movements, Collective Action, and Politics.* 3rd ed. Cambridge: Cambridge University Press, 2011.

Thom, Derrick. "The Niger-Nigeria Boundray 1890-1906: A Study of Ethnic Frontiers and a Colonial Boundary." Papers in International Studies, Africa Series, no. 23, Ohio University, 1975.

———. "The Niger-Nigeria Borderlands: A Political Geographical Analysis of Boundary Influence upon the Hausa." PhD diss., Michigan State University, 1971.

Thomas, Melissa, and Oumar Sissokho, "Liaison Legislature: The Role of the National Assembly in Senegal." *Journal of Modern African Studies* 43, no. 1 (2005): 97–117.

Tidjani Alou, Mahaman. "La dynamique de l'État post colonial au Niger." In *Le Niger: État et démocratie,* edited by Kimba Idrissa, 85–126. Paris: L'Harmattan, 2001.

———. "Les politiques de formation en Afrique francophone: École, état et sociétés au Niger." Thèse de doctorat, Université de Bordeaux I, 1992.

Tohidi, Nayereh. "Gender and Islamic Fundamentalism: Feminist Politics in Iran." In *Third World Women and the Politics of Feminism,* edited by Chandra Talpade Mohanty, Ann Russo, and Lourdes Torres, 251–267. Bloomington: Indiana University Press, 1991.

Toungara, Jeanne Maddox. "Inventing the African Family: Gender and Family Law Reform in Côte d'Ivoire." *Journal of Social History* 28, no. 1 (1994): 37–61.

Triaud, Jean-Louis. "L'Islam et l'État en République du Niger (Première partie)." *Le mois en Afrique* 192–93 (December 1981): 9–26.

———. "L'Islam et l'État en République du Niger (Deuxième partie)." *Le mois en Afrique* 194–95 (January–February 1982): 35–48.

Tripp, Aili Mari. *Women and Politics in Uganda.* Madison: University of Wisconsin Press, 2000.

Tripp, Aili Mari, Isabel Casimiro, Joy Kwesiga, and Alice Mungwa. *African Women's Movements: Transforming Political Landscapes.* Cambridge: Cambridge University Press, 2009.

Tripp, Aili Mari, and Alice Kang. "The Global Impact of Quotas: On the Fast Track to Female Representation." *Comparative Political Studies* 41, no. 5 (2008): 338–61.

Tripp, Aili Mari, Dior Konaté, and Colleen Lowe-Morna. "Sub-Saharan Africa: On the Fast Track to Women's Political Representation." In *Women, Quotas, and Politics,* edited by Drude Dahlerup, 112–37. New York: Routledge, 2006.

Trubek, David, and Marc Galanter. "Scholars in Self-Estrangement: Reflections on the Crisis in Law and Development Studies in the United States." *Wisconsin Law Review* 4 (1974): 1062–1102.

Tsebelis, George. *Veto Players: How Political Institutions Work.* Princeton, N.J.: Princeton University Press, 2002.

Tsikata, Dzodzi. "The First Lady Syndrome." *Public Agenda,* January 19, 1988, 19–25.

UN Committee on the Elimination of Discrimination against Women (CEDAW). "Initial et deuxième rapports du Niger sur la Convention sur l'élimination de toutes les formes de discrimination à l'égard des femmes." U.N. Doc. CEDAW/C/NER/1-2, November 21, 2005.

———. "Concluding comments of the Committee on the Elimination of Discrimination against Women: Niger." U.N. Doc. CEDAW/C/NER/CO/2, June 11, 2007.

UN Conference of the International Women's Year, Mexico City, Mexico, June 19–July 2, 1975, Report. U.N. Doc. E/CONF.66/34.

UN Development Program. "Recommendation by the Executive Director: Assistance to the Government of Niger." U.N. Doc. DP/FPA/PROJECTS/REC/2, March 11, 1983.

UN General Assembly. Universal Declaration of Human Rights, G.A. Res 217 (III) A, U.N. Doc. A/RES/217(III) (December 10, 1948).

UN Treaty Collection (TC). "Convention on the Elimination of All Forms of Discrimination against Women." Status as of July 10, 2013, http://treaties.un.org/Pages/ViewDetails.aspx?src=TREATY&mtdsg_no=IV-8&chapter=4&lang=en.

UPFN. *Rapport des travaux de l'atelier de restitution des résultats de l'étude sur la répudiation au Niger, Niamey du 17 au 19 septembre 2001.* Niamey: UPFN, 2001.

———. *Rapport final des travaux des sous commissions de la commission nationale chargée de l'élaboration d'un projet de loi règlementant le mariage et le divorce au Niger, mai-septembre 2003.* Niamey: UPFN, 2003.

Urvoy, Yves. *Histoire des populations du Soudan central (Colonie du Niger).* Paris: Larose, 1936.

Van Allen, Judith. "'Sitting on a Man': Colonialism and the Lost Political Institutions of Igbo Women." *Canadian Journal of African Studies* 6, no. 2 (1972): 165–81.

Van Craneburgh, Oda. "'Big Men' Rule: Presidential Power, Regime Type, and Democracy in Thirty African Countries." *Democratization* 15, no. 5 (2008): 952–73.

Van de Walle, Nicolas. "Presidentialism and Clientelism in Africa's Emerging Party Systems." *Journal of Modern African Studies* 41, no. 2 (2003): 297–321.

Van Santen, José. "'My 'Veil' Does Not Go with My Jeans': Veiling, Fundamentalism, Education, and Women's Agency in Northern Cameroon." *Africa* 80, no. 2 (2010): 275–300.

Van Walraven, Klaas. *Yearning for Relief: A History of the Sawaba Movement in Niger.* Leiden: Brill, 2013.

Villalón, Leonardo. "From Argument to Negotiation: Constructing Democracy in African Muslim Contexts." *Comparative Politics* 42, no. 4 (2010): 375–93.

———. "The Moral and the Political in African Democratization: The *Code de la Famille* in Niger's Troubled Transition." *Democratization* 3, no. 2 (1996): 41–68.

Viterna, Jocelyn, and Kathleen Fallon. "Democratization, Women's Movements, and Gender-Equitable States: A Framework for Comparison." *American Sociological Review* 73 (August 2008): 668–89.

Vreeland, James Raymond. "Political Institutions and Human Rights: Why Dictatorships Enter into the United Nations Convention against Torture." *International Organization* 62, no. 1 (2008): 65–101.

Walsh, Denise. *Women's Rights in Democratizing States: Just Debate and Gender Justice in the Public Sphere.* Cambridge: Cambridge University Press, 2010.

Wang, Vibeke. "Women Changing Policy Outcomes: Learning from Pro-Women Legislation in the Ugandan Parliament." *Women's Studies International Forum* 41, no. 2 (2013): 113–21.

Waylen, Georgina. *Engendering Transitions: Women's Mobilization, Institutions, and Gender Outcomes.* Oxford: Oxford University Press, 2007.

Weiss, Anita. "Interpreting Islam and Women's Rights: Implementing CEDAW in Pakistan." *International Sociology* 18, no. 3 (2003): 581–601.

Weldon, S. Laurel. "Beyond Bodies: Institutional Sources of Representation for Women in Democratic Policymaking." *Journal of Politics* 64, no. 4 (2002): 1153–74.

Wing, Susanna. "Women Activists in Mali and the Global Discourse on Human Rights." In *Women's Activism and Globalization: Linking Local Struggles and Transnational Politics,* edited by Nancy Naples and Menisha Desai, 172–85. New York: Routledge, 2002.

Wolbrecht, Christina. *The Politics of Women's Rights: Parties, Positions, and Change.* Princeton, N.J.: Princeton University Press, 2000.

World Bank. *Implementation Completion Report, Republic of Niger: Population Project.* Report No. 17762-NIR, May 1, 1998, Washington, D.C.: World Bank, 1998.

———. *Implementation Completion and Results Report (IDA-H309-NIR) on a Loan in the Amount of SDR6.7 Million (US$10 Million Equivalent) to the Republic of Niger for a Multi-Sector Demographic Project.* Report No. ICR1949, September 30, 2013. Washington, D.C.: World Bank, 2013. http://documents.worldbank.org/curated/en/2013/09/18367792/niger-multi-sector-demographic-project.

———. "World Bank Approves US$10 Million Grant for Niger Multi-Sector Demographic Project." Press Release 2007/457/AFR, June 19, 2007.

———. "World Development Indicators." http://data.worldbank.org/data-catalog/world-development-indicators.

Wotipka, Christine Min, and Francisco O. Ramirez. "World Society and Human Rights: An Event History Analysis of the Convention on the Elimination of All Forms of Discrimination against Women." In *The Global Diffusion of Markets and Democracy,* edited by Beth Simmons, Frank Dobbin, and Geoffrey Garrett, 303–43. Cambridge: Cambridge University Press, 2008.

Wotipka, Christine Min, and Kiyoteru Tsutsui. "Global Human Rights and State Sovereignty: State Ratification of International Human Rights Treaties, 1965–2001." *Sociological Forum* 23, no. 4 (2008): 724–54.

Yacob-Haliso, Olajumoke. "Investigating the Role of Government Legislation and Implementation in Addressing Gender-Based Violence among Returnee Refugee Women in Liberia." *Wagadu* 10 (2012): 132–49.

Yin, Robert. *Case Study Research: Design and Methods.* 3rd ed. Thousand Oaks, Calif.: Sage, 2003.

Yoon, Mi Yung. "Explaining Women's Legislative Representation in Sub-Saharan Africa." *Legislative Studies Quarterly* 29, no. 3 (2004): 447–68.

Zakari, Maïkoréma. Contribution à l'histoire des populations du sud-est nigérien : Le cas du Mangari (XVI-XIXe siècle). Niamey: Institut de recherches en sciences humaines, 1985.

———. *L'islam dans l'espace nigérien: De 1960 aux années 2000, Tome 2.* Paris: L'Harmattan, 2009.

Zald, Mayer, and Bert Useem. "Movement and Countermovement Interaction: Mobilization, Tactics, and State Involvement." In *Social Movements in an Organizational Society: Collected Essays,* edited by Mayer Zald and John D. McCarthy, 247–71. New Brunswick, N.J.: Transaction, 1987.

Zerbo, Sandra. "Everyday Heroes: Nana Aichatou Foumakoye." *Trust Africa Blog,* June 20, 2011. http://blog.trustafrica.org/.

INDEX

Collier, David, 29

Collier, Ruth, 29

colonialism: customary-cum-Islamic law in
Niger and, 29, 38–41; education under,
42; French collaboration with elites in
Niger and, 29–34; gendered effects in
Niger of, 41–43; gender equality norms
and, 14–15; history of French conquest
of Niger, 34–35; interethnic competition
in Niger and, 29–30; passive secularism
in Niger and, 47; power-sharing with
precolonial elites and, 35–43; social
elites and state entities under, 54; state
building in Niger under, 34

Colonie du Niger, establishment of, 35

Comité des Associations Islamiques
Nigériennes Opposées au Protocole, 142

Comité Nigérien sur les Pratiques
Traditionnelles (CONIPRAT), 83

Commission Electorale Nationale
Indépendante (CENI), 117–18

Commission National Préparatoire à la
Conférence Nationale (CNPCN),
exclusion of women from, 89–98

Commission on the Status of Women
(CSW), 75, 95, 109

Committee on the Elimination of
Discrimination against Women, 77, 117,
145, 149–50

Conseil Consultatif National (CCN), 94–98,
194n164

Conseil de Reconciliation Nationale (CRN),
124, 131–32

Conseil Islamique, 72

Conseil Supérieur de la Communication
(CSC), 118

Conseil Suprême pour la Restauration de la
Démocratie (CSRD), 71

consensus doctrine in Niger, gender quota
legislation and, 102–6

conservative activism: absence in gender
quota debate of, 106–8; catalysts for,
162–63; against CEDAW ratification,
126–29, 131–33; democratization and

countermobilization of, 46–47, 59–66;
family law reform in Niger and, 46–47;
Maputo Protocol and, 139–44;
one-religion discourse and, 55;
participative approach to family law
reform disrupted by, 71–74; research
methods concerning, 168; resistance
to international norms and, 77–78;
summary of research on, 153–55;
women's rights policy outcomes and,
6–7, 176n83

Constitutional Court (Niger), enforcement
of gender quota and, 88, 115–18. See also
Benin: Constitutional Court in

Convention Démocratique et Sociale (CDS),
84, 92, 95–96, 106, 115–16, 136–39

Convention on Consent to Marriage,
Minimum Age for Marriage and
Registration of Marriages, 75

Convention on the Elimination of All Forms
of Discrimination Against Women
(CEDAW): bargaining strategies in
ratification by Niger, 129–33;
conservative activists' vilification of,
74, 106–7; countermobilization in Niger
against, 126–29; democratic and
autocratic regimes and ratification of,
147–48; ideology of leadership and
party and ratification of, 148; impact
on gender equity of, 19; international
comparisons of ratification, 18, 22,
195n9; international norms and
ratification of, 145–47; Muslim-majority/
non-Muslim majority ratification
comparisons, 16–17; ratification in
Niger, 1–3, 22–25, 27, 74, 77, 120, 122–33;
reservations to, in Niger ratification,
122–33; UN pressure for ratification
of, 94

Cooper, Barbara, 13, 37, 39–40, 48

Coopération Belge, 135

Coopération Suisse, 76, 124

Coordination des Organisations Non
Gouvernementales et Associations

donor funding (cont.)
and, 124–26, 145–47; enforcement of
gender quota and, 115; family law
reform in Niger and, 76–77; impact on
gender policies of, 18; influence in Niger
of, 23–25, 70–71; for Maputo Protocol
ratification, 134–35, 145–47; women's
rights policies and, 160–61
dueling binaries, of Islamic and human
rights law, 63
Dunbar, Roberta Ann, 31, 52

Economic Community of West African
States (ECOWAS) Court of Justice, Niger
antislavery law and, 19
economy: gender participation in, 14; in
Niger, 20–22, 56, 67; women's movements
influence on policy and, 156–57
education: in colonial Niger and girls, 42–43,
180n76; gender inequities in Niger, 85
Egypt, 155; CEDAW ratification in, 17, 122;
gender quota in, 15, 109
elected office: enforcement of gender quota
and, 115–18; exclusion of Nigérien
women from, 92–94; gender quota
adoption and, 110–11; public opinion on
gender and, 112; women's representation
in Niger in, 81–119
elites in Niger: consensus doctrine and,
102–6; conservative countermobilization
and, 61; family law reforms and, 55–56;
French colonial state building and
coalition with, 34; gender quota
enforcement and role of, 116–18;
postcolonial political alliances and,
44–45, 54–56; in precolonial era, 31–34
ethnicity, African politics and, 29–30;
concerns about, 75
Europe, political ideology and gender
equity in, 19; women's movements in, 4
European Court of Justice (ECJ), women's
rights and, 19
European Union: funding, 93; women's
rights policies in, 19

évolués class: in colonial Niger, 42–43, 52–54;
postcolonial political alliances of, 43–45
executive cabinet, women in. *See* cabinet,
women in
Executive Office (Niger National Assembly),
99–100

Fall, Ousmane, 40
Fallon, Kathleen, 157
family law reforms: authoritarian regimes
of 1960–1989 and, 47–56; bargaining
strategies for passage of, 68–71; colonial
state building in Niger and, 34;
conservative activism in Niger against,
46–47, 59–66; crisis in Nigérien women's
mobilization for, 66–67; democratization
in Niger and, 5–6, 9, 56–57, 67–74;
French colonial customary-cum-Islamic
law in Niger and, 38–41; international
influence in Niger and effects of, 23–25,
75–78; mobilization of women for,
56–59; in Niger, 20, 22–27; omnibus *vs.*
single-issue proposals, 20; participative
committee for drafting of, 71–74; in
postcolonial Niger, 44–45; state-
religious distinctions in Niger and,
28–30; state-sanctioned religious
authority and, 50–52
Fédération Internationale des Ligues de
Droits de l'Homme (FIDH), 145–47
Fédération Kassaï, 95, 123, 125, 134
Felstiner, William, 90
female genital mutilation, association in
Niger against, 83
feminist bureaucrats, civil society and state
coalitions and, 5
feminist policy scholarship, women's
coalitions and, 4–11
fiqh (human understanding), French
colonial customary-cum-Islamic law in
Niger and, 38–41
Fish, M. Steven, 112
Fisher's exact test, international women's
rights treaty ratification and, 16–17

Hausa society: divorce rate in, 13; French
colonial relations with, 36; interethnic
competition in Niger and, 29–30;
women's political positions in, 41–42
Haut Conseil de la République (HCR),
56, 61
Heritage Foundation, 163
historical institutions, family law reform
and, 54
Houphouët-Boigny, Félix, 55, 78–79
Htun, Mala, 156, 175n45
human rights: Islam and, 14; law and
Islamic law, 63; norm spread, 159–60;
treaties, 120–22, 147–48
human rights organizations, in Niger. *See*
Association Nigérienne pour la Défense
des Droits de l'Homme

ideology of political parties and leaders:
19–20, CEDAW ratification in Niger and,
124–26, 148; family law reform and,
78–79; gender quota adoption and,
110–11; Maputo Protocol defeat and, 148
Idrissa, Abdourahmane, 11, 178n1
Idrissa, Kimba, 35, 37, 132
Igbo society, colonialism and gender norms
in, 14
Imuzurag family, 35
indigénat, 40, 180n60
indigène status, in French colonial legal
system, 38
Indonesia: Islamic law in, 13; women's
mobililzation in, 6
Inglehart, Ronald, 11–13
inheritance laws: conservative activism
concerning, 63–64; in modern Niger, 3,
46, 70; in Niger authoritarian regime of
1960–1989, 48, 53; in postcolonial Niger,
44–45
Institut PANOS Afrique de l'Ouest, 93, 114
international actors and institutions,
research methods concerning, 170–71
international law, impact on women's rights
policies of, 19

international norms: blocking factors in,
176n84; CEDAW ratification in Niger
and, 130–33, 145–47; disaggregation
of influence of, 160–61; expansion of,
159–61; gender quota legislation in Niger
and, 109–10, 117–18; influence on family
law reform in Niger and, 23–25, 75–78;
influence on women's rights policies
and, 17–20; Maputo Protocol defeat and,
145–47; women's rights treaties and,
120–21. *See also* donor funding
international women's rights treaties:
conservative opposition to, 141–44;
Muslim-majority/non-Muslim majority
comparisons of, 16–17
Inter-Parliamentary Union (IPU) Plan of
Action to Correct Present Imbalances in
the Participation of Men and Women
in Political Life, 96, 109, 161
Iraq, 155; gender quotas in, 111, 160
Islam: conventional wisdom about women's
rights and, 11–17; Nigérien women's
interest in, 50; in precolonial Niger, 31–34
Islamic associations, growth in the number
of, 127
Islamic barrier hypothesis: gender equality
research and, 13–15; Niger as challenge
to, 20–22
Islamic law and jurisprudence: colonial
customary-cum-Islamic law in Niger
and, 29, 38–43; family law reforms
and, 53–56, 58–59, 61–66, 71–74; in
postcolonial Niger, 44–45; repudiation,
marriage, and divorce laws and, 68–71;
state building in colonial Niger and
favoring of, 34; state-sanctioned
religious authority and, 50–52
Ismael, Cheick Oumarou, 51, 73, 132, 140
Ismael, Cheick Djabir, 73
Issaka, Roukayatou Abdou, 84
Issoufou, Abba Moussa, 53
Issoufou, Mahamadou (President), 21, 78,
86, 117; (Prime Minister), 59, 67, 72, 76;
CEDAW ratification in Niger and, 124

Niger (cont.)

66–67; politics and demographics in, 20–22, 177n99; state building during colonial era in, 34; transitional government in, 71; women's rights policies in, 1–3; 22–25

Nigeria, 5; conservative activism in, 78; divorce rate in northern, 13; expansion of Islamic law in, 10; frontier with Niger, 43; women's activists in, 4, 8

nomadisme politique, 97, 105

Norris, Pippa, 11–13

Olivier de Sardan, Jean-Pierre, 37, 40–41

omnibus reforms, 20; in Niger, 23–25, 71–72, 76, 79

ONG Dimol, 117, 133–35, 143

Opus Dei, 163

Organization of the Islamic Conference (OIC, now named Organization of Islamic Cooperation), 55, 78

Osborn, Emily, 40–31

Oumarou, Amadou (Bonkano), 56, 65, 101

Oumarou, Seyni, 72

Ousmane, Mahamane (President), 22, 59–60, 63, 66–67; lack of CEDAW ratification in Niger and, 124; (after presidency), 105

Oxfam, NOVIB, and Quebec: 76

parliament: African women's numerical representation in, 14–15; autonomy of, 174n36; gender quotas in Niger and, 87–89; legislative process in Niger and, 99–100; Maputo Protocol debates and, 136–39; reserved seats based on gender quotas in, 87; women's activism in Niger and, 9–11; women in Niger in, 81–119; women acting for women in, 57, 104–5, 123

Parti Nigérien pour la Démocratie et le Socialisme (PNDS), 78, 84, 92–94, 106–7, 115–16, 136–39, 148

Parti Nigérien pour le Renforcement de la Démocratie (PNRD), 84

Parti Progressiste Nigérien-Rassemblement Démocratique Africain (PPN-RDA), 43–45, 48, 54, 82

Parti Social-Démocrate Nigérien (PSDN), 83, 115, 136

peer pressure, women's rights policies and, 160–61

policy reforms: conservative activism and, 6–7; definition of women's rights, 25–26; doctrinal policy proposals, 20; implementation of, 164–65; judicial policy making, 19; omnibus *vs.* single-issue approaches to, 20; prolonged time frame for, 6–11; thinkability of women's rights, 5–11; women's activism and, 4–11, 156–59

political context: autonomy of state leaders and fate of, 78–79; CEDAW and Maputo Protocol and, 121–22, 148–49; gender quota adoption and, 100–102, 114–18; influence on state policies and, 17, 19–20; international norms and, 109–10; lack of family law reforms and, 74–80; Maputo Protocol debates and, 135–39; party and leadership ideology and, 78–79; in precolonial Niger, 30–34; ratification of CEDAW in Niger and, 129–33; research on, 15–16; women activists' influence on, 152–59; women's representation in Niger and, 81–119

Politique de Promotion de la Femme au Niger, 57

polygamy: abolition in Tunisia of, 19, 54, 78; in North Africa, 54

polygyny, family codes and, 50, 52; comparison of African countries with, 79

population health and control, World Bank initiatives concerning, 76–77

power-sharing arrangements: between church and state, 11; consensus doctrine in Niger and, 102–6; gendered effects of

French colonization of Niger on, 41–43; marginalization of Nigérien women from, 92–94; state building in colonial Niger and, 34–43

Précis de législation musulmane de Sidi Kahlil, 38

private member bills (*propositions de loi*) (Niger), 99–100

proportional representation (PR), 87–89, 92–94, 111

Protocol to the African Charter on Human and Peoples' Rights on the Rights of Women in Africa (Maputo Protocol): bargaining strategies in Niger and, 143–44; countermobilization against, 139–44; democratic and autocratic regimes and defeat of, 147–48; ideology of leadership and party and ratification of, 148; international norms and defeat of, 145–47; Muslim-majority/non-Muslim majority ratification comparisons, 16–17; Niger rejection of, 22–25, 27, 107, 120–22, 133–44

Provisional National Defense Council (Ghana), 19–20

public opinion: 12–14; gender quota adoption and role of, 111–12; Maputo Protocol and, 142–144; social construction of, 59, 129, 142

Qadiriyya order, 25

qadis (Muslim judges): colonialism in Niger and, 29; French colonial customary-cum-Islamic law and, 38–41; in precolonial Niger, 34; state-sanctioned religious authority and, 51–52

Rabiou, Amina, 128

Radio Anfani, 108

Radio Saraounia, 114–15

Radio Téneré, 108

Ramirez, Francisco, 18, 121

Rassemblement Démocratique des Femmes du Niger (RDFN), 57–59, 64–65, 94–96, 139

Rassemblement pour la Démocratie et le Progrès (RDP), 84, 107, 115–16, 136

Rassemblement Social-Démocratique (RSD), 84, 115, 136, 138

Rawlings, Jerry, 20

regime, definition, 173n4

régime d'exception, 21, 86

regional women's organizations. *See* Réseau Interafricain pour les Femmes, Media, Genre et Développement, Solidarity for African Women's Rights, Women and Law in Southern Africa

regional women's rights treaties. *See* Protocol to the African Charter on Human and Peoples' Rights on the Rights of Women in Africa (Maputo Protocol)

religiosity, 17

religious actors: diversity in Niger of, 25, 151–52; family law reforms and, 46–47; Maputo Protocol ratification and, 134; resistance to women's activism from, 6–7; state building in colonial Niger and coalition with, 34; state-sanctioned religious authority and, 50–52, 154–55; women's movements influence on policy and, 156–59

religious-state separation: in France, 175n45; in Niger colonial legal system, 28–29; in postcolonial Niger, 47; state-sanctioned religious authority and, 50–52; women's activism and, 9–11, 156–59

representation by women in Niger, 81–119; gender quota laws and, 87–89; mobilization for gender quota, evolution of, 89–98, 153–55; scope of underrepresentation, 82–86, 89–94

reproductive rights for women, 83, 136, 139

repudiation, 48–49, 51–52, 68–71; international donors and, 76

research methods: overview of, 22–26, 167–68; sample selection bias in, 12–13; spurious correlation and, 13–14

concerning, 167–68; silence during the 2011 family law effort of, 73–74; summary of research concerning, 151–65

women's employment in Niger, gender quota adoption and impact of, 112–14

women's representation in Niger: bargaining strategies for, 81–119; scope of underrepresentation, 82–86

women's rights policymaking: definition of, 25–26; influences on, 17–20; in Niger, 22–25

Wonkoye, Hawa Garba, 84

World Bank, 20; family law reform in Niger, 76–77; women's rights policies and indirect influence of, 160–61

World Conferences on Women: Mexico City World Plan of Action, 75; Beijing, 8, 18; CEDAW ratification and, 123, 146; family law in Niger and, 75; gender quotas and, 93–94; influence on women's rights policies of, 18; Nairobi, 50, 75; ratification of women's rights treaties and, 121

World Values Survey, 12–13

Wotipka, Christine, 18, 121

Yaro, Mallam, 36

Zada, Haoua Barazé, 84

Zarma societies: French colonization of Niger and, 37; interethnic competition in Niger and, 29–30; in precolonial Niger, 30–34

Zinder: colonial rule in, 35, 37, 42; conservative activism in, 60, 67, 140–42; family law debate in, 72; politicians representing, 22, 57, 95–96, 102, 105, 123, 138; unrest in, 67; women's activism in 49–50, 90, 151

ALICE J. KANG is assistant professor of political science and ethnic studies at the University of Nebraska–Lincoln.